NOVELL'S

Guide to Integrating
NetWare® 5 and NT

NOVELL'S

Guide to Integrating
NetWare® 5 and NT

J. D. MARYMEE, SANDY STEVENS, and GARY HEIN

Novell Press, San Jose

Novell's Guide to Integrating NetWare® 5 and NT

Published by
Novell Press
2211 North First Street
San Jose, CA 95131

Library of Congress Catalog Card No.: 99-65266

ISBN: 0-7645-4580-9

Printed in the United States of America

10 9 8 7 6 5 4 3 2 1

1B/TQ/QX/ZZ/FC

Distributed in the United States by IDG Books Worldwide, Inc.

Distributed by CDG Books Canada Inc. for Canada; by Transworld Publishers Limited in the United Kingdom; by IDG Norge Books for Norway; by IDG Sweden Books for Sweden; by IDG Books Australia Publishing Corporation Pty. Ltd. for Australia and New Zealand; by TransQuest Publishers Pte Ltd. for Singapore, Malaysia, Thailand, Indonesia, and Hong Kong; by Gotop Information Inc. for Taiwan; by ICG Muse, Inc. for Japan; by Norma Comunicaciones S.A. for Colombia; by Intersoft for South Africa; by Eyrolles for France; by International Thomson Publishing for Germany, Austria and Switzerland; by Distribuidora Cuspide for Argentina; by Livraria Cultura for Brazil; by Ediciones ZETA S.C.R. Ltda. for Peru; by WS Computer Publishing Corporation, Inc., for the Philippines; by Contemporanea de Ediciones for Venezuela; by Express Computer Distributors for the Caribbean and West Indies; by Micronesia Media Distributor, Inc. for Micronesia; by Grupo Editorial Norma S.A. for Guatemala; by Chips Computadoras S.A. de C.V. for Mexico; by Editorial Norma de Panama S.A. for Panama; by American Bookshops for Finland. Authorized Sales Agent: Anthony Rudkin Associates for the Middle East and North Africa.

For general information on IDG Books Worldwide's books in the U.S., please call our Consumer Customer Service department at 800-762-2974. For reseller information, including discounts and premium sales, please call our Reseller Customer Service department at 800-434-3422.

For information on where to purchase IDG Books Worldwide's books outside the U.S., please contact our International Sales department at 317-596-5530 or fax 317-596-5692.

For consumer information on foreign language translations, please contact our Customer Service department at 800-434-3422, fax 317-596-5692, or e-mail rights@idgbooks.com.

For information on licensing foreign or domestic rights, please phone +1-650-655-3109.

For sales inquiries and special prices for bulk quantities, please contact our Sales department at 650-655-3200 or write to IDG Books Worldwide, 919 E. Hillsdale Blvd., Suite 400, Foster City, CA 94404.

For information on using IDG Books Worldwide's books in the classroom or for ordering examination copies, please contact our Educational Sales department at 800-434-2086 or fax 317-596-5499.

For press review copies, author interviews, or other publicity information, please contact our Public Relations department at 650-655-3000 or fax 650-655-3299.

For authorization to photocopy items for corporate, personal, or educational use, please contact Novell, Inc., Copyright Permission, 1555 North Technology Way, Mail Stop ORM-C-311, Orem, UT 84097-2395; or fax 801-228-7077.

For general information on Novell Press books in the U.S., including information on discounts and premiums, contact IDG Books Worldwide at 800-434-3422 or 650-655-3200. For information on where to purchase Novell Press books outside the U.S., contact IDG Books International at 650-655-3021 or fax 650-655-3295.

Trademarks: Novell, NetWare, GroupWise, ManageWise, Novell Directory Services, and NDPS are registered trademarks; Novell Press, the Novell Press logo, NDS, Novell BorderManager, ZENworks, and Novell Distributed Print Services are trademarks; CNE is a registered service mark; and CNI and CNA are service marks of Novell, Inc. in the United States and other countries. All brand names and product names used in this book are trade names, service marks, trademarks, or registered trademarks of their respective owners. IDG Books Worldwide is not associated with any product or vendor mentioned in this book.

John Kilcullen, CEO, IDG Books Worldwide, Inc.
Steven Berkowitz, President, IDG Books Worldwide, Inc.
Richard Swadley, Senior Vice President & Publisher, Technology

The IDG Books Worldwide logo is a registered trademark or trademark under exclusive license to IDG Books Worldwide, Inc. from International Data Group, Inc. in the United States and/or other countries.

Marcy Shanti, *Publisher, Novell Press, Novell, Inc.*

Novell Press and the Novell Press logo are trademarks of Novell, Inc.

Welcome to Novell Press

Novell Press, the world's leading provider of networking books, is the premier source for the most timely and useful information in the networking industry. Novell Press books cover fundamental networking issues as they emerge — from today's Novell and third-party products to the concepts and strategies that will guide the industry's future. The result is a broad spectrum of titles for the benefit of those involved in networking at any level: end user, department administrator, developer, systems manager, or network architect.

Novell Press books are written by experts with the full participation of Novell's technical, managerial, and marketing staff. The books are exhaustively reviewed by Novell's own technicians and are published only on the basis of final released software, never on prereleased versions.

Novell Press at IDG Books Worldwide is an exciting partnership between two companies at the forefront of the knowledge and communications revolution. The Press is implementing an ambitious publishing program to develop new networking titles centered on the current versions of NetWare, GroupWise, BorderManager, ManageWise, and networking integration products.

Novell Press books are translated into several languages and sold throughout the world.

Marcy Shanti
Publisher
Novell Press, Novell, Inc.

Novell Press

Publisher
Marcy Shanti

IDG Books Worldwide

Acquisitions Editor
Jim Sumser

Development Editor
Kurt Stephan

Technical Editor
J. D. Marymee

Copy Editor
Larisa North

Production
IDG Books Worldwide Production

Proofreading and Indexing
York Production Services

About the Author

J. D. Marymee began his computer life with TRS-80s back in the good old days of 16K RAM and cassette program loading. Upon finding the computer industry was in need of knowledgeable people, and because the college instructors knew less about microcomputers than he did, J. D. began working full-time at a computer distributor circa 1983. After several bouts with technical support and sales, he began teaching Novell classes in 1985 and joined Novell's Education Division in 1988. This continued (along with some consulting) until 1990 when J. D. was asked to head up a new part of Education based in Provo, Utah. After completing this task, he jumped into Systems Engineering with the infamous Corporate Integration Manager group. There J. D. was routinely beaten up (and enlightened) by customers of all shapes and sizes. Severely scarred, he moved to the marketing organization, which mandated instant lobotomies. J. D. now has responsibilities that include O/S integration efforts (such as Windows NT), platform products (including NetWare), and distributed services (such as BorderManager).

Like J. D., **Sandy Stevens** has been involved in computers since the early days. Sandy ventured into PC networking in its infancy. Taking the abundance of practical knowledge she gained from the School of Hard Knocks and the small amount of practical knowledge she gained in college, Sandy became a CNI and CNE and, in 1989, she began a career of teaching and consulting in the San Francisco Bay Area. Sandy later joined Novell, was beamed to Utah, and became an instructor for the prestigious Novell Technology Institute. The desire to become more involved with Novell's products prompted a move to the NetWare product team. There, Sandy was a technical marketing manager and, later, a product manager for NetWare 3, NetWare 4, NDS, and other distributed services. Today, Sandy prefers an entrepreneurial lifestyle to corporate chaos, so she works as a freelance writer and consultant.

Like J. D., **Gary Hein** started working with the TRS-80 and Apple IIe in the early 1980s. While earning his electrical engineering degree from Arizona State University, Gary became involved with Novell software as a NetWare 3.11 server administrator for ASU's public television station, KAET 8. After graduating from ASU in 1992, Gary moved to Utah and started working in Novell's technical support division. Over his seven-year career at Novell, Gary has worked in technical support, consulting services, marketing, and engineering. When he's not working, Gary enjoys snow skiing and water skiing.

Preface

When we first thought about writing the previous edition of this book, the idea came from a need to have systems working heterogeneously. Simply put, many IS shops had to integrate two or more systems and have them work as seamlessly as possible. The number of new companies and products currently being made available on the market is not surprising. Many IS managers just want their users to be capable of doing their jobs without becoming computer experts. This job, in and of itself, is quite a task when you have only *one* small system. Imagine how it multiplies when you mix in a totally different system and attempt to get it to work! How much actually gets accomplished is amazing!

When it comes to making two worlds work as one in the networking space, there is so much to discuss. UNIX users and PC networks have been trying to coexist for years with some measure of success, although it *does* take an enormous amount of effort. In the IBM/SAA mainframe space, the same can be said. The promise of dual-management utility that a PC could provide by being used as a PC machine (and all its productivity applications), as well as an entry point to the mainframe, was worth the hassle of maintaining dual IS staffs to maintain two dissimilar back end systems.

Today's systems administrators more than ever want to have a seamless way of tying two or more systems together both for administration and user consumption. The cost of maintaining a system of this complexity becomes prohibitive, especially when technologies change as rapidly as they do today.

This new edition is fully revised for NetWare 5 and features full coverage of LDAP v.3, pure IP, contextless login, NDS for NT 2.0, NDS for Solaris, and much more. In addition, you'll find all the latest information on NDS, including a detailed description of Z.E.N.works in Chapter 10.

What You'll Find in This Book

This book attempts to bring together in one cohesive work as many of the ways to integrate two popular platforms — NetWare and Windows NT (Server and Workstation) — as possible, and to create a seamless (or nearly seamless!) environment in which administrators and users can be productive. The Holy Grail of single login/single administration can finally be approached without having to create special tools or utilities.

Following is a summary of each of the chapters you'll find in this book.

▶ *Chapter 1: Why Integrate?* — In this chapter, we begin by examining today's heterogeneous networks and some of the challenges faced when managing and using these networks. We then discuss how NetWare and Windows NT are commonly implemented and the benefits of integrating two environments, and then we look at what *not* integrating is costing you.

▶ *Chapter 2: The NetWare Operating System* — This chapter provides you with an overview of the NetWare operating system. It provides a foundation to assist you in determining the main differences between NetWare and Windows NT and in learning how best to integrate the two operating systems.

▶ *Chapter 3: NT Server Networking* — In this chapter, we discuss NT Server and how it operates in a normal NT-only system. The information presented in this chapter builds on the foundation presented in the previous chapter, which enables you to understand how to integrate NT services best into a NetWare environment.

▶ *Chapter 4: Addressing Integration in the Heterogeneous System* — In this chapter, we address the typical integration challenges that appear in a mixed network. Our approach is addressing what problems you may be trying to solve — and mapping the possible technologies you can use to solve them.

▶ *Chapter 5: Integrating NT Workstations* — In this chapter, we discuss integrating Windows NT Workstations in a NetWare environment. We cover the NetWare Client for Windows NT in detail. The chapter also covers integrating NT Workstations in a network with both NetWare file servers and Windows NT servers.

▶ *Chapter 6: Synchronizing Network Directories* — This chapter discusses the use of NDS as a Meta-Directory in a mixed NetWare and NT environment and the synchronization products available to provide integration of this environment. Specifically, this product provides detailed information on the installation and use of the Novell Administrator for Windows NT and NetVision's Synchronicity for NT.

▶ *Chapter 7: Integrating with Novell's NDS for NT* — This chapter discusses replacing the native security system inherent to Windows NT with NDS. It covers Novell's NDS for NT product in detail: how it is architected and how it almost completely eliminates all administrative burdens of NT Domains.

▶ *Chapter 8: NDS Cross-Platform* — In this chapter, we discuss the architecture, purpose, and use of NDS on multiple platforms. We discuss the entire NDS cross-platform strategy that allows NDS to run on Windows NT, IBM MVS, IBM AIX, Sun Solaris, Fujitsu, SCO UnixWare, NetWare, and other platforms.

▶ *Chapter 9: Deploying Emulator Services in the Network* — This chapter deals with an emulator approach to providing client functionality and server access. It provides examples of when you may want to deploy emulator services and the network emulation options available to a heterogeneous network. The emulator options covered include Microsoft's File and Print Service for NetWare (FPNW), and Microsoft's Gateway Services for NetWare.

▶ *Chapter 10: Managing NT Workstations through NDS: Z.E.N.works* — This chapter examines the administrative challenges encountered when integrating Windows NT workstations into your Novell network. It focuses on Novell's solution to ease the administrative burden of NT Workstations: Z.E.N.works. We discuss the features, installation, and configuration of Z.E.N.works.

▶ *Chapter 11: Scripting an Integrated Environment* — This chapter details how scripting can be used to automate the access to network resources in an integrated environment. The purpose of this chapter is to provide you with a basic understanding of common problems in an integrated environment and to suggest ways to overcome those problems. In addition, we provide you with examples of real-world scripting solutions.

▸ *Appendix A: NDS versus Domains* — Appendix A takes an objective look at the main differences between NDS and NT Domains. It discusses the differences between a true directory service (per X.500) and a name service, where NDS and NT Domains fit in this classification, and what difference it makes in your network.

▸ *Appendix B: Solutions Guide* — Appendix B provides you with a guide to help you determine which integration products you should implement in your environment and which chapter in the book to refer to for more information on each product.

▸ *Appendix C: Microsoft Active Directory Services* — Appendix C provides a cursory overview of ADS and what it offers to Windows NT. In addition, we briefly discuss possibilities of integration with NetWare networks going forward.

Acknowledgments

As we embarked on our journey to write this edition, we were unaware of the many hours of sacrifice and the blood, sweat, and tears that would be shed before we finally saw a printed copy. We were not alone in our journey, though. This book would not have been possible without the sacrifices and hard work of many other people, some of whom we'd like to thank here.

To Jim Sumser, thank you for talking us into doing this book, and then for being ever-so-patient as we struggled our way through writing it. Thanks for always being nice to J. D. when the pressure was on. And please give us a month or two before you ask us to write another book! Thanks also to Kurt Stephan, Larisa North, Susan Parini, and everyone else at IDG Books Worldwide who helped make this edition possible.

To Marci Shanti at Novell Press, thank you for making this book possible and for continuing to put quality information in the hands of our readers.

And to all the others—editors, illustrators, secretaries, janitors, and FedEx delivery people who either directly or indirectly helped us get this book published—you may not be mentioned by name, but your efforts are truly appreciated. Thank you all.

Contents at a Glance

Why Integrate?

"**W**hy integrate?" This is a question many network administrators have asked in the last year or two. With the evolution of Windows NT Workstation and Windows NT Server, many Information Systems (IS) shops have had to face the challenge of integrating NetWare and Windows NT into a single network. Some may even approach the solution from a single operating system perspective: Throw out or minimize one (NetWare or Windows NT) and make a go of it with just one operating system to maintain. Although this is one solution to the integration task, we don't recommend it as the most economical one.

Although integrating the two isn't an impossible task, many administrators have hesitated to attempt an integration project, partially because there aren't many technical people with a detailed knowledge of both operating systems.

A variety of tools exist to assist in the integration task. The problem is one place doesn't exist where you can look and find all the tools. That's what we'll do for you.

What we'll explore are the many ways to integrate Windows NT and NetWare. The degree of integration varies depending on how much you want to integrate and how much effort you want to expend doing it. Ultimately, integration ends up being a combination of one or more of the technologies we'll describe.

Because integration is the topic of this book, the following are some terms we'll use:

> *Best-of-breed.* When most people go shopping, they usually look for the best product (the most quality) for the money they can spend. In computing systems, this holds true as well. Although you can somewhat guarantee a floor wax will work when you get it home, no guarantee exists that a piece of software will work in your computing system. Ideally, we would all like to buy software/hardware and have a level of assurance it will work in our system. (This is where standards come in.) The ability to buy the best-of-breed available component (such as an accounting or management package) for our computing system is desirable, although no assurance exists it will work when we get it installed into our system!

> *Homogeneous system.* This hearkens back to the days of "Big-Blue" shops (all IBM equipment). In a homogeneous system, one vendor provides the majority of software, hardware, and support. The benefit is one-stop shopping, making

system administration convenient. The downside is the inability to add services from someone other than the vendor you're locked into.

▶ *Heterogeneous system.* This is a system composed of a variety of services from an array of vendors. The benefits include the ability to choose what components are best for the system, meaning the ability to buy from different vendors. The downside is that not nearly as much cooperation exists among these vendors as we all would like. As a result, more effort is necessary to make the multitude of services integrate well.

Many companies like the idea of a mixed (heterogeneous) system while preserving a homogeneous feel. A user's exposure to the system ideally should be a homogeneous one, although the network may be a heterogeneous design.

Heterogeneous Systems Integration

Most networks today are a hodgepodge of dissimilar components, including UNIX, Windows NT Server, Windows NT Workstation, NetWare, OS/2 Warp, LAN Server, and so on. Throw in the mainframe and you really have a mess! Unfortunately, this kind of network (a very heterogeneous one) is typical in today's networking environment.

In an ideal situation, all networks would be homogeneous (one operating system — one vendor). At least, this is what we're led to believe. The visions of the old IBM shop days come to mind. Most IS shops end up choosing a best-of-breed environment in which to run their software because of the diversity allowed by choosing multiple vendors for a complete network solution.

NOTE

When we say IS shop, we're referring to a company's networking operations. Much like the old computing centers at a company have been called an *IBM shop* (a computing infrastructure composed mostly of IBM equipment), *IS shop* is a generic term for a company's computing central.

Components of a Heterogeneous System

All the elements of an integrated dissimilar system usually appear as the network evolves. The main building blocks of the system are not ordinarily a corporate-wide decision, contrary to what most CIOs would like to believe. This is because most IS managers take what is on hand (what has solved or is solving a problem) and attempt to integrate it. One vendor alone usually cannot solve all the information processing needs of a medium- or large-sized company. This is evidenced by what we find in many networks, such as:

▶ *Application servers.* These are operating systems (such as Windows NT, NetWare, and UNIX) that host services over and above basic systems services (such as file, print, and directory services). An application server is the place where a network service may reside.

▶ *Network Operating Systems (NOS).* These operating systems provide the basic services (file, print, and directory services). These may also be providing application server services. The NOS may run on an Intel platform (such as Windows NT and NetWare) or on others (such as Windows NT on the Digital Alpha processor).

▶ *Directory (naming and security) services.* These have traditionally been part of the NOS, but this is changing with the advent of Novell Directory Services being ported to multiple platforms, such as UNIX and Windows NT.

▶ *Client services.* These are the clients required for the NOS or for the application services (such as a SQL client).

▶ *Network applications.* These are the consumers of NOS and Application server services (for example, Microsoft Word or an accounting package using SQL). The network application usually runs on an application server of some sort (Windows NT or NetWare).

Common combinations of these components are evident in IS shops today. Because we are mainly addressing Windows NT and NetWare networking, Table 1.1 shows a few combinations of services you might see.

TABLE I.I *Service Combinations*	COMBINATION	DESCRIPTION
	Primary NOS NetWare/ Microsoft Clients	NetWare as the main file, print, and services solution with NT Workstation as one the desktops of choice along with Windows 95, Windows 3.1, Windows for Workgroups, OS/2, DOS, and so on. NetWare still enjoys a large following. More than 60 percent of the installed network operating systems today are still NetWare.
	Primary NOS NetWare/ Peer services using Microsoft Clients	NetWare and some flavor of workgroup solution using a combination of NT Server and NT Workstation. In this scenario, local resources are shared among users in a peer-to-peer fashion. NetWare provides the centralized file and print service.
	Dual NOS System/ Mixed services and clients	NetWare and NT Server running side by side providing file and print services. NetWare may be providing server-based services (such as IP/IP gateway services, routing, or Border Services) and NT may be providing database (MS-SQL Server), Web server (MS IIS server), or specialized applications (such as SAP or PeopleSoft applications). This configuration also will have a mixture of desktops similar to the previous.

Application Servers

When most people think of Windows NT Server, they usually think in the context of an application server. This means different things to different people. Usually, an application server is some middle area where some business logic is run. In a mainframe environment, this means the mainframe runs all the application logic and users consume all the available bandwidth of the mainframe. Enter a Client/Server environment like the UNIX environment. Under UNIX, the possibility exists of having an application split up between an application server running logic on the back-end (the service) and the other piece running on a client station (the client). This can be a database, an accounting application, or other CPU-intensive application. The shared logic can be placed on a high-performance machine, while the client consumers reside on a variety of workstations. NT or NetWare servers can fulfill this role if the application back-end service is written to run on either platform.

NOTE Many databases have been built around this model. As a result, many of the database services today (such as Oracle, Sybase, and Informix) run on either NetWare or Windows NT, not to mention a host of UNIX versions.

Security and the Network Operating System

Every NOS has some form of security within it. NetWare and Windows NT are no exception. The goal when integrating the two is to make the Windows NT Server and NetWare appear as seamlessly integrated as possible.

When dealing with a heterogeneous system, naming becomes a key challenge when integrating the two. Ideally, when two systems are thrown together, a common naming system between the two would be ideal. This would enable each person to find things a standard way, and then use them. Unfortunately, this hasn't been the case. What we'll show you are some ways to do this (especially with Novell's NDS for NT product—see Chapter 6).

NetWare and Windows NT have some different ideas when it comes to security. This presents another challenge when attempting to integrate the two. This section discusses some of the differences. Chapter 2 delves into the details of NetWare security, and Chapter 3 follows up with Windows NT. This should provide a good understanding of the capability of each operating system. From this understanding, you can begin to see how to make the two fit together.

NT Network Security

Every NT operating system, regardless of whether it is a server or workstation, has a security database called the Security Accounts Manager (SAM), which is the central repository of pertinent user and group information in the NT network. To gain access to the system and to use resources (such as file and print), you must be created in the SAM first (in other words, you must be created as a user in the Windows NT security system— SAM).

When you are created as a user, you get a unique user ID that identifies your account throughout the system. When access is granted, your user object ID is written with the resource showing the operating system that your account can use the resource and to what extent the resource can be used. That concept holds true whether you are using a single server, a workgroup, a Domain, or a Multi-Master Domain Implementation. Chapter 3 discusses the ramifications of each.

NT Domain Model

Windows NT enables an administrator to designate a group of NT Servers and Workstations into a logical entity called a Domain. This Domain has a defined set of users and groups it maintains to allow user authentication and access to resources. Because these Domains typically are arranged by workgroup, they tend to be rather small. To join two or more Domains into a larger workgroup, you must use a feature called trust relationships. Trust relationships allow two Domains to act as one system. If set up properly, a user can be authenticated in one Domain, and then access resources in another. The burden becomes evident when an administrator must find out what trust relationships exist and who trusts whom.

Novell Directory Services (NDS)

Novell Directory Services (NDS) does not have the concept of trust relationships. Instead, all servers are treated as one system, and users can be given rights to any available resource in the system. The trust is inherent when the system is built. A user (or administrator) never sees it and, therefore, those relationships never need to be managed.

What Novell is doing with products such as Novell Administrator for NT and NDS for NT is to provide a way to marry the two systems into one apparent homogeneous system with a heterogeneous mix of products. This is the best of both worlds — a single naming system (NDS) with a range of choices for system components. This also means one security system to deal with for logging in users and managing accounts. We'll discuss the differences in more detail in the following chapters.

NOTE

A significant difference exists between a naming system (such as a Domain or a Bindery) and a directory service. For a detailed comparison, see Appendix B.

Multiple Security Systems Administration

Supporting multiple security architectures complicates things for the administrator because a user must be created under NT Server Domains (covered in significant detail in Chapter 2) as well as Novell's Directory Service (also covered in Chapter 2). The user, in effect, must have a minimum of two logon names to gain access to the network and resources. As long as they are in synch, things work out. When they are not in synch, the user must help reconcile the situation.

Multiple Client Support

One of the biggest issues in a mixed environment is you must use at least two clients to access resources. For example, a system supporting NetWare, NT Server, and a service, such as an Oracle database, would need the clients shown in Table 1.2.

TABLE 1.2	CLIENT	DESCRIPTION
Multiple Client Support	NetWare Access — NetWare Core Protocol (NCP) Client	Novell provides a 32-bit client used to access NDS, as well as file and print services shared on a NetWare server. Microsoft also provides a limited functionality NCP client with Windows 95 and NT.
	NT Server Access — Server Message Block (SMB) Client	This is the native client that comes with NT Server, NT Workstation, and Windows 95. It enables browsing of Domain and Workgroup services (file and print) provided in NT and Windows 95.
	Services Client — such as Oracle Database SQLNet Client	This could be any client that users need to access any services deployed on NetWare or NT. In this case, an Oracle SQL client would be deployed on clients where users need database access. Authentication to the service depends on what security the service has implemented. In the case of Oracle, when running on NetWare, NDS authentication is used. When running on NT Server, Domain (SAM) is used.

NOTE

Not all clients will need access to all services. Some clients may only need NetWare file and print services and Oracle services; others may need only NT file and print services. The type of services the user needs will dictate what clients must be deployed.

If you have roaming users, it may be necessary to deploy all clients to support the needs of the roaming users. Another potential solution might be using Novell's Application Launcher (NAL) technology (now part of Novell's Z.E.N.works product) discussed in Chapter 10.

Benefits of Integration

Most IS departments don't want a purely homogeneous environment. This dates back to the days of IBM domination in most IS shops. The primary drawback to a single-vendor solution is being totally locked into a single vendor's products. Best-of-breed technology is sacrificed in lieu of simplified support.

Integrating the systems allows more freedom when choosing add-ons to the network. Some of the advantages of integrating include:

- ▸ Freedom of a heterogeneous system with a homogeneous feel

- ▸ Taking advantage of services available to the client from a variety of platforms

- ▸ Freedom as to which operating system will host services deployed in the network (Windows NT or NetWare)

- ▸ The ability to choose the best platform (OS) that will host a service (such as file, print, database, and so on)

Heterogeneous Solution/Homogeneous Look and Feel

As we previously noted, an IS manager's dream is to choose any service (such as a new database) and place it into a network without having to worry about integration. Existing users can log in and start to use the new service without any training, and the IS manager can count on the new service automatically integrating with all existing systems.

This means the ability to choose a best-of-breed solution and, once installed, to have it appear homogeneously to users (one login name and password to access it, use of existing client software, and so on). Although we can't promise this in every case, integrating Windows NT and NetWare can provide this capability in many cases (such as with Microsoft BackOffice components).

Leveraging Client/Server Computing

The promise of client/server computing was that a server of choice could be used to place a common service many people use. Consider the example of Lotus Notes: Say we place a Notes server on a Windows NT Server. If we log into NDS, in a nonintegrated system, we must log in to a Windows NT Server as well. And we must know which Windows NT Server hosts the service.

If the system is integrated, when we must use the Notes server, we ask for it (by way of a directory such as NDS), it is found, and we start to use it. Single login to the whole system means we do not have to log in to the server where Notes is hosted. Nor do we need to know where the Notes server resides. The directory can look it up for us.

Freedom of Choice for Platforms

In today's market, a multitude of software/hardware choices exist. Traditionally in the software market, a sound piece of advice is to choose the best software available, and then choose the hardware and operating system that supports the chosen software package. Today, many software packages are designed to run on Windows NT or UNIX, while many services (such as database or Internet services, such as Novell's Border Manager) run best on NetWare.

In a nonintegrated system, many IS managers must choose the best software/hardware that works with what their infrastructure is, not what is the absolute best solution for the company. Having an integrated system enables an IS manager to choose the software first, regardless of the platform.

NOTE
NetWare is notoriously fast for running services because of the thin layer between the operating system and the hardware. Running Java services is no exception. Novell now has a free, downloadable Java Virtual Machine (JVM) for NetWare. This gives the IS administrator a choice of where a Java service should be run — NetWare, UNIX, or NT.

Distributed File and Print

Built into NetWare, Windows for Workgroups, Windows 95/98, NT Workstation, and NT Server is the capability to share disk and printing resources. In the Windows for Workgroups, Windows 95/98, and Windows NT environments, users can share part or all of their hard disks at their discretion. This is an almost impossible thing to manage as an administrator, but it can be a useful function in small groups.

As a network grows larger, the sharing of files and printers becomes a necessary function that must be centralized. When you decide to do this in an all-NT network, an NT Domain becomes necessary. Domains take the concept of sharing resources further by enabling an administrator to design and deploy such services in a centralized way. To understand this, you must understand how NT works and scales. (Chapter 3 discusses NT networking in detail.)

For several years, NetWare has been the fastest platform for file and print services. This translates into a reduced cost of deploying these services in the network. NetWare has not traditionally been the application service platform of choice (such as running an accounting system). With the advent of a Java Virtual Machine for NetWare, this preference may change when administrators are deciding where to run server-side services.

Integrating the two systems enables an administrator to host shared files and printers on NetWare (the fastest place to host it), while hosting application services on Windows NT (one of the most flexible places to run applications). If the administrator chooses, he or she can allow limited support for file and print services on the Windows NT Servers running applications. This choice of where to host file and print (as an example) is transparent to the people using them. One login allows trusted access and the ability to distribute where data is stored.

Challenges of Integrating Heterogeneous Systems

Multiple desktop and network operating systems have been available for some time now. NetWare has been available since 1983. UNIX has been around in different flavors for much longer. Windows NT has been around (if you count LAN Manager) since 1989. So why hasn't integration been easy?

User Management with Multiple Systems

When combining two systems, with two administration models, naturally the issue of user management will occur. This includes user creates, deletions, moves, changing user information, and so on.

Multiple User Account Management

If you have a user who needs resources from both systems, one approach is to create the user using each system's tools in each of the security systems. In the case of an NT/NetWare system, this means using User Manager to create an NT/Domain user and then NWAdmin to create a NetWare user. This also means entering in the same user information twice and keeping the passwords synchronized.

In short, this means doubling the effort of the administrator to maintain two systems (such as NetWare and Windows NT).

NOTE

Novell deployed NDS internally circa 1990. Before then, Novell had a "user virus" problem. When a new employee (such as Kyle) joined Novell, he was placed on two or more servers. The longer Kyle stayed, the more servers he was created on. If Kyle left the company, half the struggle would be to find his user account on all the existing systems and ensure the account was deleted for security purposes. Such a problem is symptomatic of Domain- or Bindery-based systems. In a true Directory, the user exists in only one place. Therefore, user creation/deletion is trivial.

Pseudo-Single Login

Fortunately, clients provided by Novell and Microsoft allow for a pseudo-single login. The client will attempt to authenticate a user to each client (NetWare and NT LAN Manager) if the user requests access. Two logins actually happen, but it appears to the user as if only one login occurred. This is because the user only had to provide one login name and password to the client operating system.

For example, say user SallyS logs in to the workstation first thing in the morning. Her username and password is kept locally after she enters it. When SallyS logged in, her login script attached her to the NetWare server VECTOR. She then browses the Network Neighborhood and sees server SABRE (an NT Server).

When SallyS double-clicks the SABRE icon, she will be authenticated to the SABRE server via a background process. This will only occur seamlessly if her username and password is the same on both systems. If it is not, SallyS will be denied access and she must supply a valid username/password pair to login. This also assumes SallyS has both NetWare and NT LAN Manager clients installed on her workstation.

This presents a challenge to the administrator. If the client name/passwords are not exactly the same on both systems (NetWare and Windows NT) pseudo-single login will not happen. The client OS asking for a second username and password will confuse the user.

Maintaining Multiple Users

When a user is deleted, care must be taken to ensure the user no longer needs access to either system. For example, if user Gary needs access to sales information on the NT Server, but no longer needs access to the SYS: volume on a NetWare server, an administrator may unwittingly delete the Gary account from both systems. Without a central place to store this information, a user's object may be potentially erased, even though the user still needed it.

Login Scripts and Application Launching

When a user logs in, he or she usually has a script that runs and sets the user environment properly. Which system's scripts should run? Especially when resources must be mapped for the user to both systems. In addition, perhaps some applications need to be run during login (such as desktop inventory software). Where should they be stored?

Access to Existing Services

Most users don't care where or how the service is provided, as long as it works when it should. Most people would love to get their job done and not worry where the application or data is coming from. This is the administrator's job. Ideally, once the system has been set up, there should be a minimum level of intervention from the administrator for users to consume services. If a person uses a service and doesn't know where it came from, one of the design goals for the system will have been met.

Security Integration

With two or more systems comes the dilemma of security. What if one system has stronger security than the other? What if one system has different naming? When the user names and passwords are matched between the two, if a breach occurs on one, the other is also compromised. This is of critical importance to consider when implementing a C2-Security class system. If one or both have not been C2 evaluated, then no guarantee exists, other than from the vendor, that each system is network secure.

As solutions evolve, the impact of security will be minimized as more systems converge on common, reliable security systems. This may be accomplished using Certificates (RSA or Kerberos) or some other shared asymmetrical security system.

Cost of Dual System Administration

Many companies may employ a multiple system strategy today to get the best-of-breed environment. This may require (especially in larger enterprises) employing two complete IS staffs to administer the network of services. This also means the expense of keeping both staffs current on the latest technologies and patches for each of the different systems.

In addition, supporting two naming systems (such as Windows NT Domains and NDS) may require additional hardware in order to host the name databases. Since the naming function would be redundant in this type of scenario, an additional server may be needed to host primary and backup copies of the name database.

NOTE

This may be the case when Windows NT is involved. Each copy of the Domain name database must be kept on a separate server. See Chapter 3 for a detailed description of the Domain architecture.

For many smaller companies (and some larger ones), this is far too costly. The benefit of integrating two or more systems into one is an idea with significant appeal.

The Cost of Not Integrating

As is the case in the networking and computing industry, new products and services evolve at a rapid pace. Because of this, businesses are constantly looking for better ways to streamline the business process and to get a better return on the computing infrastructure.

Part of the success of NT has highlighted the need for integrated solutions. Most people concede that NetWare has the fastest file services whether native or exported (such as NFS support on top of NetWare). NDS is by far the best X.500-based directory available today. NT allows a stable platform for deploying services (such as SQL Servers). To maximize the return when using best-of-breed applications and services, integration must first be possible. As mentioned previously, getting the best return on investment may require the need for two IS support staffs. Indeed, several companies have gone this route to accomplish the integration objective.

Unless vendors of best-of-breed solutions work together to solve administration issues, however, this option will most likely be relegated to companies with large IS budgets. As integration tools emerge (such as the ones discussed here), smaller IS departments will be able to take advantage of a truly mixed environment, as well.

Summary

In this chapter we have explored the many ways to integrate Windows NT and NetWare. We have discussed the reasons you may want to consider integration, the benefits to integration, and the challenges faced when attempting to integrate these systems. We have also looked at the consequences of not integrating, which boils down to the need to employ two complete IS staffs to administer the combined network. This is a costly and unnecessary solution.

Now that we have some reasons for integrating, let's look more closely at each operating system to understand better how the two could be integrated and where it makes sense.

CHAPTER 2

The NetWare Operating System

Novell has long provided the industry with some of the most comprehensive networking solutions available. In fact, until Microsoft's release of Windows NT Server, NetWare was practically the only game in town.

This chapter provides an overview of the NetWare operating system — beginning with a quick look at how NetWare has evolved over the years, and then moving on to NetWare today.

The information presented in this chapter provides a foundation to assist you in determining the main differences between NetWare and Windows NT and in integrating the two operating systems best. This chapter focuses on NetWare; Chapter 3 discusses Windows NT.

The majority of this book addresses NetWare 5 — Novell's most current release of the NetWare operating system.

The Evolution of NetWare

Since the earliest versions of NetWare, Novell's main product objective was to enable organizations to share resources. The early 1980s marked the first releases of NetWare. If you've been in the industry a while, you may even remember NetWare packaged in blue and gray boxes — S-Net and 68b. These two products provided basic file and print sharing, which, at the time, were revolutionary. However, not only did Novell offer these products as software solutions, the company also manufactured the server boxes that were required as part of the network.

NetWare 2

Novell didn't take long to drop the hardware aspect of the solution after it recognized customers needed freedom of choice in hardware. The first 2.*x* versions of NetWare enabled customers to use any PC that met the hardware requirements as their file server. These early 2.*x* releases did, however, require the installation of a serialized "key card" in the server. These key cards were later replaced by software serialization which, over time, evolved to the software licensing found in NetWare today.

With each release of NetWare, more functionality beyond basic file and print sharing was added. The 2.1x versions of NetWare introduced Value Added Processes (VAPs), which could be linked in with the operating system to add additional functionality (such as an external print server or Macintosh support). Support for the Macintosh and flexible (at the time) printing services were two other key features added in NetWare 2.1x.

NetWare 3

In the late 1980s, Novell completely "re-architeched" NetWare and introduced a modular operating system they called NetWare 3. This again revolutionized the industry, moving away from the NetWare 2.x operating system architecture that required all components (such as LAN and disk drivers, printing, and other services) to be hard-coded into the operating system file. Instead, NetWare 3 used NetWare Loadable Modules (NLMs), software modules that load into a generic operating system file (SERVER.EXE). In this way, LAN drivers, disk drivers, printing, and other services can be added to a system on the fly, by simply loading or unloading the NLM at the file server.

NetWare 3 also provided increased client support. With this release, Novell introduced the Open Data-Link Interface (ODI) — an interface that, through the use of multiple frame types, enables a single network adapter to support multiple protocols. This allows for support of not only Internet Packet Exchange/Sequenced Packet Exchange (IPX/SPX), but also Transmission Control Protocol/Internet Protocol (TCP/IP), AppleTalk, and other protocols on a single wire. Before ODI, each protocol required a separate physical network. So, to support the Macintosh in a NetWare 2 environment, the file server required a network adapter for the DOS (IPX) clients and a second adapter for the Macintosh (AppleTalk) clients.

Providing further client support, NetWare 3 also introduced multiple name space support, which enabled NetWare to store natively not only DOS files on server volumes, but also Macintosh, Network File System (NFS), and OS/2 files in their native formats.

The NetWare 3 reign lasted through the late 1980s and well into the 1990s. The product still has a tremendously large installed base today.

NetWare 4 and IntranetWare

The year 1992 marked the next major release of NetWare — NetWare 4 featuring Novell Directory Services (NDS). Once again, Novell revolutionized the industry by providing an operating system that could truly support enterprise networking. With NDS, networks shifted from server-centric to global entities. Instead of users logging in to a specific file server as in earlier versions of NetWare, with NDS they log in to the entire network with a single login. This provides the global access to the network resources the users need from wherever they are, without having to maintain multiple login IDs and passwords. From the administrator's perspective, NDS enables management of the entire network from a single location. NDS is discussed in greater depth later in this chapter.

In 1996, Novell repackaged NetWare 4 to mold it into the Internet/Intranet paradigm. In doing so, they created a brand-new product — IntranetWare. Intranet-Ware was simply NetWare 4.11 with the addition of a Web server, an IPX to IP gateway, a multiprotocol router for WAN connections, and a few other features that enable organizations to set up internal or external World Wide Web (WWW) sites.

NetWare Today

NetWare has come a long way from the early days of basic file and print sharing. Novell's latest offering, NetWare 5, builds on the NetWare history by including pure TCP/IP support, desktop management, the Netscape FastTrack server for NetWare, and Oracle 8. Today, NetWare 5 provides a comprehensive network solution, delivering robust file, print, directory, security, management, messaging, and Web services. However, NetWare is no longer the only game in town. Other companies, primarily Microsoft, have delivered networking solutions that rival NetWare. Since its release, Microsoft's NT Server has gained significant mind share, as well as market share.

But NetWare does have three characteristics that set it aside from all other network offerings on the market. Those characteristics are:

- ▸ Novell Directory Services (NDS)

- ▸ NetWare file system

- ▸ A design that meets C2 (Red Book) government security specifications

The remainder of this chapter discusses each of these characteristics and identifies the areas unique to NetWare.

Novell Directory Services (NDS)

Novell Directory Services is a key component of NetWare that makes it easy to access, use, and manage network resources. By integrating your NT networks with NetWare, these benefits extend across both platforms. We'll tell you how this is so, as we discuss NDS in greater depth in this section.

What Is NDS?

For the sake of those who may be unfamiliar with NDS, here's a quick overview. We'll cover these concepts in greater depth later in this chapter.

NDS is a network resource database that maintains information about every resource on the network — including users, groups, printers, volumes, applications, fax servers, computers, and nearly any other device attached to the network. This information is stored in a single, logical database that provides users with a global view of all network services and resources. In an NDS environment, users log in to a multiserver network and view it as a single system, instead of as a collection of individual servers. This provides users with access to network services and resources through a single login, regardless of the user's location or the location of the resources.

To help you understand NDS and other concepts in this book better, we will provide examples using a fictitious company called Scuba Divers Unlimited (SDU). SDU is a chain of dive stores located in prime diving destinations throughout the United States and the Caribbean. SDU has stores in San Diego, Catalina Island, Maui, and Curacao. Each store is a retail establishment, as well as a training and dive guide facility.

Figure 2.1 shows an example of the NDS tree for SDU. When SDU users log in, they do not log in to a specific file server (as they would with NetWare 2.x or NetWare 3.x). Instead, they log in to the NDS tree shown in this figure. The users can then access any resource to which they have rights, regardless of where the resources are located.

FIGURE 2.1

NDS provides a single, global view of the entire network. This provides users with access to all network resources and services through a single login from anywhere on the network. It also provides administrators with a central point of administration.

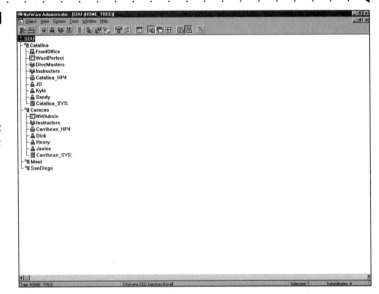

Here's an example of how NDS simplifies access to network resources. Referring to Figure 2.1, assume that user Kyle in Catalina needs to send a document to user Dick in Curacao. Rather than sending it by traditional means (such as by mail or fax), Kyle simply selects the printer in Curacao (Carribean_HP4) and prints the document directly to it. No additional login or password is required.

NDS also provides administrators with significant time-saving benefits. First and foremost, NDS eliminates the redundant administration typical in multiserver environments.

In the previous example, Kyle selected the Caribbean printer in his application and the print job was sent off to Curacao. Because NDS users are global, no additional login or password was required. NDS simply performed a background security check to ensure Kyle had rights to the printer at the time it was selected.

In a non-NDS environment, the administrator would have been required to set up a user account for Kyle on the server in Curacao for him to access the resources there. Without NDS, if a user needs access to resources on five different file servers, the administrator must create an account for that user on each file server. Or, in the case of NT Server, a trust relationship must be established (this is described in greater detail in Chapter 3).

The previous example demonstrates how NDS eliminates this redundant administration by requiring only one user account per user for the entire network. This is a key factor in integrating your Windows NT networks with NetWare. The single point of access and single point of administration provided with NDS can be extended to Windows NT environments, as well as to other platforms.

NDS is the enabling technology that allows this integration. Table 2.1 gives a brief description of the NDS-based utilities provided by Novell that tie your Windows NT and NetWare environments together. Each of these is covered in greater detail later in the book.

TABLE 2.1

Integration Utilities
Enabled by NDS

AREA OF INTEGRATION	UTILITY	DESCRIPTION
Network Application Management	Z.E.N.works	Works with NDS to simplify administration of network applications by allowing the administrator to manage and deploy network applications centrally to user workstations across the network. (See Chapter 10 for details.)
Administering Windows NT Server Domains or NT Workgroups	Novell's NDS for NT	Provides NDS synchronization with NT Server Domains or NT Workgroups. This enables administrators to manage users and groups of these environments centrally through the NDS administration utility NWAdmin. (See Chapter 6 for details.)
Administration of NT Workstations	Z.E.N.works	A component of the NetWare Client for Windows NT allows the NT Workstation's local SAM and user policies and profiles to be managed through NDS. This eliminates the need to deploy NT Server Domains. (See Chapter 8 for details.)

The previous table and examples give you a brief overview of NDS and the role it plays in the integration process. To understand how NDS provides a platform for integration of dissimilar systems, the structure and underlying architecture of NDS must be discussed. These concepts are summarized, and covered in greater depth, in the sections that follow.

▸ Hierarchical Directory Tree. The NDS database is composed of objects organized in a hierarchical fashion to form a Directory tree. This hierarchy provides a method of organization of network resources that makes them easy to locate, use, and manage. The Directory tree provides users with a single global view of the entire network.

▸ Distributed Replicated Database. The NDS database is a distributed database, which means it is broken into manageable pieces called partitions. These partitions are stored on various file servers across the network to provide optimal performance and fault tolerance. NDS partitions can also be replicated (copied) on to multiple file servers to enhance performance and fault tolerance further.

The NDS Directory Tree

The most common analogy used to describe NDS is one of a telephone book or a building directory. As with looking for information in a telephone book or building directory, users locate resources in NDS by browsing or searching for the resource by resource type, name, or location. To make finding services or resources on the network easy, NDS presents these resources in a hierarchical structure.

This hierarchical structure is referred to as a Directory tree. Generally, an organization arranges its Directory tree according to the way people access and use company resources. In this way, NDS acts as a repository of information based upon the specific needs of the organization.

Objects and Properties

Network resources are represented in the NDS Directory tree as objects. Each NDS object has a set of associated attributes called properties. The two main types of objects defined in NDS are as follows:

▸ Leaf objects. These objects generally represent the actual network resources. Examples of leaf objects include Users, Groups, Printers, File Servers, Network Applications, and so on.

▸ Container objects. These objects can contain other objects in the Directory tree and are used to organize network resources in a hierarchical fashion. Container objects can contain leaf objects and other container objects. Examples include Country, Locality, Organization, and Organizational Unit.

One additional object, called [Root], is located at the topmost part of the tree and is identified by the icon. Its purpose is to allow trustee assignments that grant rights to the entire Directory tree.

Container and leaf objects create the hierarchical Directory tree. Containers are used to create the "branches" of the tree, while the leaf objects represent the network resources. This is shown in Figure 2.2.

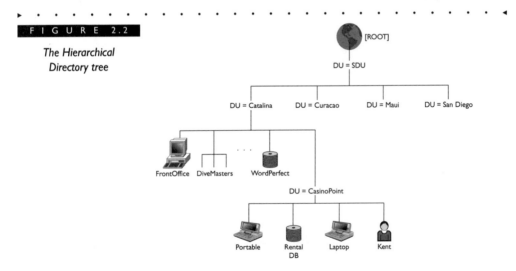

FIGURE 2.2

The Hierarchical Directory tree

Figure 2.3 shows the view of an NDS tree from the administration utility NWAdmin.

Referring once again to the Directory tree of SDU, Figure 2.3 shows the two main types of NDS objects. The container objects in this tree can be identified by the directory icon that precedes each container's name. The container objects shown in this tree are SDU (an Organization object), and Catalina, CasinoPoint, Curacao, Maui, and SanDiego (Organizational Units). All other objects shown in this tree are leaf objects. Because leaf objects represent resources on the network, their icons vary, but they generally depict the type of resource. For example, the icon for a printer object depicts a printer.

Notice the hierarchy of the tree shown in Figure 2.3. At the top of the Directory tree is the Organization object SDU, which represents the company's name, Scuba Divers Unlimited. SDU contains all the Organizational Units that represent the various cities where Scuba Divers Unlimited is located. Note the Organizational Unit (CasinoPoint) under the Catalina container. The tree in this illustration provides a visual overview of the rules of NDS object containment. These rules are detailed in Table 2.2.

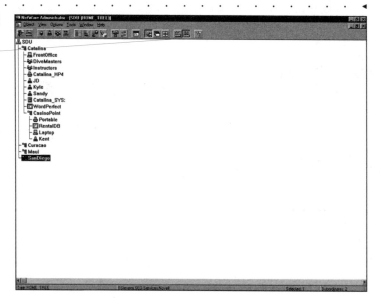

FIGURE 2.3

Resources in the NDS tree are referred to as objects. The two types of NDS objects are leaf objects (which typically represent network resources) and container objects (which are used to organize the Directory tree). This figure shows the hierarchical nature of NDS.

NOTE

The containment rules shown in Table 2.2 refer to the NDS default. They do not take into consideration extensions to the NDS Schema. The NDS Schema is discussed later in this chapter.

TABLE 2.2	OBJECT	CONTAINMENT RULES
NDS Object Containment Rules	[Root]	Can contain Country, Organization, and Alias objects.
	Country	Can contain Organization, Application, and Alias objects.
	Organization	Can contain Organizational Unit and leaf objects.
	Organizational Unit	Can contain other Organizational Units and leaf objects.
	Leaf object	Cannot contain any other objects.

The numbers and types of objects in an NDS tree will vary depending on how the tree is structured and the various network resources represented in the tree. NetWare 4.1x and NetWare 5 include a set of base NDS objects that addresses the basic needs of most networks. These objects are listed in Table 2.3.

TABLE 2.3	CONTAINER OBJECTS	LEAF OBJECTS
Base NDS Objects	Country	AFP Server
	Organization	Alias
	Organizational Unit	Computer
	Directory Map	
	Group	
	NetWare Server	
	Organizational Role	
	Print Queue	
	Print Server	
	Printer	
	Profile	
	Template	
	User	
	Volume	

Table 2.3 lists the basic objects included with NDS. The names of these objects generally provide a description of the use of each object type. For example, the User object is used to create network users, the Printer object is used for network printers, and so on.

NDS is extensible, which means additional object types can be added to NDS to represent various network applications or services. For example, Novell's NT integration solutions add objects to the NDS database that enable management of the integrated environment.

Adding new object types to NDS is described in greater detail later in this chapter.

Properties   As mentioned previously, every object has a set of attributes associated with it, which define the characteristics of that object. Each object type has a set of properties defined by the NDS Schema. We'll discuss the Schema in greater detail later but, for now, let's look at the properties of a User object. We are highlighting the User object in this example because it is the most basic type of NDS object and it will exist in every environment. User objects are created in an NDS tree to represent network users. Remember, each object type (User, Printer, File Server, and so on) has a unique set of properties, and the types of objects in a Directory tree will vary based on the needs of each network.

Figure 2.4 shows the property of a user object as viewed with NWAdmin, the NDS management utility.

As you examine Figure 2.4, notice the buttons on the right-hand portion of the screen. Each of these buttons represents pages of properties of the User object. By selecting a button, you can move into that page and change data contained in the properties there. The data contained in an object's properties are referred to as values.

Generally, the following are the three types of properties:

- ▸ Optional properties. Properties that do not require data, such as the Other Name property shown in Figure 2.4.

- ▸ Mandatory properties. Properties that must have data in them. An example of a mandatory property is the Last Name property shown in Figure 2.4. Although the figure shows no indication this is a mandatory property, a User object cannot be saved if no data has been entered in the Last Name property.

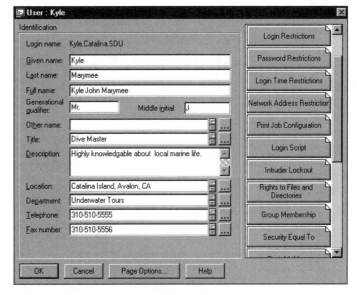

FIGURE 2.4

Each NDS object has a set of attributes (known as properties) associated with it. A partial list of the properties of a User object is shown on the right side of the screen. They include Login Restrictions, Password Restrictions, Login Time Restrictions, and so on.

▶ *Multivalue properties.* Properties that can contain more than one entry. In Figure 2.4, multivalue properties are identified by the drop-down buttons that follow them. For example, the Telephone property is a multivalue property, enabling more than one telephone number to be entered for a user.

Object Naming Each object in the NDS tree is required to have a unique complete name. The complete name of an object is comprised of its name, or Relative Distinguished Name (RDN), plus its location in the hierarchy of the Directory tree. NDS objects are named from the least significant object to the most-significant object in the hierarchy. To understand this better, refer to Figure 2.5.

In Figure 2.5, the full name of the printer Hawaii_HP4 is as follows:

```
HAWAII_HP4.MAUI.SDU
```

The naming convention used in this example is referred to as typeless naming. This type of naming does not use object name attributes to define the object types. The following are the common NDS name attributes used in object naming:

C   Country

O   Organization

OU   Organizational Unit

CN   Common Name (used to identify leaf objects)

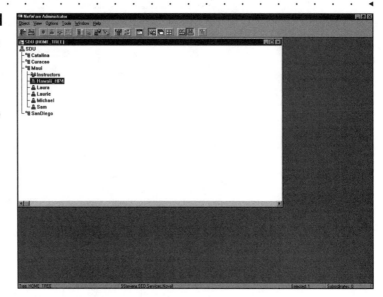

An object's full name in the Directory tree is a combination of its name and location in the NDS tree. Objects are named from the bottom of the tree up. The full name of the printer object in Maui is Hawaii_HP4.Maui.SDU.

Using these object name attributes to name objects utilizes the NDS naming convention known as *typeful naming*. To name an object using typeful naming, precede each object name with the appropriate object attribute using an equal (=) sign to separate the attribute and value. This is shown in the following example of typeful naming.

```
.CN=HAWAII_HP4.OU=MAUI.O=SDU
```

In most cases, typeless naming can be used when referring to an object but, in a few instances (in certain NetWare utilities, for example), you may be required to use typeful naming.

Flexible Object Management   NDS is flexible when it comes to object management. Objects can be easily modified with a simple point-and-click or drag-and-drop. In Figure 2.5, for example, the user Michael in Maui is transferred to the Catalina store. In a non-NDS environment, this would create a somewhat large administration task. The user would have to be deleted from one location and completely re-created (including login scripts, trustee assignments, and any other properties) in another. With NDS, the task is accomplished simply by clicking the user in the Maui container, and then dragging-and-dropping the object to its new location in Catalina. (This method also works with moving groups of objects.) When an object is moved in NDS, all its associated attributes are moved as well (login scripts, trustee assignments, and so on). This is a significant time-saving feature of NDS that is unavailable with other network operating systems.

The NDS Schema

The NDS Schema determines the type of objects that can be stored in NDS. The Schema is a rules system that regulates the structure of the NDS database. It determines what objects are defined, what attributes can be associated with objects, what properties each object inherits, and what position objects occupy in the Directory tree.

The best part about this system is that the NDS Schema is completely extensible. What this means is the base Schema supplied with NetWare can be modified to customize NDS to fit your organization's specific needs. For example, if you want to store personal information about employees in NDS (such as social security numbers or spouse names), you can do this by modifying the attributes (or properties) of the NDS User object.

Another example of how extending NDS can be beneficial is in integrating new services into NDS. Software developers or independent software vendors (ISVs) can modify the Schema to add new object types to NDS to support their applications or services. By doing so, the service or application becomes a part of the NDS tree and receives all the benefits of NDS — single point of access, single point of administration, security, and so on.

In addition, applications can use the NDS database instead of having to maintain a separate user/authentication database. This not only saves software developers time in writing their applications, it also saves the administrator time because he or she is not required to administer multiple databases. A prime example of this is a messaging service. This service could either use the NDS database as its messaging database or it could synchronize with NDS. Either way, the administrator would only be maintaining one database.

The ability to extend the NDS Schema is significant to integrating Windows NT into your NetWare networks. It allows NDS to be the central repository of all company information and resources, regardless of device type or platform on which the device is running. To most administrators, especially those who manage more than one platform, this translates to total network nirvana — a single login and a single point of administration for not only NetWare environments, but also for every platform on your network.

Distributed, Replicated Database

Now that you understand what makes up the NDS database and its structure, let's talk about its design.

NDS is a distributed, replicated database, which was designed this way to provide fault-tolerant login and administration from anywhere on the network. What this means is, even though the NDS network is global, a downed file server or wide area network (WAN) link won't affect the operations of the remainder of the network.

NDS accomplishes this through the following features:

▸ Partitioning

▸ Replication

▸ Synchronization

Partitioning

The NDS Directory tree can be divided into manageable pieces called partitions. Partitions are created at the Organizational Unit level and can include any subordinate Organizational Units. However, a partition cannot include more than one Organizational Unit at the same level.

NDS partitions are stored on multiple file servers across the network, thus providing fault tolerance by eliminating a single point of failure. For example, if the entire NDS database was stored on a single file server and that server went down, no one could access the network or its resources — even if other servers were still up. By partitioning the NDS database and storing it across multiple file servers, this single point of failure is eliminated. If one server goes down, access to the network is still possible through the other servers that stored NDS partitions.

Figure 2.6 shows an example of NDS partitioning.

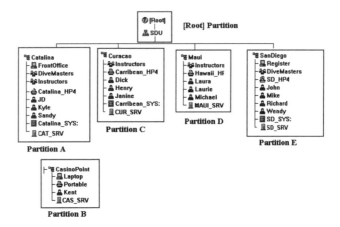

FIGURE 2.6

The NDS database is divided into manageable pieces, called partitions. These partitions are stored on file servers across the network to provide fault tolerance and to eliminate a single point of failure.

In the example in Figure 2.5, the NDS tree for SDU is partitioned based on workgroup boundaries. Each branch of the Directory tree that represents an SDU location is partitioned and stored on a server in that location. For example, Partition E shown in Figure 2.6 contains all the resources typically used by the users in the San Diego store. The partition is physically stored on the San Diego server, SD_SRV.

Partitioning the NDS database as described previously and storing those partitions on servers close to the users who use the resources speeds access to network resources. When a user in San Diego makes a request to use the SD_HP4 printer, the local server services the request. Again, from the fault-tolerance perspective, if the WAN link that connects the San Diego site to the rest of the network goes down, users still have access to their local resources.

Flexible Partition Management   As with managing NDS objects, NDS is flexible when it comes to managing partitions. NDS allows a company's Directory tree to change as the organization changes. So, if the Casino Point store in Catalina is closed, its partition (Partition B in Figure 2.6) can simply be merged into the parent partition (Partition A). Or, if the store was moved to San Diego, the entire subtree can be moved to that location in the tree.

NDS also allows the merging of two separate Directory trees into one. If SDU buys out a competitor (who happens to have NetWare and NDS installed), the two trees could easily be merged. This would eliminate the need to create all the new users and resources of the new store in the SDU tree.

Replication

NDS adds additional fault tolerance through replication of NDS partitions. Replication is simply the process of making one or more copies of a given partition and storing them on different file servers across the network. By replicating the NDS database, if a file server containing a copy of an NDS partition is down or, for some reason, is unavailable, users can still gain access to the resources in that branch of the tree through a replica stored on another server elsewhere.

NetWare file servers can store multiple replicas, but each individual server can store only one replica of any given partition. To store an NDS replica, a file server must be installed in the NDS tree where the replica is created. In addition, file servers cannot be installed in more than one tree and, therefore, can only store NDS replicas of a single tree. A new replica can be copied to a server at any time, and does not require the server to be taken down or re-installed. This flexibility is unique to NDS.

NDS partition and replica management is performed through the NDS Manager Utility, as shown in Figure 2.7.

The following are the three main types of NDS replicas:

▶ Master

▶ Read/Write

▶ Read-Only

Master Replicas   For every NDS partition, one replica of the partition is designated as the Master replica. Each partition has only one Master; all others are either Read/Write or Read-Only. Master replicas are writable copies of the database, which means they can be used for authentication to the network, as well as for the creating, modifying, and deleting of objects. Master replicas are the only replicas that can be used in partition operations (such as partition moves, merges, or splits). Because the Master replica is used as a locking or semaphore mechanism for replica operations, the Master replica must be available before partitioning operations are started.

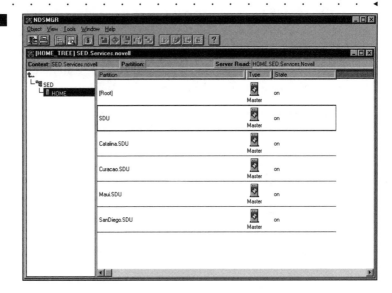

FIGURE 2.7

Management of NDS partitions and replicas is done through the NDS Manager Utility.

Read/Write Replicas   Read/Write replicas are similar in nature to Master replicas. They are writable, can be used for authentication to the network, and objects can be created, modified, and deleted using a Read/Write replica. The two main differences between Master replicas and Read/Write replicas are:

▶ Multiple Read/Write replicas can exist (whereas only one Master can exist).

▶ Read/Write replicas cannot be used for partition operations (such as partition moves, splits, or joins).

With the exception of performing partition operations, all writable partitions (Masters and Read/Writes) are created equal. If one writable copy of a partition is down or not immediately available when a request for login or a change to NDS information is made, another writable replica will automatically take over in its place—no administrator intervention is required. This is another capability unique to NDS.

In addition to fault tolerance, the capability to make changes to any NDS partition provides location brokering by allowing administration of, and access to, resources from a local replica. In the case of SDU, if administration of the San Diego container is done at the Catalina site, a Read/Write replica of the San Diego partition should be stored on the server in Catalina. In addition, if the San Diego users frequently work at the Catalina store, when they log in to the network from that location, they are authenticated through the local Read/Write replica. If the Read/Write replica of San Diego did not exist in Catalina, authentication of those users would have to take place across the WAN link.

Read-Only Replicas   As their name implies, these replicas are read-only. Users cannot use Read-Only replicas to authenticate to the network, nor can users make changes to the network through Read-Only replicas. This is because both of these activities update the NDS database. Updates to the NDS database must be done through a writable replica.

Changing Replica Types   The replica type of any Read-Only, Read/Write, or Master replica can be changed with the simple click of a button in the NDS Manager utility. For example, assume the server containing the Master replica of a partition was being taken down for maintenance purposes. A Read/Write or Read-Only instance of that partition can be upgraded to Master status, on the fly, with the simple click of a button.

Synchronization

To ensure all replicas of a particular partition are current, NDS automatically synchronizes any changes made to a replica. As mentioned previously, updates can be made to any Read/Write or Master replica. To ensure replicas of a given partition are consistent — at a predetermined interval — all the servers holding copies of the same partition communicate with each other to determine who holds the latest information for each object. This is done based on time stamps, which record information about when and where an object was modified. Using these time stamps, the servers replace the old information with the new.

NDS Utilities

One of the compelling features of NDS is that few utilities are required to administer it. In fact, all daily administration of NDS can be done through a single utility — NWAdmin. NWAdmin supports a snap-in technology that enables other applications and services to add functionality to it. For example, a fax server could not only extend the NDS Schema to integrate its services with NDS, it could also add options to administer the fax server entirely through NWAdmin. NWAdmin provides a single utility for just about everything you need to do on the network.

In addition to the NDS administration utilities, Novell also provides tools for repair and maintenance of the NDS database. These include NDS Manager, DS TRACE, and DS Repair.

Table 2.4 summarizes the available NDS utilities.

TABLE 2.4 *NDS Administration Utilities*	UTILITY	DESCRIPTION
	NWAdmin	A Windows-based utility that enables administration of the entire NDS database (including network users, security, file services, printing, and other network devices) and services that use the snap-in architecture.
	NDS Manager	A Windows-based utility that enables administration of NDS partitioning and replication services, provides NDS diagnostics and repair features, and provides NDS version-update capability. This utility snaps in NWAdmin and can be accessed from the Tools option of the NWAdmin menu bar.
	DS Migrate	A Windows utility that enables administrators to model NetWare 2 and 3 bindery information and migrate it across-the-wire to NDS. This utility snaps in to NWAdmin and can be accessed from the Tools option of the NWAdmin menu bar.
	DS Repair	A file server console utility that enables the repair of inconsistencies in the NDS database.
	DS Trace	A file server SET command that provides NDS statistics for troubleshooting and diagnostics.

NetWare File System

NetWare has always been an exceptionally fast platform for running network services. This is because little exists between the operating system and the hardware (for example, no graphical interface). This design makes NetWare's file system the fastest available.

In addition, the file system includes a number of features that make it versatile in all types of environments. These features include:

- Optimal use of disk space

- Multiple name space support

- Robust file system security

Optimal Utilization of Disk Space

The NetWare file system provides features that enable you to minimize file server hardware costs by ensuring optimal use of file server hard disk space. These features include:

- File compression

- Disk block suballocation

- Data migration

File Compression

File compression is a feature of NetWare that allows the compression of files stored on file server volumes. Enabling file compression on server volumes can provide as much as a 50 percent to 60 percent increase in available disk space.

When file compression is enabled, files that have been unused for a specified period are compressed automatically. Compressed files are automatically decompressed when the files are accessed. Compression and decompression take place transparently to the user. In addition, the entire process runs as a background task and does not affect file server performance.

Disk Block Suballocation

Disk block suballocation is another file system feature that saves significant hard disk space. Disk block suballocation does this by subdividing volume blocks into 512 byte units, thereby eliminating the possibility of wasting disk space in partially used disk blocks.

Without disk block suballocation, when a file stored on a server volume is smaller than the disk block size, the entire disk block will be allocated for that file. For example, if the disk block size of a volume is 4K and a file 1K in size is saved, the entire 4K will be allocated for that file. This results in 3K of wasted disk space. With suballocation enabled, the remaining 3K of disk space is suballocated into 512-byte segments, which can then be used for storing other files.

Organizations that have upgraded to NetWare 4 or NetWare 5 from previous versions of NetWare have realized up to a 50 percent savings in disk space through this feature alone.

Data Migration

NetWare also includes a data-migration feature that enables the automatic migration of infrequently used data to inexpensive storage devices. This frees the primary disk space for commonly used files. Any file that has been migrated still appears to the users as part of the file system directory structure. When a user accesses a migrated file, the system automatically de-migrates the file from the secondary storage device.

Multiple Name Space Support

Traditionally, NetWare volumes were designed to support only the DOS filename convention (that is, filenames with the 8.3, or an eight-character filename with a three-character extension). Early on, Novell recognized the need to store non-DOS files on NetWare volumes and released the original name space support modules with NetWare 3.*x*. These modules provided support for Macintosh, OS/2, and NFS (UNIX) files on NetWare volumes.

Today, more and more operating systems have evolved beyond the 8.3 naming conventions of DOS, including Windows 95 and Windows NT. To offer support for the extended name spaces of these environments, NetWare provides the following name space support modules:

▶ LONG.NAM. Provides support for OS/2, Windows 95, Windows 98, and Windows NT files.

▶ MAC.NAM. Provides support for Macintosh files.

▶ NFS.NAM. Provides support for NFS files.

To add long-name, Macintosh, or NFS file support to your volumes, you must manually add name space support for those file systems to your volumes. This is accomplished by loading the appropriate name space NLM (LONG.NAM, MAC.NAM or NFS.NAM), and using the ADD NAME SPACE console command to configure the volumes to support the filenames.

NOTE

You only need to use the ADD NAME SPACE command once to add a name space to a volume. However, name space support modules must be loaded each time the file server comes up. This is generally automated through the AUTOEXEC.NCF file.

When adding name space support to a volume, understanding how the operating system keeps track of the various file types is important. NetWare uses directory entries to keep track of basic information about files and directories stored on server volumes. This includes the file or directory name, the owner, the date and time of the last update, and the location of the first block of data on the hard disk. Directory entries are stored in the Directory Entry Table (DET) of each volume.

Distinguishing file system directory entries from NDS is also important. Although the term directory is used in both, the directory entries in the DET are part of the file system, not NDS. The DET does, however, provide a link between the NDS directory and the file system by storing information about both.

When name space support is added to a volume, another entry is created in the Directory table for the directory and file-naming conventions of that name space. For example, if you add Macintosh name space to a volume, every file will have two directory entries: one for DOS and one for Macintosh. A volume with DOS, Macintosh, and long-name support would result in three directory entries per file.

As you can imagine, these directory entries add up quickly. Earlier versions of NetWare 4 supported up to 2 million directory entries per volume. Originally, this seemed more than enough directory entries to support customer needs. When customers began supporting many different name spaces on a single volume, however, some were actually using up all the available directory entries before their volumes were full. The result was, even though disk space was available, no additional information could be stored on the volumes because no directory entries were available. With NetWare 4.11 and beyond, insufficient directory entries are no longer an issue. Each server volume can now support up to 16 million directory entries by default.

File System Security

File system security in NetWare is granular, which means access rights can be assigned all the way down to the smallest possible unit in the file system — a file. Eight rights are used to control access to files and directories stored on server volumes. These rights and their descriptions are detailed in Table 2.5.

TABLE 2.5	RIGHT	DESCRIPTION
NetWare File System Rights	Read	Provides the ability to open and read files, and to open, read, and execute applications.
	Write	Provides the ability to open, write to, and modify a file.
	Create	Provides the ability to create new subdirectories and files.
	File Scan	Provides the ability to view file and directory names in the file system structure.
	Access Control	Provides the ability to add and remove trustees and change rights to files and directories.
	Erase	Provides the ability to delete directories and files.
	Modify	Provides the ability to rename directories and files and to change file attributes.
	Supervisor	Implies all other seven rights.

File system rights can be granted to users, groups, or container objects. File system rights assignments are done through the NWAdmin utility. Figure 2.8 and Figure 2.9 show two methods of granting file-system rights.

FIGURE 2.8

NWAdmin is used to administer file system rights. This figure illustrates granting rights for user JD (as indicated at the top of the screen) to the SYS:\DATA directory on the Catalina server. JD is being granted all rights but Supervisor in this figure.

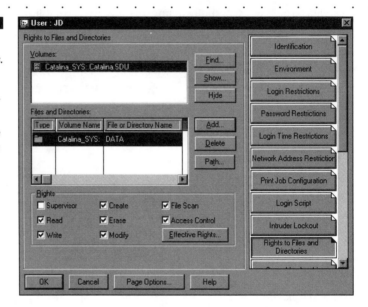

FIGURE 2.9

This figure illustrates an optional method of granting file system rights in NWAdmin. In this example, the file SYS:\DATA\ WPDOCS\LETTER.WPD has been selected and the group Instructors is being granted all rights but Supervisor to the file.

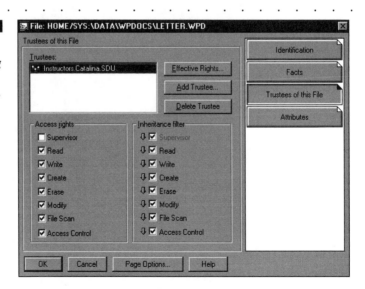

Figure 2.8 illustrates one method of granting file system rights in NWAdmin. In this illustration, we have simply selected the User object in the NDS tree, and from the Details page, selected the Rights to Files and Directories property. We then selected the volume and directory to which we wanted to give the user rights and selected the desired rights. JD has been granted all rights but Supervisor in this figure.

Figure 2.9 illustrates an optional method of granting file system rights. In this case, we have chosen a specific file in NWAdmin, and then chosen the object to which we wanted to grant rights (the Instructors group).

Users can be given rights to a specific file or directory through five different methods:

- Explicit trustee assignments

- Group memberships

- Security equivalencies

- Directory inheritance

- Container inheritance

User rights are *additive*, which means a user can obtain rights from any or all of the items listed here. For example, a user's rights to a give resource is the sum of explicit trustee assignments, group memberships, security equivalencies, and so on.

Explicit Trustee Assignments

Explicit trustee assignments are the most basic form of granting rights. The user object is selected and explicitly given rights to a specific file or directory. As you can imagine, if this were the only method of granting rights, setting up file system security would be a huge task. Generally, file system rights are granted using one of the methods described in the following sections.

Group Membership

Granting user rights through group membership is fairly straightforward. Access rights are granted to a group and any users who are members of the group receive the rights of the group.

Security Equivalencies

A user in the NDS Directory tree can be made equivalent to another user in the tree. When this is done, the second user will receive all the rights of the first user. Any changes to the rights granted to the original user will reflect on all equivalent users.

Directory Inheritance

Directory inheritance is a feature available in NetWare that saves significant time in granting file system rights. The concept is simple. Rights granted at a directory or subdirectory level flow down to all subdirectories and files below.

For example, consider the file system directory structure shown in Figure 2.10.

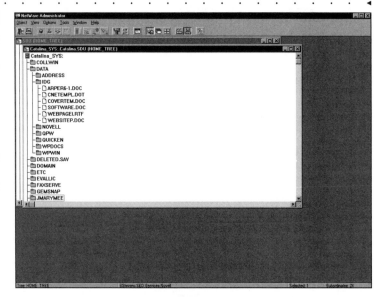

► · ◄

F I G U R E   2.10

File system rights granted at a directory level flow down to all the subdirectories and files below. So, if rights were granted to a user at the Catalina SYS:\DATA level, the user would have those same rights to the Catalina SYS:\DATA\IDG subdirectory and all its files (as well as the other subdirectories and their files).

In this figure, if the user Kyle were granted the Read, File Scan, Write, Create, and Erase rights to the Catalina SYS:\DATA directory, he would have those same rights to all the subdirectories (Address, IDG, Novell, QPW, and so on) and their files.

Let's assume the administrator does not want Kyle to have access to the SOFTWARE.DOC file located in the Catalina SYS:\DATA\IDG directory. The inheritance of the rights could be blocked either by giving Kyle an explicit assignment of no rights to that file or the Inherited Rights Filter (IRF) for that file could be used to block the rights. The IRF is a filter that determines what rights can be inherited from parent directories. Granting rights explicitly only affects the user to whom the rights were granted, while the IRF affects all users, except those with the Supervisor right. The IRF for the file SOFTWARE.DOC is shown in Figure 2.11.

► • ◄

FIGURE 2.11

The Inherited Rights Filter determines what rights can be inherited from parent directories. The IRF for SOFTWARE.DOC indicates all rights can be inherited from SYS:\DATA\IDG and all directories above.

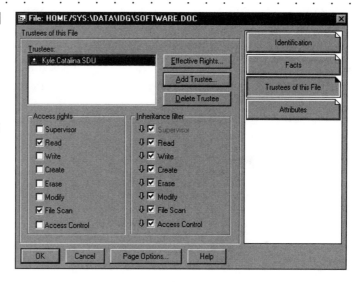

Figure 2.11 shows all rights are allowed to flow through from parent directories. So any user who has rights to the parent directory IDG, to DATA, or to the Catalina SYS: volume also has those rights to SOFTWARE.DOC. A right in the IRF that is not preceded by a check mark would indicate the right has been blocked. To prevent rights from flowing for Kyle or any other user, each right would need to be selected to remove the check mark.

Notice also in Figure 2.11 that the Supervisor right is dimmed. This is because the Supervisor right cannot be blocked by an IRF. Any user with this right has rights to all directories and subdirectories below, regardless of the IRF.

Container Inheritance

The final way users can obtain rights is through Container inheritance. Container inheritance is a method of granting rights that are unique to NetWare and NDS. By granting rights to an NDS container, all the users in that container (and the containers below, unless blocked by an IRF) automatically receive those rights.

In most organizations, users (or at least workgroups) typically all need similar access to files and directories. From this, the terms Rules-based administration and Management by exception have stemmed. These terms indicate managing on an NDS container level, and then only granting rights explicitly when an exception to the rule exists. For example, user JD may require the Supervisor to the Catalina SYS:\APPS directory to install applications, while the rest of the users in that container only require Read and File Scan access. In this situation, rights are administered at the container level and an explicit assignment is made for JD. This form of network administration saves significant time in administering networks.

C2 (Red Book) Security

If you are like most Information Systems (IS) managers, a secure network is important. This is becoming especially important today with the expansion of corporate networks to the Internet and the World Wide Web (WWW). To ensure Novell networks are secure, the company designed NetWare 4.1x and NetWare 5 to meet the security standards of the National Computer Security Center (NCSC).

The NCSC evaluates network operating systems to ensure conformance with two network security standards:

- Trusted Computer System Evaluation Criteria (TCSEC)

- Trusted Network Interpretation (TNI)

These security standards were originally defined by the Department of Defense, but are being used today by many other government and commercial organizations as standards to ensure the information within their organizations is secure.

TNI Class 2 Rating

To receive an TNI Class 2 rating, the following three components of the NetWare network are being/have been evaluated:

- ▸ Server

- ▸ Client

- ▸ Complete network

Novell's objective is to evaluate the network architecture, as well as the various components of the network. This will assure customers that any client or server component labeled as "Enhanced Security Approved" will be part of the evaluated configuration.

In the initial evaluation of NetWare by the NCSC, the client component of the complete network solution is being evaluated with the Cordant Assure EC product as the trusted workstation. However, the evaluated network architecture allows other trusted workstations to plug into the network without requiring complete reevaluation.

NOTE

Cordant Assure EC is an IBM-compatible personal computer (PC) workstation that provides controlled access to the network and to local storage and peripherals. It operates as a DOS and Windows application platform and allows DOS and Windows applications to run unmodified. This product is available from SISTEX, Inc.

IntranetWare/NetWare 4.11 was the first general-purpose network operating system to receive a TNI Class 2 security rating. An operating system meeting the TNI criteria also meets the TCSEC criteria, as described in the following sections.

C2 Red Book vs. Orange Book

Significant confusion exists in the industry about C2 security evaluations. The root of this confusion is that two different C2 security evaluations are available: Red Book and Orange Book. NetWare 4.11 and NetWare 5 have been evaluated by the NCSC as C2 Red Book certifiable networks. NT Server and workstation have been evaluated as C2 Orange Book.

The Trusted Computer System Evaluation Criteria (TCSEC) provides criteria for evaluating the security of a standalone system — a workstation or a server. This is what is known as C2 Orange Book. The Trusted Network Interpretation (TNI) is a subset of the TCSEC that covers the network component. This is what is known as C2 Red Book. Systems evaluated under TNI also meet the criteria of TCSEC.

Here's the caveat: C2 Orange Book systems are not evaluated in a networked environment, so C2 Orange Book ratings become invalid the minute the device is placed on a network.

Windows NT Server and NT Workstation both have been evaluated as C2 Orange Book devices. Unfortunately, the minute the systems are placed on a network, the rating is invalid. NetWare, on the other hand, was evaluated under the NTI interpretation of the TCSEC and meets the criteria of a class C2 secure network.

NetWare Enhanced Security

For a NetWare network to meet the requirements of a Class C2 secure network, NetWare Enhanced Security must be implemented. NetWare Enhanced Security is a set of security components that allow NetWare networks to meet the Class C2 requirements.

NetWare Enhanced Security encompasses the entire network — from file servers and workstations, to the interconnection devices (routers, bridges, and repeaters), and network media that ties everything together. The objective of NetWare Enhanced Security is to provide a trusted system that protects all information stored on the network.

NetWare includes the following features to enable NetWare Enhanced Security:

▸ An auditing utility called AUDITCON that enables C2-compliant auditing.

▸ Secure audit log files that are represented as NDS objects in the Directory tree. These files are controlled through NDS security.

▸ A group of SET parameters that allow a NetWare server to be configured as an Enhanced Security Server.

To have a NetWare file server configured automatically as an Enhanced Security server, use the following SET parameter:

```
SET Enable SECURE.NCF
```

The SECURE.NCF file contains a set of script commands that configure a server as an Enhanced Security server.

For more information on implementing a Class C2 secure network and using NetWare Enhanced Security, refer to the following sources:

- ▶ Novell *Application Notes* April 1994 — "Building and Auditing a Trusted Environment with NetWare 4"

- ▶ Novell *Application Notes* August 1994 — "An Introduction to Novell's Open Security Architecture"

- ▶ *Security Features User's Guide*

- ▶ *NetWare Enhanced Security Administration* manual

- ▶ *NetWare Enhanced Security Components* manual

- ▶ *Auditing the Network* manual

- ▶ Novell's WWW site at: `http://www.novell.com/security`

Summary

NetWare has come a long way from its original roots. It is now one of the most robust, feature-rich operating systems you can buy. NetWare today has a full-service directory, an advanced file system, and has been designed as a C2 (Red Book) secure network platform. All these characteristics of NetWare make it the most widely installed network operating system on the market. Where NetWare was once the only option when it came to network operating systems, Windows NT Server is now becoming just as popular as NetWare. Chapter 3 describes NT Server in detail. Once we've laid the foundation in these two chapters, we'll move on to integrating the two environments.

CHAPTER 3

NT Server Networking

This chapter discusses NT Server and how it operates in a normal NT-only system. Understanding this, you can then move forward to integrating NT services into a NetWare environment. Cross-references will be made when possible to contrast the difference. A good source of this information can also be obtained by reading the NT Resource Guide 4.0.

► • ◄

The Evolution of Windows NT and LAN Manager

NT Server had its beginnings in LAN Manager, which was an effort between Microsoft and IBM circa 1988–1989 to capture the network operating system market by placing a network services engine (LAN Manager) on top of a general-purpose operating system (OS/2). Ultimately, that ended with IBM marketing OS/2 on their own (with LAN Server) and Microsoft taking the services forward with Windows NT (see Figure 3.1). A part of the operating system work made it into Windows NT, but Windows NT also has had a considerable amount of additional operating system technology pioneered into it.

► • ◄

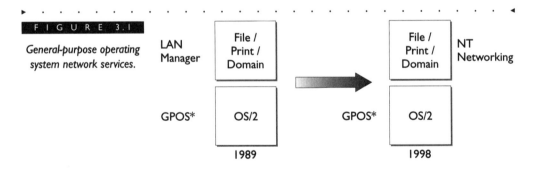

FIGURE 3.1

General-purpose operating system network services.

LAN Manager | File / Print / Domain

GPOS* | OS/2

1989

File / Print / Domain | NT Networking

GPOS* | OS/2

1998

* General Purpose O/S

Because of the LAN Manager beginnings, much of the user management and connection of workgroups was inherited by Windows NT from LAN Manager. Even the Application Programming Interfaces (APIs) used in NT today are prefaced by an LM_, because the primary networking components in Windows NT are still LAN Manager. This is slowly changing as Microsoft adopts additional security and naming technologies (such as directory services).

The Beginnings of NT

Originally, Windows NT began as a new operating system, wholly owned by Microsoft, as opposed to sharing a common code base with IBM. Some of the original work done by Microsoft as part of the OS/2 development was rolled into NT and is still partly maintained in releases of NT. This includes the capability to run some character-based OS/2 version 1.3 applications.

The first version of NT started with 3.1, named after the current version of Windows (16-bit) 3.1. The difference was NT was a 32-bit operating system and Windows was a 16-bit operating system. In addition, the two flavors of NT were NT Advanced Server and NT Workstation. Microsoft designed a new operating system with the advent of Windows NT, but maintained the networking components inherent to OS/2 and LAN Manager. This is why you still see components of LAN Manager in Windows NT today, including:

▸ A Domain-based security system

▸ Text-based Host file (similar to a UNIX hosts file) as one way to resolve station names

▸ NetBIOS broadcasts to resolve station addresses

▸ A nonhierarchical (flat) naming system

▸ A noninheritance-based Access Control List (ACL) file system

With the advent of Windows NT 3.5 came the ability to have trusts (described later in this chapter) between Domains, as well as the Windows Internet Naming Service (WINS) as a better way to find resources.

Version 3.51 followed, but this was mostly a revision update, along with some utility enhancements.

Windows NT Server and Windows NT Workstation Today

When Microsoft initially released NT, it was stratified into two different platforms:

▶ NT Advanced Server. Primarily used for several functions, such as file and print, application services, and a platform for BackOffice services, such as SQL server.

▶ NT Workstation. Used as a power users' platform, as well as lower-end application services. Microsoft has limited certain licensing in this version to prevent people from using NT Workstation in ways Microsoft had instead intended for NT Server.

Starting with version 3.5, Windows NT iterations were named Server and Workstation, respectively. The current version of Windows NT (Server and Workstation) is 4.0, with the next version, known as Windows 2000, expected by fall of 1999 or later.

Differences Between Windows NT Server and Windows NT Workstation

Microsoft has spent a considerable amount of time emphasizing that NT Server and NT Workstation are two different products. As it turns out, the two are similar, from the base operating system up. The only real differences are the applications bundled with NT Server and several registry settings (not to mention the licensing restrictions on NT Workstation). So for all intents and purposes, NT Server and NT Workstation are basically the same. For integration, some capabilities exist that NT Server has that Workstation does not have (one of these is the user database).

Because Windows NT Server and Windows NT Workstation are basically the same, we'll cover what's involved with supporting a network using Windows NT technology. Items we'll cover include:

▶ The Windows NT Security Accounts Manager (SAM) database

▶ Using the SAM to create Domains

▶ Fault tolerance in the Windows NT security system

. . . . .

- ▶ Using trust relationships in a multi-Domain network

- ▶ How the Domain works as a naming system (compared to NDS)

- ▶ Microsoft-recommended deployment strategies

- ▶ How file-sharing and print-sharing work with Windows NT

- ▶ Security and Windows NT

- ▶ Microsoft and third-party product security integration

- ▶ Network management utilities

- ▶ Windows NT and Security (NCSC) ratings

Understanding how Windows NT works is essential to understand how integration can be accomplished.

NT SAM — Security Accounts Manager

Every NT operating system provides an authentication database called a Security Accounts Manager (SAM), as shown in Figure 3.2. SAM is used to authenticate people when they first access the system. Just like UNIX has a user name/password scheme and NetWare uses NDS, NT uses SAM.

SAM exists on all NT operating systems, regardless of whether you are using NT Workstation or NT Server. In fact, even when NT is part of a larger network (called a Domain) you will still have a local SAM database present. This is because the Domain is built using SAM as the security-storage mechanism. A user must have a SAM user name and password to log in to the system, whether it's a user on a single station or a thousand users logging into a Domain.

When that user name and password are stored on a central machine (known as a Domain Controller), then the machine acting as the Domain Controller is using its SAM database as a master user database on that network (see Figure 3.3). This doesn't mean the other machines do not have a SAM database; this merely means they will ignore their local database in favor of a master database.

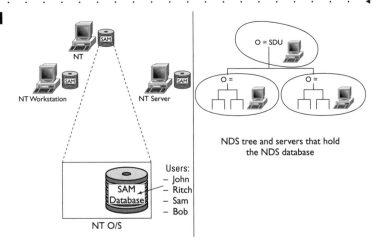

FIGURE 3.2

NT has SAM on every O/S. NetWare uses NDS as the global database.

NDS tree and servers that hold the NDS database

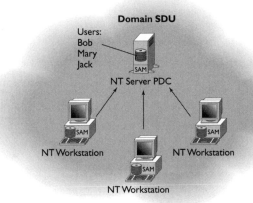

FIGURE 3.3

You can use one SAM database as the master security database. All NT stations still have a local SAM, but they look to the main one as the master.

If, for example, user Mike cannot login to the master database (Domain), then he may be logged on locally using cached credentials if he has logged on at least once before. If Mike has not, then he may log on locally if a user name and password have been created for him in the local SAM.

The SAM database is a fairly static database and is nonextensible. That is, you cannot create a new object type, such as Fax Server, within the database. For special cases, where a custom server or user is needed, a separate database must be created. This is the case with Microsoft SQL Server, Exchange, and other third-party services running on NT. The base object types the SAM can host include Servers, Users, Global and Local Groups, and Printers, as shown in Figure 3.4. On a User account, it includes basic information such as Description, Full Name, Password, and account restrictions.

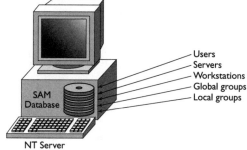

FIGURE 3.4

SAM is limited to five object types — Users, Servers, Workstations, Global groups, and Local groups.

Users
Servers
Workstations
Global groups
Local groups

SAM Database

NT Server

The lack of extensibility applies even when a SAM is used as a Domain Controller security database. SAM, at that point, is a focal data store for security, but the structure and limitations of the data store still hold.

NT Networking and the Domain System

The Windows NT networking Domain system architecture is a carryover from the LAN Manager system designed and implemented by Microsoft and IBM in the late 1980s. Its basic structure is one of a master/slave relationship. This system is geared toward centralizing management and administration of user accounts by creating a central Domain Database.

In a Domain, all workstations and servers refer to a Domain Name that specifies a home network (see Figure 3.5). A person may not be part of more than one Domain. To access multiple Domains, a user account may be duplicated or may gain access through a special Domain relationship known as a trust.

► · ◄

F I G U R E 3.5

NT Networking Domain SCUBA Divers Unlimited.

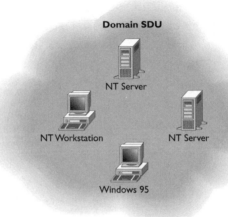

Domain SDU

Primaries and Backups

In any type of networking system, security always is a major aspect of the operating system; NT is no exception. NT Server provides a way to validate users against a central security database. This master database pointer, called a Primary Domain Controller (PDC), is illustrated in Figure 3.6.

► · ◄

F I G U R E 3.6

When using a Domain, at least one domain controller will always exist. This domain controller is called the Primary Domain Controller (PDC).

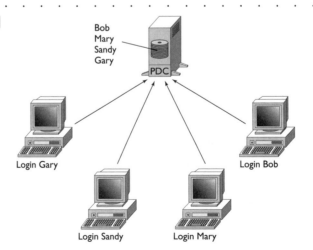

The PDC's security database is used whenever a user is created, deleted, or updated. In addition, when a user authenticates, the PDC is often consulted. What if the PDC goes down? Because the PDC is the central repository of all user information in the Domain, a catastrophic loss of the PDC SAM would result in the loss of all security information. This is where the Backup Domain Controller (BDC) comes in.

BDCs act as a secondary repository of security data. All the account information kept in the central SAM database (PDC) can be replicated to a BDC. If the PDC goes down, a BDC can be manually promoted to a PDC, and the network continues normally. For purposes of login, BDCs can also act as an authentication point. If the PDC is busy, this can offload a significant amount of work from the central machine (see Figure 3.7). A BDC cannot act in place of a PDC for management reasons, however. If a PDC goes down, you cannot create, delete, or modify user information in any way (including password changes) unless an existing BDC is promoted to a PDC or the existing PDC comes back online.

▶ · ◀

FIGURE 3.7

You can backup the PDC by designating a Backup Domain Controller. Users can authenticate to it or to the PDC.

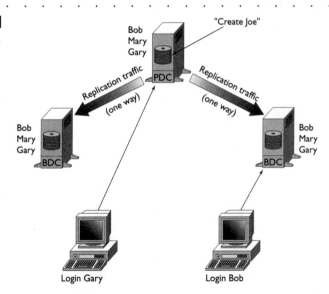

When NT networking is being deployed, care must be taken to ensure users can always log in to the system. This means placing backup copies of the security database strategically, so any given failure will not result in a denied login.

This becomes even more critical when WAN links are involved. The nature of NT networking implies all administration will be centrally managed (details on implementation are discussed later in this chapter). This usually means the PDC will be placed at a central site (such as corporate). If a WAN is used, users at the WAN site will be authenticating over the WAN to the corporate PDC, unless a backup database is deployed at the remote site. If the WAN link goes down, users must still be able to log in. Therefore, placing a backup of the PDC (in the form of a BDC) at the remote WAN site makes sense (see Figure 3.8). This does require another machine at the remote site to house the BDC replica, because an NT operating system can only host one copy of any Domain Controller (DC) database at one time. This also means all user accounts will be replicated to the remote site's BDC database. If 5,000 users are in the PDC at corporate, all 5,000 will be replicated to the remote BDC. Fortunately, only changes to the database are synchronized to the remote site.

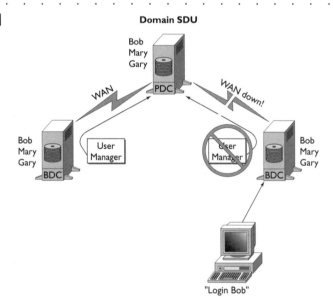

FIGURE 3.8

If a WAN design is used, a BDC can be placed at the remote site to help with authentications. If the WAN goes down, users can authenticate, but user changes cannot occur.

Domain SDU

When authentication occurs at the remote site, the BDC information is used to log in the user. Management of the user can only take place at the PDC, so user changes cannot take place (see Figure 3.8). In essence, this means authentication can be load-balanced, but user management cannot. In fact, if the WAN link goes down, and the PDC cannot be contacted from the remote office, management is not possible. User creations, deletions, name changes, and such are not possible until a new PDC is available.

Trust Relationships and Domains

As stated previously, a user may only be part of one domain at a time. You can create duplicate user names on multiple Domains, but these are technically separate accounts and may have different passwords and rights in the system.

The challenge comes when users from one Domain must be given access to resources in another Domain. One option is to create a duplicate account. A less redundant way is to create a trust relationship.

A trust is a way of having one Domain allow access to a user who does not exist within the Domain where the resource resides. For example, take Domain Maui and Domain Catalina for SDU. In the Domain Maui, a shared disk exists with all kinds of skydiving pictures. User Sam in the Domain Maui wants access to the pictures. The administrator of Domain Catalina and Domain Maui can agree to create a trust between the two Domains. Once completed, user Sam in the Domain Maui can be granted access to the shared disk in Domain Catalina (see Figure 3.9). User Sam then logs in and requests access to the directory shared on server UW-Photos under Domain Catalina. When the share is requested, a pass-through authentication occurs through the trust and access is granted.

NOTE Creating a trust does not grant *any* user privileges by default. Creating a trust merely provides the *capability* of granting a foreign user access rights to a local resource.

Trusts by nature are one-way. If one Domain (such as Maui) trusts another Domain (such as Catalina), users in Domain Catalina can be granted access to resources in Domain Maui. Users in the Maui Domain, however, cannot, unless another trust is created from Domain Catalina to Domain Maui (see Figure 3.10).

▶ · ◀

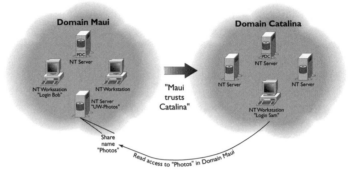

FIGURE 3.9

You can link Domains by using trusts. Domain Maui trusts Domain Catalina, so user Sam can be given access to the files on server UW-Photos.

▶ · ◀

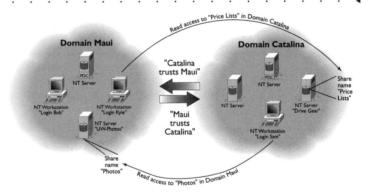

FIGURE 3.10

Another trust must be created from Maui to Catalina for the users in the Catalina Domain to access files on server DiveGear.

In addition, trusts are not transitive. If Domain Curacao trusts Domain Maui and Domain Maui trusts Domain Catalina, Domain Curacao will not automatically trust Domain Catalina (see Figure 3.11). This option may change with the advent of Windows NT 5.0 and Active Directory Services (ADS), Microsoft's forthcoming directory service.

Directory Naming Within the Domain System

Naming within the Domain system is based on a flat system of objects. In other words, because no hierarchy exists, names cannot be duplicated. If two users named Sandy exist, both user names must be unique within the Domain. Perhaps one could be named SandyM and the other SandyS (see Figure 3.12). Ultimately, Microsoft is proposing a hierarchical naming system with ADS to eliminate this problem.

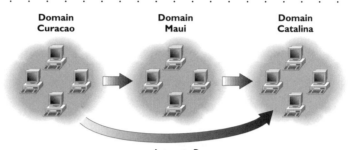

FIGURE 3.11

In the current implementation of NT Server, trusts are not transitive. A separate trust must be set up between Curacao and Catalina.

Domain Curacao   **Domain Maui**   **Domain Catalina**

A trusts B
B trusts C
A does **not** trust C!
Separate trust needed

FIGURE 3.12

Because the Domain database is a flat structure, you cannot have duplicate user names.

No duplicate user names in a flat structure

User Manager - EXCEL_DOMAIN

User   View   Policies   Options   Help

Username	Full Name	Description
Administrator		Built-in account for administering the comp
Guest		Built-in account for guest access to the con
JD		
JMarymee	JD Marymee	Main User
KMarymee	Kyle John Marymee	
KProws		
SandyM	Sandy Marymee	
SandyS	Sandy Stevens	

Groups	Description
Account Operators	Members can administer domain user and group accounts
Administrators	Members can fully administer the computer/domain
Backup Operators	Members can bypass file security to back up files
Domain Admins	Designated administrators of the domain
Domain Guests	All domain guests
Domain Users	All domain users
Guests	Users granted guest access to the computer/domain

Unlike NDS, another current limitation of Domains is the possibility of creating custom object types in the Domain Database. For example, a third party wishes to create a fax server for NT. Under NDS, a fax server object can be created and referenced (see Figure 3.13). Under NT, a new object cannot be created.

Therefore, any control information about the object must be kept elsewhere. Usually this means the software developer must create a separate database to keep information about the fax server.

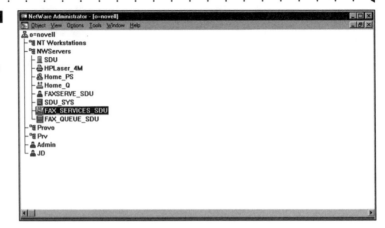

FIGURE 3.13

Under NDS, new object types can be created dynamically by applications to simplify administration.

So, why would the ability to create a fax server object, for example, be useful? Having the fax server reference a common naming system has several benefits:

▸ The information regarding the fax server object goes in the same database as other network information and can, therefore, be backed up at the same time.

▸ Because the fax server object and User/Group objects are part of the same database, access controls can be granted. (User has rights to use the Fax Server object.)

▸ The Fax Server object can search the directory for other objects it may need (perhaps a Modem object).

Another example of where a nonunified directory approach can be seen is with Microsoft SQL Server. User access information is kept in a special, separate database created just for SQL Server (see Figure 3.14). SQL Server can look at the Domain database for purposes of authentication, but it must reference its own database for all other information. This means the two must be kept in relative synchronization if a smooth, single-login approach is desired. For example, if user Mike exists in the Domain, Mike must also be created as a SQL Server user in the SQL Server database. Otherwise, Mike will be unable to access SQL Server data.

► . . . . ◄

FIGURE 3.14

Under the Domain system, services usually create their own database to store user information, as does MS-SQL Server.

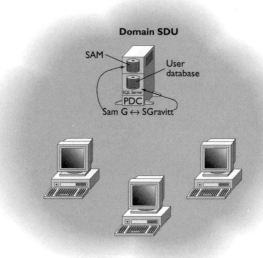

Contrast this to using an extensible directory such as NDS. Instead of creating a new database for each new service, the directory can be extended to support new service (object) names in the existing directory. This means less redundancy in the system, because the information needed regarding the service is only kept in one database — the Directory.

NOTE

Several of the Domain-based applications, such as Exchange and SQL server, will dredge users from the existing domain. Other applications, such as Exchange, actually enable you to create users in the domain by using the Exchange management tools. From initial inspection, Exchange and SQL server appear integrated with the domain, but these are only integrated through the user-based utilities and pass-through authentication.

► . . . . ◄

Domain Options for the Network

NT networking offers a variety of ways to deploy the system. This section discusses several ways that the typical system is deployed and highlights advantages/disadvantages of each. Note the advantages and disadvantages in each option where the user information is stored (the Master database or PDC/BDC pairs, for example).

While Microsoft recommends several ways to deploy Domains, Novell does not recommend multiple deployment options for NDS. The reason is NDS deployment recommendations concern directory partitioning and replication, yet usually only one Directory tree exists. Domain deployment requires careful consideration to have a workable system. This is because Windows NT is still based on a Domain model until Windows NT 5.0 is released with a directory system.

Microsoft recommends several ways to deploy Domain-based systems. Three are recommended and one usually happens by accident! The options are:

- ► Complete Trust

- ► Single Domain

- ► Single Master Domain

- ► Multiple Master Domain

Complete Trust

In the Complete Trust scenario (see Figure 3.15), every Domain (or most Domains) will trust all the other Domains, and vice versa. This allows great flexibility in granting rights and maximizing the NT servers at hand, but it is an administrative nightmare. The user must also have some knowledge of where resources are located. For example, an NT administrator may have 20 Domains available, but which one supports the HP LaserJet 5M? Where is the shared hard disk with all the games? The administrator won't know unless he or she is actively browsing all the Domains looking for resources. Another method is to write down where all the resources are located.

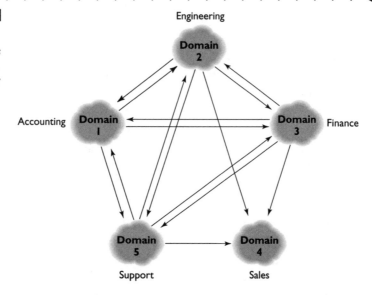

In a Complete Trust implementation, all Domains trust all the other Domains. This enables any user in any Domain to be given rights to resources in any other Domain.

NOTE

Domains and Workgroups have no inherent way to search for objects, such as printer and file shares available in the network. Browsing is possible on a Domain-by-Domain basis. This may be rectified when Active Directory becomes available, which should be in the first half of the year 2000.

Typically, this is not the first recommended solution when using Domains. In fact, Microsoft usually recommends against it for the following reasons:

▸ Trusts are notoriously hard to administer.

▸ When you have a large number of trusts, you have an n(n-1) number of trusts to administer (where n is the number of domains participating).

▸ No graphical way exists to view all the trust relationships. These must be drawn out by hand.

▸ Any time a server name changes, all trusts to (and from) that server will be invalidated.

▸ Control of the network is totally decentralized and cannot be managed efficiently.

As you can see, a Complete Trust is usually the least desired solution. Unfortunately, this is often the most common implementation by default. The reason for this is human nature. When a new Domain workgroup is installed (such as Maui), people will naturally use it (see Figure 3.16). As the content (data) grows in Domain Maui, other people will want to share and use it (such as users in Domain Catalina). At that time, the Domain administrator of Maui may create a trust relationship with Domain Catalina, either one-way or bidirectional (see Figure 3.17). If another Domain group (Curacao) wants to join, because Domain Maui has good data that relates to Domain Catalina, the users in Domain Curacao will want access to both Domains. Now, two new trusts are created between Maui, Catalina, and Curacao. They may be either one-way or bidirectional (see Figure 3.18). The question is, who owns the administration of that network? No central administration exists because each Domain administrator controls his or her Domain. If any server names change, all the trusts in place are broken.

▸ . . . . ◂

F I G U R E   3.16

Domain Maui in a single workgroup Domain.

Domain Maui

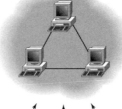

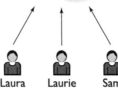

Laura   Laurie   Sam

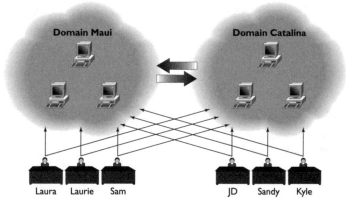

FIGURE 3.17

The Domain Catalina wishes to share information between the users. Therefore, a bidirectional trust is created.

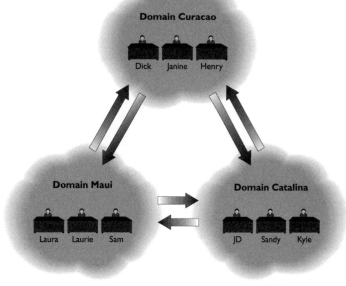

FIGURE 3.18

A third Domain, Curacao, joins in. Because all users want to share among the Domains, bidirectional trusts are created among all three.

One of the goals of integration with NetWare is to simplify the administration of the network. Chapters 6, 7, and 8 discuss implementation strategies, which may either reduce or eliminate trust relationships.

Single Domain

In a Single Domain, all resources and users are placed on one named Domain. This makes administration much simpler, because only one location exists for all resources and users. In a small workgroup, this is a workable solution (see Figure 3.19).

F I G U R E   3.19

A single Domain contains all users, groups, and resources. It contains a PDC and should contain a BDC as well for fault tolerance.

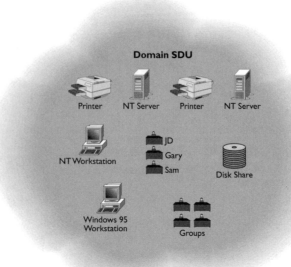

When the Domain scales larger than a small workgroup, a Single Domain begins to suffer. If a WAN link is involved, it becomes difficult to provide access to the resources intelligently. Consider SDU again, as an example. Three locations exist: Corporate in Catalina, San Diego, and Curacao. People in San Diego have printers and files shared on servers, as do users in Curacao. The Catalina office is where administration occurs. In a Single Domain, only one Domain will be created (perhaps called Domain SDU). At the remote site in San Diego, a BDC will be placed (because the PDC will probably be held at Corporate). A BDC will also be placed in Curacao. All data from the PDC will be replicated down to each BDC because you cannot distinguish what data gets replicated to a BDC. This isn't the most efficient way to manage resources in a geographically disbursed system (see Figure 3.20).

FIGURE 3.20

Single Domain SDU geographically deployed.

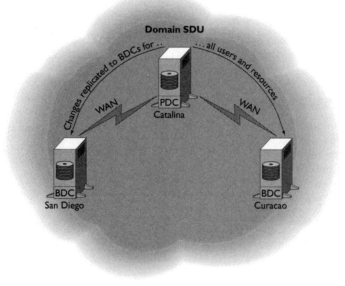

The benefits to a Single Domain are:

▶ Because everything is in one Domain, no trusts exist to maintain.

▶ Users will always authenticate to one Domain. In a multiple Domain network, a roaming user may select the wrong Domain when logging in from a foreign system.

▶ Only two systems are required: one for the PDC and one for the BDC.

NOTE

Migrating from a Single Domain to a Single Master or Multiple Master is one of the most difficult transitions in NT networking. Either shares (and, hence, user data) must be moved to a Resource Domain (explained later in this chapter) or users must be deleted and created in the new Master Domain. Either way, planning and work are required.

Single Master Domain

Single Master Domain introduces the concept of managing users and resources separately. A new element called a Resource Domain is used to deploy resources in the network. Single Master Domains also use trusts to accommodate linking the Resource Domains into the Master (see Figure 3.21).

▶ . . . . ◀

F I G U R E   3.21

Single Master Domain configurations consist of one Domain deployed as the Master and any number of Domains deployed as Resource Domains linked by a one-way trust.

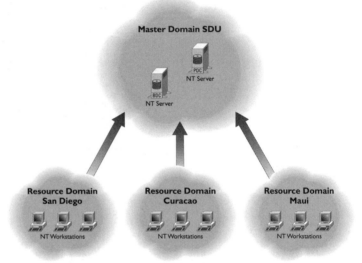

NOTE

A Resource Domain is *exactly* the same as a regular Domain, except it is only used to store resources in the network. Semantically, Master Domains (Users and Groups) and Resource Domains (Printers and File Shares) exist. In reality, there is no technical difference. A Domain is a Domain. The model is used solely to simplify the managing of the network.

Single Master Domains also introduce the concept of Global Groups and Local Groups. The main difference is Global Groups can be members of Local Groups. The manner in which they're used is discussed later in this chapter.

Deployment for SDU would be as follows (see Figure 3.22):

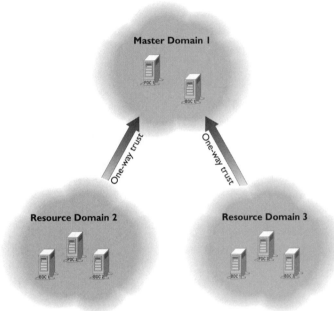

The SDU company with a Single Master setup. Note, each filed site has a resource domain complete with a PDC/BDC pair for fault tolerance. Note, too, each remote site also has a BDC of the Master Domain to assist in authentications.

- ▶ A Master Domain would be deployed at Corporate (Catalina). Users would be created only in the Master Domain. This includes all users, even at the San Diego and Curacao sites. The PDC for the Master would be located in Catalina. At least one BDC would be deployed in Catalina as well for fault-tolerant reasons. If the PDC failed, a BDC could be manually promoted as the new PDC.

- ▶ A Resource Domain would be created at the San Diego and Curacao sites. Printers, file shares, and other services (such as SQL databases) would be created/installed in each local Resource Domain. No users would be created in either Resource Domain, except those created by default (such as Guest and Administrator).

- ▶ The Resource Domains each have a PDC and a BDC for fault tolerance. This means at least two machines must be deployed at each site.

► A one-way trust would be created between each Resource Domain and the Corporate Domain (Resource trusts the Master only). This enables users to log in to the Corporate (Master) Domain and to be granted access to resources respective to their local Resource Domain.

► Usually, a BDC of the Master Domain would be placed at each remote site. This enables users to log in from either San Diego or Curacao, and to be authenticated to a local BDC. This prevents authentication over the WAN link. In addition, if the WAN link fails, users can still log in. Changes to existing user accounts, or the creation of new user accounts, however, could not occur until a new PDC is available or the WAN link comes back online again.

► Global Groups would be created in the Corporate Domain. An example would be an Instructor or a Dive Master group (see Figure 3.23).

► An Instructor or Dive Master Local Group would be created at each Resource Domain Site (see Figure 3.24).

► The Global Groups would be given access to the Local Groups in each Resource Domain.

► Users would be created and given membership to a Global Group. That Global Group should be a member of one or more Local Groups in a Resource Domain.

► Groups are granted access to shares, printers, and services the users need.

NOTE   **Local Groups have some inherent problems when used in a Domain environment. In Single Master deployment, Local Groups are not always required. You can create Global Groups in the Master Domain and grant the global groups rights required for the users to access resources in the Resource Domains. Using the Global/Local Group model is helpful if the network will be migrating to a Multiple Master design eventually.**

FIGURE 3.23

Global Groups are used at the Master Domain to simplify user management. A Global Group will become a member of a Local Group in the Resource Domain or it can be given specific access to resources in a Resource Domain.

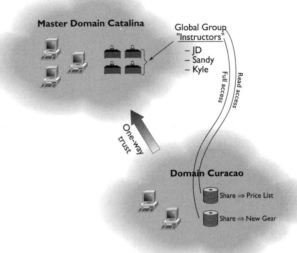

FIGURE 3.24

Local Groups can be created in the Resource Domains and can be given specific access to local resources. User gains access to these resources as a member of a Global Group that is a member of the Local Group.

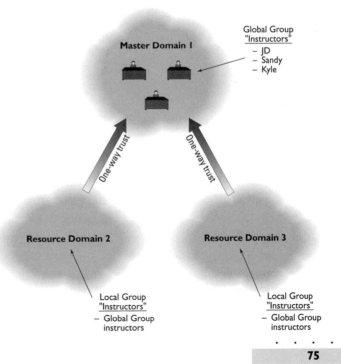

Multiple Master Domains

When the system has grown substantially, migrating to a Multiple Master Domain network may be necessary. The number of users and geographical requirements usually dictate when this is necessary.

Microsoft has stated that a single Domain can have as many as 40,000 objects (users, servers, and groups) per Domain. Real-world implementations have shown actual numbers of objects per Domain are much smaller. The actual number may be as low as 100 or 200 per Domain, or perhaps 1,000 or 2,000, depending on what performance requirements you have and what services are residing on the Domain Controller servers.

Multiple Master Domains use trust relationships to a greater extent than even in the Single Master deployment, mostly because more than one Master Domain exists in the network. Each user in each Master Domain should be able to have access to any Resource Domain. Aside from sheer user numbers, the other reasons for using Multiple Masters are as follows:

▸ In a building or multiple buildings within a campus, you may need to have each Master Domain administered separately.

▸ There are several geographical areas to the corporate site (for example, in SDU, perhaps one in Catalina and the other in Two Harbors).

▸ The network may evolve from several Single Masters or Single Domains/Workgroups to a consolidated network of Multiple Masters.

In the example of a Single Master, one-way trust relationships exist from the Master to the Resource Domains. In the Multiple Master, two-way trust relationships exist from each Master to the other Masters. (This enables any user to log in from a Domain and be part of a group that exists on another Master Domain.) This is an example where a Complete Trust is required.

For the Resource Domains, a one-way trust relationship may exist between each Master Domain and each Resource Domain to facilitate access. The number of managed trusts is expanded significantly in this deployment, but provides the most scalable solution in NT networking. An example of a Multiple Master resembles Figure 3.25.

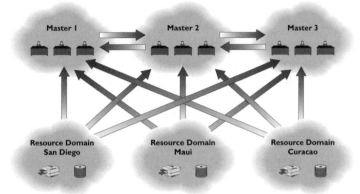

FIGURE 3.25

A Multiple Master is like a Single Master tied together into a large network. Many trusts may exist, depending on how accessible the resources must be to all the users.

NOTE

In deployments, the number of trust relationships varies. In some situations, creating trusts as they become necessary is better. The downside is one administrator may need to call another to set up the trust. If one central administration authority exists, then he or she can create the trust, because there are no other administrators.

Because Multiple Master deployments usually grow out of Single Master networks, usually more than one administrator exists. This requires that the administrators cooperate to manage a Multiple Master effectively.

What Does This All Mean to You?

When it comes to managing an NT network, the most difficult part is the administration of Domains. In fact, no one ever buys and implements NT networks solely on the basis of NT Domains and trusts. Numerous products are emerging now to facilitate administration of NT Domains and trusts, some of which are discussed in this book. Most companies buy NT for several reasons:

- Services running on NT Server and/or Workstation, This includes databases (such as Oracle or SQL Server), or third-party applications (such as human-resource applications like PeopleSoft or SAP).

▸ Applications that only run on a Windows platform. This includes spreadsheets, word processors, and e-mail.

▸ Developing to the NT platform. Because NT and Windows 95 have such a rich development set available, many companies have standardized on WIN32 as the main development environment for in-house development.

Sharing Resources Under NT Networking

The two main items that can be shared in an NT network are printers and file services. Other shared resources (such as databases and e-mail) are discussed later in this chapter.

File Sharing Under NT

In an NT network, each NT (Workstation and Server) operating system and each Windows 95 workstation has the capability of sharing part or all of its local hard disks. When a hard disk is made available for others to use, it is called a share.

Shares can be an entire hard disk, or just part (such as from C:\SYS\GAMES and below). When sharing the file system, access rights can be granted to a group or a user under NT. Under Windows 95, you share based on a common password, or by user and group (see Figure 3.26). Sharing in Windows 95 and NT does have differences:

Windows 95

Sharing can be turned on per workstation. Once enabled, you can share files and printers by creating a share and providing access. The access can be either by password only or by user names and group names. The security on Win95 is minimal. Access levels consist of either Full Access or Read-Only.

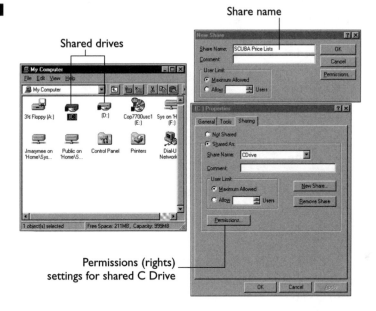

On an NT or Window 95 machine, shares can be created using the My Computer icon. Several layers of shares can be within a single hard disk.

Share name

Shared drives

Permissions (rights) settings for shared C Drive

NT Workstation/Server

Under NT Workstation, you can share files similar to Win95. The main difference is the access levels you can assign. Another option NT has that Windows 95 doesn't is permissions under the NT File System (NTFS), if it is installed.

Basic file access rights under a share are:

▸ *No Access.* This option is used to block access from a user or group.

▸ *Read Access.* This option enables the user to read or execute a file.

▸ *Change.* This option enables a user to change share permissions affecting other users and groups.

▸ *Full Control.* This option enables a user to take ownership of the file, as well as execute the other accesses.

Extended access rights are only available when using the NTFS file system. Access rights (permissions) include the following:

- ▸ Read

- ▸ Write

- ▸ Execute

- ▸ Delete

- ▸ Change

- ▸ Take Ownership

The file system is not shared to general users as a default in NT. This means to use NT as a file and print server, you must at least set up one share for every volume you want to make available. To centralize administration of shares, usually NT Workstation volumes may not be shared (although this is possible).

NTFS permissions will be unavailable unless the volume where the permissions are set has been shared first. In addition, shares take the highest priority when it comes to rights, as shown in Figure 3.27. For example:

1. A share is created on NT Server SeaBass on Drive C:. The share is called CDRIVE.

2. A share access of Read is set on the share to group FISHERS.

3. An NTFS permission of Change is granted to the group FISHERS to volume C:.

4. Users of the group FISHERS log in and attempt to write to the file.

The users in this example can only execute Read-Only access because this is the highest level of access the share allows them to do. Had the share been Full Control and the NTFS permission set to Change, the highest level a user in a group GAMERS could have executed would have been Change. The only other way a user would have access is by granting direct access to the volume through a separate share access.

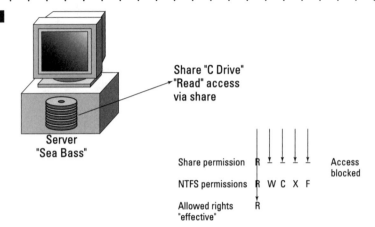

FIGURE 3.27

Users cannot use any remote hard disks unless they are shared first. Permissions for the share take highest precedence, even over NTFS permissions.

NOTE

Many NT shops do not use NTFS permissions in favor of using share permissions only. Several reasons include documenting and managing multiple level permissions. A good in-depth exploration of NTFS permissions can be found in the *NT Resource Guide*. When it comes to co-managing NetWare and NT, the file shares or NTFS permissions will still be applied the way they are in an all-NT solution.

Printer Sharing Under NT

When sharing printers under NT, a share for a printer port is created. Any desired access for a user or a group is then given on a server-by-server basis. Printers do not entail many rights by nature. There is either the ability to print to a shared device or not.

Once the printer has been shared, it can then be managed using Printer Administrator.

What Does All This Mean to Me?

We've discussed the various ways NT allows sharing of resources in an NT network. The hard part comes in when you attempt to provide access to these resources in a heterogeneous environment.

Because access is based on a user or a user as a member of a group, if you want to share resources between NT and NetWare, some user-access mapping must exist between the two. Several of the tools you may already be using under NT you will still use because, to date, no tools exist that cross both environments in all possible areas. The areas where you will still need to use NT tools include:

▸ Creating file shares

▸ Assigning share and NTFS permissions

▸ Creating printer shares

▸ Managing printers shared under NT

Integration points (discussed in Chapter 4) will enable single user/group creation and management thereof, but not permissions. Ideally, having a single user/group creation tool on the desktop, as well as tools to manage shares and permissions, would simplify most management challenges.

Sharing Other Services Under NT Networking

NT inherently allows basic sharing of networking resources. One of the main reasons for implementing NT is the variety of services that have been created to run under NT. This is where the real value of NT becomes apparent. NT is an excellent platform to host these types of services because of hardware support and the rich development environment in which to create these services.

The following two styles of applications (see Figure 3.28) run under NT:

▸ *Client/Server*. In a client/server environment, a service is running on NT that provides some sort of service. A client can connect to the service and ask for whatever this service is providing. In this case, shared service code is running on an NT Server or Workstation. The client may be running on just about anything (UNIX, Win95, NT, and so on), depending on protocol. Examples include SQL Server, Oracle Server, Novell GroupWise, and Lotus Notes. This option usually requires a specific client to consume the service.

► *Monolithic*. The application runs in total on a client (such as NT, Win95, and so on) and the data is available through a file share. The application may be downloaded first from a server, and then executed, or the application may have been pre-installed on the desktop. This is the traditional application sharing in most networks. Examples include Microsoft Word, Microsoft PowerPoint, and Quattro Pro.

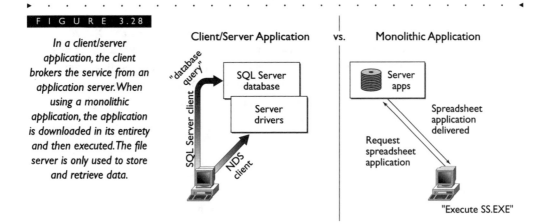

FIGURE 3.28

In a client/server application, the client brokers the service from an application server. When using a monolithic application, the application is downloaded in its entirety and then executed. The file server is only used to store and retrieve data.

Because most people are familiar with Monolithic applications (traditional word processing, spreadsheet, and such), we'll look in detail at client/server options.

Client/Server Services Under NT

When NT is used as the platform to host these types of services, several considerations exist:

1. How will the users authenticate to the service to consume it?

2. Where will the service store its user information?

3. What additional clients (that consume the service) must be deployed at the desktops?

Services Security Access Under NT (Server Add-Ons)

Here's an example to illustrate: When Microsoft SQL Server is installed on NT Server, authenticating users is a real requirement. You don't want just anyone accessing the data in the accounting database. Services such as Microsoft SQL Server have a built-in authentication service to accommodate this, which includes a separate database used to track the user information needed for the service. This is necessary because the Domain database (SAM) is nonextensible and cannot store the information needed by the service.

NOTE

NDS (Novell Directory Services) was created based on the X.500 specifications for a network directory. As a result, the NDS database is extensible to allow for custom data to be stored in the directory for this purpose. Network services, such as Oracle, take advantage of this capability to reduce development time and to provide login and administration of the service.

Using a separate authentication database requires that a user first log in to the network, and then log in to the SQL Server. This means the user must supply a user name and password to use the network and a separate name and password to use the SQL database service. The ability to solve this dual login is the Holy Grail for many administrators; this is usually referred to as a single sign-on environment.

Integrating Service Security

Microsoft has reduced some of the administrative effort by providing a way to form a loose link between the network and the service under NT networking. Services, such as Microsoft SQL Server and Microsoft Exchange, can create a user name mapping between the custom service database (hosted on the NT Server) and the NT Domain Database (SAM). This means a user named Sandy Stevens may have the name of SStevens under the NT Domain and have a separate name of SandyS under the SQL Server database. The SQL Server database keeps a mapping of the two (SStevens ⇨ SandyS). When Sandy logs in to the network, she will be authenticated as SStevens. When she then attempts to access the SQL Server, the SQL Server will check to see if she is authenticated to the network. If she is, access is granted to her based on the SandyS account under the SQL Server database (see Figure 3.29).

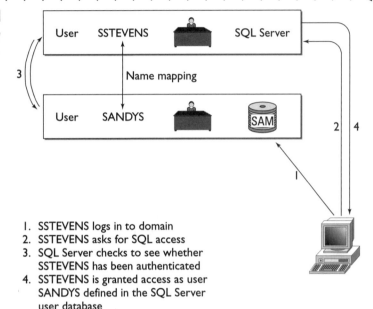

FIGURE 3.29

User names can be mapped between the service and an NT Domain. This way, when a user logs in, the same authentication can be used by the service to validate the user.

1. SSTEVENS logs in to domain
2. SSTEVENS asks for SQL access
3. SQL Server checks to see whether SSTEVENS has been authenticated
4. SSTEVENS is granted access as user SANDYS defined in the SQL Server user database

User creation is also synchronized between the two. If a user named KProws is created in the Domain, then KProws can be automatically created in the SQL Server database, as well. This reduces the time required to manage both the service of the network and the services, because they appear as one.

NOTE

Novell's NDS for NT also accomplishes this task using NDS instead of SAM. The benefit is Domains and trusts are no longer needed, thereby simplifying administration. Users must still have a SQL Server client, of course, to consume SQL services.

Third-Party Service Integration

Many applications are now emerging for NT Server and Workstation. Some of these use the same security mapping as Microsoft services, and some do not. If no integration exists, then users are forced to provide two logins to use the service: one for the network and one for the service. This is livable in some implementations, but in some, it isn't.

NOTE

The security integration of existing services may be changing as Microsoft moves toward *Active Directory Services* (ADS). This may break existing third-party service integration because of its radical departure from traditional Domain Services. Microsoft has stated that its own services (such as Exchange) will be re-engineered in a future release to use ADS. The other BackOffice services probably will follow.

▶ · ◀

Administration Tools for NT Networking

An entire suite of tools can be used to manage NT Server and services. When integrating the two systems together, it's important to know which tools must be available and deployed to manage both systems. We'll refer to the different tools when we talk about integrating NetWare and NT. Table 3.1 shows these NT networking utilities.

TABLE 3.1	UTILITY NAME	PRIMARY USE
NT Networking Utilities	USER Manager	Create users, create Global Groups and Local Groups, create or change policies, add/delete users from groups, change passwords, create trust relationships between Domains.
		This is the main entry point into the Domain SAM database. When used on an NT Workstation, no Domain management options exist.
	Server Manager	View Domains and servers within a Domain. Enables you to look at shares in use and disconnect users. Enables some tuning of the server.
	Policy Manager	Create User Policies. These can be extremely useful to control the desktop. Enables the administrator to remove the Run option from Windows, remove the Network Neighborhood, set custom desktop bitmaps, and so on.
		This utility is only available on NT Server. It can be run on NT Workstation or Windows 95.

T A B L E 3.1	UTILITY NAME	PRIMARY USE
NT Networking Utilities	My Computer icon	Enables (with proper access) the ability to create shares of the file system (hard drives, CD-ROM drives, and so on).

If you use other services, you may use other utilities as well. Some of those more common to NT are:

- ► SQL Server

- ► SQL Server Admin

- ► Exchange Server

- ► Exchange Manager, Planning Tool

- ► IP Networking

- ► DNS Manager

- ► DHCP Manager

- ► WINS Manager

► · ◄

Summary

Windows NT has evolved considerably from its LAN Manager roots. Microsoft has continually added features to evolve into a full-featured, general-purpose operating system.

NT networking has a rich set of services to offer to the network, specifically in application services. As the network grows, management of an NT network must be carefully planned to keep the system manageable.

NT provides File and Print Sharing as a core part of the system and allows other services to dovetail off the Domain. Some services are well-integrated, while others are not. NT has emerged as a good place to host network services, such as database, e-mail, and special-purpose client/server services.

Let's now look at ways to integrate some of these services (both Microsoft and others) into the NT network to get a better understanding of how the system works. This will also give you better insight when it comes to integrating into a NetWare system.

CHAPTER 4

Addressing Integration in the Heterogeneous System

When addressing the integration issue, we typically tend to think in terms of the technologies involved and not necessarily the problems we want to solve. This almost seems like putting the cart before the horse! Maybe we can integrate certain network systems well, but did the integration solve a particular perennial problem?

Perhaps a better solution is to define the typical challenges we currently face when we try to get everything to work together. Most Information Systems managers and CIOs agree we live in a heterogeneous world, one that fosters many best-of-breed solutions, but defines no clear way to use them properly. The appearance of lackluster integration pales at the prospect of using the solution only because you may actually create more work for yourself (and your users!) in the process, due to poor integration of the "better" product.

With challenges such as these in mind, we'll address the typical integration challenges that appear in a mixed network. The approach we take in this chapter is one of addressing what problems you may be trying to solve and mapping to the technologies that you can possibly use to solve them. Once you see what technology you may need, you can then go to the technology-specific chapter and begin.

The Integration Challenges of Information Systems (IS) Managers

Ours is a tough computing world. Just as things start to work (from a system perspective), another new technology comes along (always better and revolutionary) that needs to be added to the current infrastructure. A system integrator's job is usually not one to envy, whether corporate-based or independent consultant. If one thing strikes fear in the heart it's hearing a new technology needs to be deployed and made available to most, or all, of the current user base.

We talk to many customers in the job we're in, and many times we see the same questions pop up again and again. They usually pertain to large systems, but they can apply to smaller systems, as well. These questions translate to challenges many IS managers must face. They include:

- ▸ Single directory possibilities

- ▶ Meta-Directory options

- ▶ Single sign-on to the network

- ▶ Single user account management

- ▶ Integrating resource access

- ▶ Leveraging access management

- ▶ Integrated Application sharing

Now we'll address these challenges. (Hardly anything is really a problem. The only things money or time—or good coding—can't solve are truly problems. Death, for instance, is a problem).

Single Directory Possibilities

One of the most common challenges we've seen is the amount of directories in use today—and how few integrate well with others. This is because a directory standard hasn't been available to which software developers can write. Lotus Notes, for example, had several years of development, some of which were dedicated to creating a directory robust enough for Notes to count on.

Here are a few of the directories available today:

- ▶ Novell Directory Service (NDS)

- ▶ Lotus Notes Directory

- ▶ Domain Naming Service (DNS)

- ▶ Microsoft Domain (for NT Server networking)

- ▶ Netscape Directory Server

▸ Banyan StreetTalk

▸ Internet Directories — Four11, Bigfoot

▸ NIS and NIS+ (Network Information Service)

And so on.

We won't go into detail on each one of these, because it's beyond the scope of this book. Most of these directories have been designed with a specific goal in mind: to help make resources locatable and useful when deployed. Few have been engineered to provide such services to the whole of the infrastructure.

Why a Single Directory?

So many directories (like computing standards!) exist from which to choose, why choose at all? Well, the option exists simply to support many separate directories. Some clear benefits exist, though, of supporting a single directory or Meta-Directory structure, such as the following.

Single Location of Data

A clear example of where a single, unambiguous lookup service is not evident is the DNS and the World Wide Web. Domain Name Service (DNS) — a host lookup protocol on the Internet — as a host location protocol (where are those darn Web servers?) works well. As a service locator (where is that printer?), it leaves much to be desired. For example, where is the unambiguous starting point for a resource search? Usually you start with Yahoo! or another search engine. A single directory ensures a starting point exists (Figure 4.1) and a level of reliability that you have found the right person (Figure 4.2). This is accomplished in a directory by referencing an object's (like a user) Distinguished Name. A Distinguished Name is a full reference to an object in the directory. It's much like referring to a person by his or her full name. Two people named John are easier to distinguish if you use their first, middle, and last names.

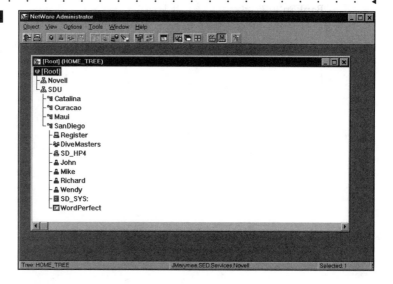

FIGURE 4.1

At the top of the tree is an unambiguous root, which is the ultimate reference for all searches and naming in the NDS tree.

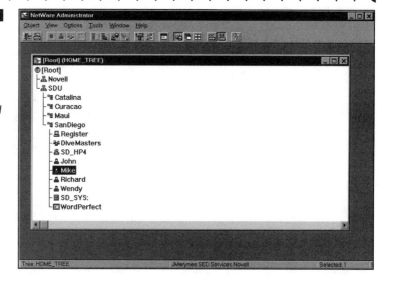

FIGURE 4.2

Note, at the bottom, the user Mike.SanDiego.SDU cannot be confused with another user (even a user whose name is also Mike) because of his distinguished name.

Leverage Knowledge of Each User

If you have a single place to go for reliable and responsive information, this means you must look in fewer places to find the network information. Nearly every user account you may have ever seen has a telephone number and mail information. How many times is this data replicated today (see Figure 4.3) in your network? If you provide a single location to go for data, common data will need to be entered in fewer places. Note, each application needn't use the central directory to store all that data (a need may still exist to store it in its own database), as long as the data can initially be placed in the directory and either a) be synchronized to the external database or b) only be placed in the directory and the application accesses it natively.

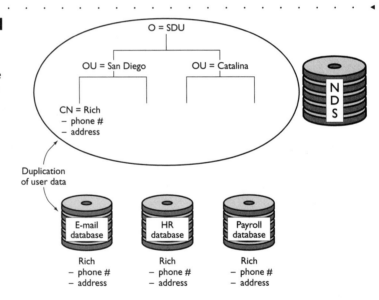

FIGURE 4.3

In many networks today, a user's name and mail address information may be replicated many times due to many nonoverlapping directories or databases.

Single-User Account Creation/Deletion

A common problem with multiple directories is single-user account management. Ironically, it may not be the account creation, as much as deletion, causing most of the heartache. Both deal with the capability of identifying a single unique object that must be managed (even if management means deletion!).

A good example is one Novell used to deal with before NDS. When a user was created under the NetWare 3.x Bindery network, there was an established list of servers on which a user was created, based on his or her job function. Over the years, that same user (let's say JMarymee, for example) was added to many other servers based on needs. If IS didn't track all those user additions, how would they know from which servers to delete the JMarymee account when he left? In a single directory network, a single user deletion would accomplish the task.

Unambiguous Reference of Data

Another useful aspect of a directory is the ability to reference useful data for a variety of reasons. One example would be a remote user (Figure 4.4). When the user is local, the directory knows it by the network address he or she is using. When the user goes remote (Figure 4.5), the directory will again know the user is not at his or her local node and can react appropriately. Such information could enable the system to:

▸ Forward faxes to the user's new location

▸ Forward phone calls

▸ Establish e-mail routing to the nearest post office automatically

▸ • ◂

FIGURE 4.4

When the user Mike is local to the network, NDS will have an address stored when he logs in that tells NDS he is now locally attached.

Logical NDS layout

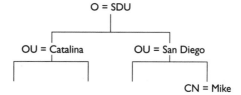

O = SDU

OU = Catalina   OU = San Diego

CN = Mike

Physical layout of network

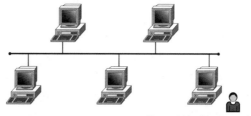

"Login Mike.San_Diego.SDU"

This type of knowledge leveraging makes the overall system easier to manage and, therefore, more fault-tolerant to system breakdowns due to misinformation. A wealth of information exists on automating this type of system in Chapter 10.

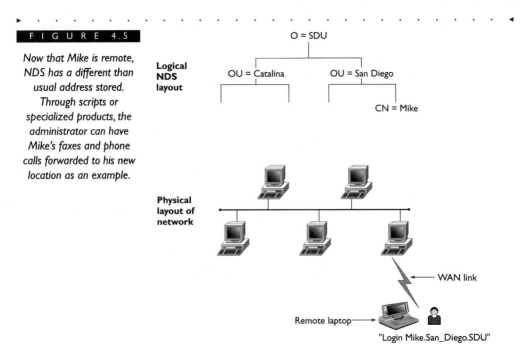

F I G U R E   4 . 5

Now that Mike is remote, NDS has a different than usual address stored. Through scripts or specialized products, the administrator can have Mike's faxes and phone calls forwarded to his new location as an example.

Integration of Multiple Directories

If you do not have a single directory as an option (which many networks do not), what is the next best alternative? This is where the Meta-Directory comes in.

A Meta-Directory can best be defined as a Directory of Directories (Figure 4.6). As we described earlier, you usually do not have a choice as to which directory a product will use. Lotus Notes is fundamentally tied to the Notes Directory. SAP (Human Resources/Business Management software) products use their own naming and authentication directory. Even Microsoft's own BackOffice products (such as SQL Server and Exchange) maintain their own directories, but use the Domain Directory for authentication checks.

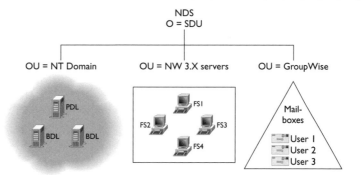

FIGURE 4.6

A Meta-Directory acts as a central point from which to manage other directories. Multiple directories will always be in the enterprise. A Meta-Directory approach provides many of the single directory benefits.

NOTE You may already be using Meta-Directories and you may not even know it. As mentioned, Microsoft BackOffice products do not use a single directory natively (the Domain). Instead, *each* BackOffice product has its own directory of user names and passwords for access. The Domain acts as a Meta-Directory in that a user created under User Manager can be synchronized to each BackOffice service that has the Domain tie-in (the only two are Exchange and SQL Server. SMS uses SQL server). Novell's GroupWise product does likewise. Any user objects created and mapped to a Post Office are synchronized down to the GroupWise database of users.

The Meta-Directory approach has several benefits: First, you needn't make a choice as to which directory to use. Simply keep each separate directory synchronized to a common main directory. Second, integrate the application directly into the directory. This reduces the number of managed directories, but requires directory-aware applications. And third, a less-explored option, allow one directory to act as two, effectively getting the best of both worlds. For example, we'll explore the option of replacing Windows NT Domain security with NDS. Domain-aware applications make calls to the domain, which get redirected to NDS. NDS applications use NDS natively.

With these as the most visible three options, let's look into them in more detail.

Integration of Applications

This approach requires writing new application code, no matter how you look at it. If you are going to integrate applications, you must choose a directory that can fulfill your needs. At best, these needs may be:

- Extensible Directory that allows custom object types and data attributes (a fax object, for example, and its related data needs).

- Scalable — It will need to be expandable enough so all users can benefit (whether local or worldwide).

- Rich Functions — Support of Query, Enumerate, and Cataloging are a few needed, especially with a large number of data.

- Ubiquitous — If you have to install the chosen directory each time the application is deployed, it may be too costly to use the directory. If the directory comes with the platforms on which your service runs, all the better!

Native Implementation of Applications

Once the needs have been defined (from a directory standpoint), applications can be written to take advantage natively of a particular directory. The benefits of such an integrated approach include:

- The interface into the directory will tend to be richer. Whenever a standard is defined that addresses multiple implementations (such as LDAP for directories), the application codes to a least-common denominator. This may mean giving up some functionality.

- The native implementation is usually faster. When using a single interface to multiple directories, redirection is what allows this to function. A native implementation doesn't go through a redirection layer.

- Security tends to be stronger. In the standards today, security is still wanting. If you code to a native layer (like NDS or Domains), security is usually inherent to the directory model.

So, pros and cons exist to using a directory natively. But wait! What about a directory Access Standard? If a standard existed to which everyone could write, then the problem would be solved, wouldn't it? Well . . . .

LDAP — Lightweight Directory Access Protocol

The only real standard (group of people who decide what will be best for the rest of us!) today for Directory Access is LDAP. Note the emphasis on Access. LDAP, in and of itself, does not define a directory (Figure 4.7); it is merely a way to access one (and now, potentially, how one LDAP-enabled directory can synchronize with another LDAP-enabled directory in v3 LDAP).

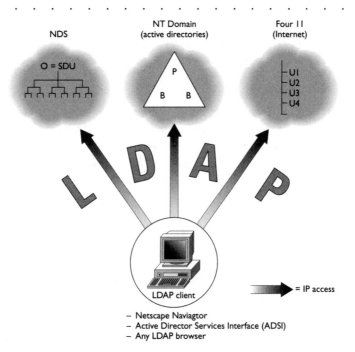

F I G U R E   4.7

LDAP is merely a way to access one or more directories. Here we can access NDS, Domains, and the Internet Four 11 Directory, all via one protocol LDAP.

To take advantage of LDAP, the application must be written to an LDAP API. Existing applications that do not use LDAP will incur no benefits from implementing LDAP access to your existing directory in your network. But take heart! Several emerging applications use LDAP to access a directory for information, such as e-mail addresses. GroupWise (from Novell) and Exchange (from Microsoft) are two such examples.

The Merging LDAP Standard

One of the reasons LDAP applications haven't emerged rapidly is the limited functionality LDAP v2 provided. LDAP v2 lacked security and offered a limited set of verbs for querying a directory and dealing with directory schemas. Version 3 of LDAP provides a richer set of security and directory access verbs, which should enable development of useful applications that can leverage a common access protocol. However, LDAP v3 is not yet complete. LDAP will continually evolve, providing even more verbs for improved security, common ACL access, and a standard replication scheme between LDAP-enabled directories (LDUP).

NOTE

Novell's NDS currently supports LDAP as an access protocol. When loaded where NDS resides, a client can use the published LDAP SDK from the University of Michigan and Netscape to create applications that leverage the directory. All the hard issues (such as replication, partitioning, and fault tolerance) are handled by NDS as the invisible directory LDAP accesses. The LDAP-enabled application can take advantage of all the information already stored in NDS (provided he or she has authorized access) such as Last/First name, mail address, phone number, and so on.

Synchronization of Directories

If you don't have the capability to create new applications or to change the existing ones, you're left with synchronization as the other alternative (or discard the idea of integration altogether — usually not an option!).

The idea behind synchronization is you can leave the current applications alone (from a development perspective) and, instead, create junctions, where possible, that enable single location management, single user account creation, and so on. In other words, glean most of the benefits of having single-directory integrated applications.

Some considerations exist when taking this approach:

▶ You may still require more than one client on the workstations and you will definitely require more than one on the administrative stations. This is because you must authenticate to the Meta-Directory (for example, NDS) as well as the other directories that are subordinately managed (such as NT Domain) to do complete account management (such as password administration).

▸ You are synchronizing two or more directories. If they get out of synch, problems may arise (such as users' ability to get access to a service). For example, an NDS user is created but the new user isn't synched to the NT Domain, so the new user cannot single sign-on to SQL server.

▸ If the synchronization tools used do NOT bidirectionally synchronize, then an administrator using a tool in a subordinate directory (such as NT Domain) may make changes that won't synch upwardly to NDS automatically.

▸ On the same note, it may be a benefit that administrators trained on the old tools may still be able to administer the subordinately managed directory. Then changes can be synched up as necessary to the Meta-Directory.

A few tools enable this sort of synchronization, which we'll discuss in subsequent chapters. One is available as a third-party product (NetVision Synchronicity) and another is a free product provided by Novell (Novell Administrator for Windows NT). Table 4.1 provides a short summary of each of these products, which we will cover in detail in Chapter 6.

TABLE 4.1	TOOL	DESCRIPTION
Tools for Synchronizing NT and NetWare Directories	Novell Administrator for NT	Runs as a service on NT and NetWare One-way synch (NDS to NT) Enables password synch Free add-on from Novell
	Synchronicity by NetVision	Runs as an application on NT Uses a Global Event System for updates Two-way synch (NDS <-> NT) Add-on product

Native Security Replacement

Another option exists for which many administrators have been waiting. This allows NT to provide what it does best, while using the best of NDS.

If we look at NT, what does it do best?

▸ Provides an Application Services Platform

▸ Provides a development platform

▸ Provides a generic easy-to-follow graphical interface

To quote one IS executive, "No one ever bought NT because of Domains. The purchasing decision was not because we love domains. We hate them. However, we bought NT because of the platform OS that it is and the services that run on it."

In the same light, what does NDS as a directory provide?

▸ Scalable, replicated, fault-tolerant directory

▸ Naming and location of resources (services like File, Print, Gateway, SQL server, Exchange, and so forth)

▸ Secure authentication (RSA public/private key authentication)

Many customers have asked Novell for the capability of combining NDS with NT to provide the best of both worlds: NDS naming and authentication with NT as a services and development platform.

As it turns out, architecturally, NT enables a developer to write a security package that replaces the native Domain/SAM authentication. Novell has designed a product (NDS for NT) that replaces the native security system (SAM) with NDS naming and authentication. Because it acts as another security provider in the network, all the BackOffice applications function normally. This means only ONE directory (NDS) exists, yet users still get to single sign-on to the network and use BackOffice applications as usual. One of the benefits is the capability to reduce or remove Trust Relationships (which most NT administrators hate), and the user truly only has one user name.

In the Domain environment, a unique user name isn't guaranteed. If you're using a Multi-Master Domain model (see Chapter 3), a user PREINER may be in Domain A, and a user PREINER in Domain B. How do you know which one is which? In NDS, you may have two users named PREINER, but they are distinguished by the following names: PREINER.SALES.PROVO.NOVELL and PREINER.CONSULTING.PROVO.NOVELL. By name alone (consulting vs. sales) you know exactly which user you mean.

► • ◄

Single Sign-On with Microsoft BackOffice Today

The way NT BackOffice applications appear to provide single sign-on today is by mapping the Service user's name and the Domain name together in a table. For example, user Sstevens in the Domain is mapped to user SandyS in the SQL server database user name table. Then, when SandyS tries to use SQL server, SQL server will look up the corresponding name (SSTEVENS) and see if SSTEVENS is, in fact, authenticated to the Domain (Figure 4.8). If she is, then she is allowed access to SQL server. The difference with NDS replacing Domains is, when SQL server checks to see if SSTEVENS is logged in (through a SAM API), the API call is redirected to NDS. If she is logged into NDS as SSTEVENS, then she will be allowed access to SQL Server (Figure 4.8).

► • ◄

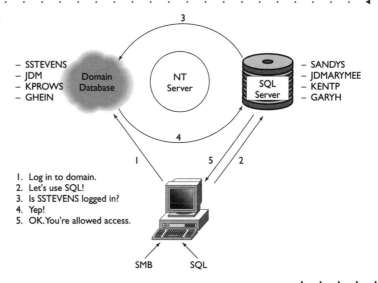

FIGURE 4.8

SQL Server as a BackOffice application can verify users' identifications when they wish to use SQL server. With this procedure, users can have a sort of single sign-on to the domain, and then use SQL server without a second logon.

- SSTEVENS
- JDM
- KPROWS
- GHEIN

Domain Database

NT Server

SQL Server

- SANDYS
- JDMARYMEE
- KENTP
- GARYH

1. Log in to domain.
2. Let's use SQL!
3. Is SSTEVENS logged in?
4. Yep!
5. OK. You're allowed access.

SMB   SQL

With this arrangement, the best of both worlds are served. Some considerations still exist with this approach:

▶ Tools must still exist to manage users in the SQL server name table, Exchange table, and so on. Novell attempts to solve this challenge with new NWAdmin Snapins.

▶ Passwords become more valuable because one gets you access to most resources a user has.

All in all, for most networks, this is the most integrated the two systems can get.

User Single Sign-On

This is the Holy Grail of many administrators. If one thing exists that a vendor could deliver to satisfy the masses, it would be a complete sign-on solution. Several emerging technologies aid in this (such as certificate managed access), although few, if any, complete solutions are available today.

True Single Sign-On

To have a complete single sign-on solution, all applications (or network services) must agree upon a single way to authenticate users to network services (such as single security method for login). For example, my e-mail, File and Print, and Web services all must use a single security. Because this is not yet the case, what's available?

▶ Native security replacement — This is what the Novell NDS for NT does by replacing the SAM-based authentication. A single NDS login is needed to access other services running on NT (see Chapter 7).

▶ Applications written to a single standard — This is what Novell has done with some of their own products, such as IPX/IP Gateway services, Border Services, and so on. This solution requires that NDS is installed and running properly. Microsoft does the same with NT, in that NT BackOffice Services use the Domain/SAM for single sign-on to the NT Server and the BackOffice Services.

Unfortunately, this may not work for all your network services, so a pseudo single sign-on may be necessary.

Pseudo Single Sign-On

If you pursue a synchronization strategy (NDS and NT Domains being synched via Novell Administrator for NT or NetVision's Synchronicity), then you still have two directories. The only thing accomplished is simplification of the administrator's job. The administrator can create a user and have this user creation synched to one or more other directories (such as the Domain/SAM directory).

For this to work, several things must be done:

▸ Each service you wish to login to transparently must have a client deployed on the user workstations. If you wish to use SQL Server, NT File, and Print and Oracle database services running on NetWare, you must have a SQL Server client, an SMB/LAN Manager client, and an Oracle SQL client installed on your workstation.

▸ Passwords, in addition to user names, must be kept in synch. If not, the user will be presented with multiple requests for user name/password combinations.

▸ The client must be capable of receiving one user name/password pair and supplying it to all clients who need user authentication. For example, if all three clients (SQL, SMB, and Oracle) have user names and passwords synched, it won't be useful if the client cannot supply the entered user name/password to all three clients.

One positive last thing is having a client who will enable a user to change a password and have it synched to all the clients to maintain the pseudo single sign-on.

Simplifying User Login

Ideally, in your network, each user will only have a single account name and password to worry about. This minimizes the amount of information the user needs to login. The downside is, the amount a user must know to login is minimal! If a user has one user name and password to get into anything, and if that user name/password pair is given out to another user, the network will be compromised. This is usually a worthwhile trade-off, as long as administrators apprise the users of the risk.

▶ . . . . ◀

Single-User Account Management

Ideally, when a new user must have access to the network and all its resources, only one account should have to be created. In a perfect world this would include the database, e-mail, file, print, and so on.

In many cases, a good integration can appear as if only one database were involved. This may mean relying on synchronization to keep several user databases in synch, perhaps by using some common administration tool. The benefit should be clear: less administration effort on behalf of the IS department.

A good example would be a network comprised of Novell's NDS for NT product and NetVision's Synchronicity for Notes. The first product truly enables the use of one database for user accounts on the network; the second product keeps those user names in synch with the external Notes user directory.

Once user accounts have been created (in more than one user database), maintenance of passwords and resource access becomes the next issue. The two main subjects we need to discuss in those areas are:

▶ Maintaining passwords

▶ Managing Groups and access to services

Maintaining Multiple Passwords

As we stated earlier, the ideal situation is to use several external services that have their own directory, but to have it integrated into the main directory (such as NDS) as the Meta-Directory.

This means you can create an account, but what about passwords? When you create the user, you can assign a password at the same time. After the fact, if a user changes his or her password and it isn't synchronized, what do you do? The problem is one security system cannot read passwords from another (Figure 4.9). If one system was synchronized and the other wasn't, you may have to set new passwords for both systems. This can be a potentially messy task if it happens often.

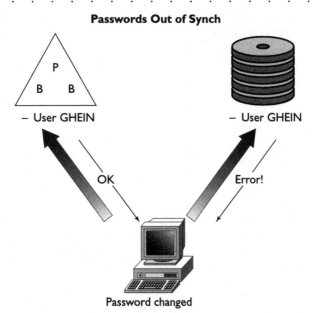

FIGURE 4.9

When synchronizing passwords, if an error occurs, you cannot recover the previous password (unless you are the one who set it and you remember it). Keeping passwords is a messy chore when using a synch strategy.

Passwords Out of Synch

Group Membership Management

Typically, the way most administrators design the network is around the Group Membership model.

1. Groups are created to model generic job functions.

2. Groups are given rights to services the group members will need (files, printers, faxes, databases, and such).

► . . . . ◄

Administrator Tip!

The recovery of lost passwords has caused administrators a significant amount of headaches. As a result, many inventive solutions have been implemented to minimize the recurrence of this problem. One such legend (by the name of SAM G.) had a large cookie jar on his desk and a fund jar next to it. Every time a user forgot or compromised his or her password, a quarter was donated to the "Oreo Fund" before the new password was issued. Everyone then benefited when the resulting fund was large enough to fill the cookie jar with cookies to share! When it becomes possible for passwords to get out of synch, this could be a helpful practice.

3. Users are created as members of groups necessary for their job function.

4. Users are given any specific rights they need separate from the other group members.

Ideally, when you have an integrated network (synched or single sign-on) you should be able to create and manage groups from multiple systems. Unfortunately, this just isn't so. Once the groups themselves have been created and given rights, you can then usually govern user membership (this is the case with Novell Administrator for NT, for example). Because much of the rights capabilities often come from group membership, this is usually a livable solution. Administrators tend to create groups and grant the Group rights, instead of each individual user. This minimizes the management aspect of the network by reducing the number of rights granted to objects by the administrator.

One benefit to Single Directory/Security Replacement is the reduced amount of space needed to support multiple services. If you have a network server (File and Print) plus a database service and e-mail, that may be at least three user accounts. This requires additional storage space to accommodate multiple user accounts per user. When one directory is used, you don't have this problem because only one directory exists (instead of using the Meta-Directory model). This is true whether you are replacing the native directory (Novell's NDS for NT) or creating or using all new applications that use one directory (native NDS or LDAP development).

Technologies That Aid Integration

Table 4.2 describes some of the technologies that will allow a degree of integration. What you will use depends on the applications you'll use as well as the level of integration that you desire. If your needs are fairly simple, you may just need a dual client. If you have a more aggressive integration project, you may need multiple technologies to accomplish sufficient integration.

TABLE 4.2 *Tools for Integrating with the Client*	TOOL	FEATURES	FOR MORE INFORMATION
	NetWare Client for Windows NT	Pseudo single sign-on	See Chapter 5
		Password synch from the client	
	Novell's Z.E.N.works	Manages local NT accounts	See Chapter 10
		Pseudo single sign-on	
		Automatic client updates	
		NT Group membership	
		WS configurations (profiles and policies)	
	Z.E.N.works	Software distribution	See Chapter 10
		Automatic application launching based on NDS information	

Integrating File and Print (Resource Access)

We typically talk about services such as database, but what about the mainstay of networking? What about file and print access? Most Network Operating Systems have some level of file and print sharing. How should those be integrated?

Integration of File and Print resources is a bit trickier than simply synchronizing two directories. When you share file and print services on the network, you must be able to consume those services through some kind of client. To sum up what kinds of things the clients provided, Table 4.3 provides some examples.

TABLE 4.3	CLIENT TYPE	FEATURES
Client Types and What They Provide in the Network	NCP Client	Used by NetWare clients to access:
		File Services
		Print Services System Services, such as locking and message passing
		Novell Directory Services (NDS)
	SMB Client	Used by LAN Manager, LAN Server, and NT Networking clients to access:
		File Services
		Print Services
		System Services
	SQL Client	Used by clients to access a SQL database such as:
		Oracle
		Sybase
		SQL Server
	Custom Requester	Used by services such as PeopleSoft to access custom client/server services

As shown, you must have both clients if you wish to use services from each Network operating system (NetWare and NT Server). In this case, you end up with a scenario that looks like Figure 4.10.

This is a synchronization strategy, possibly, where the user name/password pairs must be identical to get a semblance of single sign-on. Another way of providing services exists, however.

► • ◄

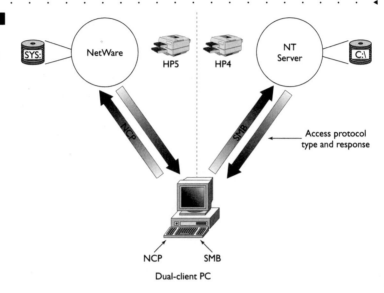

F I G U R E   4.10

If your clients need to access File and Print from both NT Server and NetWare servers, you'll need both the SMB and NCP client requesters.

Emulation Services

If one architecture is used as the main file and print infrastructure, yet you need to provide some file and print access from the other NOS, a way exists to accomplish this using emulation. For example, say you have an all-NetWare network, yet you use NT to host the network databases. Some extra disk storage exists on each of the NT Servers that you wish to make available. You have two choices:

► Add dual clients to every system to which you wish to have access both systems (Figure 4.10).

► Use an Emulator to provide basic file and/or print services to the native system. This only requires one client requester (Figure 4.11).

Integrating using two requesters will be discussed more in Chapter 5. Emulation services are discussed in Chapter 9.

FIGURE 4.11

When using emulation services, you may only need one client to use services from both operating systems. You may not get all the features of both services, though.

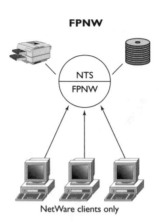

FPNW

NetWare clients only

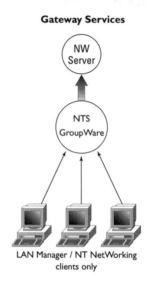

Gateway Services

LAN Manager / NT NetWorking clients only

Managing File System Rights as a Whole

Alas, no major technologies exist here to speak of. When integrating two separate file systems like NetWare and NT, it proves rather difficult. There are several reasons for this:

- NetWare uses an inheritance-based model of rights administration. Rights granted higher in the tree flow down to lower levels unless filtered (see Chapter 2 for details).

- NT uses UNIX-like ACL stamping that is done at each level of the file hierarchy.

- NetWare has eight file rights (Read, Write, Create, Erase, Modify, Filescan, Access Control, Supervisory).

- NT has (RWCDXAF).

▶ · ◀

ACLStamping in the File System

In the Windows NT file system, Access Control Lists (ACLs) are stored in the file system itself. The same is true for the NetWare file system. In Windows NT, though, a user's rights are calculated only at the current directory (ACL stamping). The NT OS won't walk up the file directory to see if any ACLs have been applied at a higher layer, unlike NetWare. As a result, managing the NT file system tends to be less manageable due to the current set of tools provided by Microsoft.

The closest you can manage the two via one interface (either the NT management tools or NetWare) is through emulation. Emulation provides the ability to see the other file system through the eyes of another (such as seeing NT volumes as NetWare volumes and assigning file rights as such). The only other choice is to manage each file/print system using the native tools.

NT File/Print Management Tools

Windows NT provides several tools to manage their file and print systems. In Windows NT 3.51, a separate tool for administering shared file resources actually exists. In Windows NT 4.0, the tool is integrated with the My Computer icon on the desktop. This is the explorer interface. Following are the tools needed for File/Print administration under Windows NT:

Explorer Interface	Used to create Shares and assign permissions on NTFS volumes. Without NTFS, Shares govern what rights a user can execute.
Printers/Control Panel	Used to create printers and share them on the network.

NetWare Management Tools

NetWare also provides several tools for administration. Like Windows NT, some of this functionality is integrated into the desktop operating system (like Windows NT does under Explorer). The two main tools provided for complete administration include:

| NWAdmin | Graphical tool used for most administration. Used to grant trustee assignments to user/group/container objects. |
| FILER | DOS tool to assign trustee rights to user/ group/container objects in the NDS tree. |

NOTE

When using emulation to grant rights, the mappings between NetWare and NTFS may not always map the way you want. Be aware of the effects of using one system to manage another before you do this in production. See Chapter 9 for details on emulation management options.

Leveraging Resource Management (Management by Exception)

What most managers would love to see is a way to package the basics of the network administration and allow those rules to preside when doing basic network functions (such as create/delete/move a user). Even when integrating two networks, such as NetWare and NT, NDS can provide some of this as a side benefit.

Putting Knowledge in the Tree

A simple analogy might prove useful. The first day you come on board with company SDU, you are given a key to the San Diego office. Inside is a fax, a printer, the network server, and so on. In addition, you are given a user name and password to the corporate network. Then you are made a member of the group SCUBA Divers.

Now you are dragged and dropped to Maui. You turn in your key to the San Diego office and receive a new key to the Maui office. The new Maui key enables you to get in and access the local resources there, just like in San Diego. And you still are a member of the Scuba Divers group. In other words, you only need access to resources local to you. You don't need access to a fax in San Diego anymore; you only need access to the one in Maui.

Modeling the Real World in NDS

NDS enables a similar management option to occur. When a user is given access to the network resources, he or she can gain access to those resources several ways:

- As a member of a group

- As an object contained within an area of the tree (a certain OU, such as San Diego, for example)

- Explicitly granted rights to my user object

Therefore, if resources are granted to a container (like OU=Maui), and I am part of that container, then when I am moved, I will lose the access I received being part of that container and I will possibly gain new accesses being part of a new container. If I am a member of one or more groups, that group membership will stay with me until I am explicitly deleted or my membership is removed.

In this way, access to resources can be given to a container (such as file, print, database, fax server, and such) and I will gain access. When I am dragged-and-dropped into a new container, I will lose my container rights and potentially gain rights being part of another.

Automating Client Update and Application Launching

Another issue when managing network resources, or just in the daily operation of the network, is that updating clients on the network may be necessary. This is part of general resource access management. If an application isn't available for launching, then users can't get their jobs done. In addition, automating client resource updates may need to be done for several reasons:

- A new version of the client is released with new features

- A new version of a client is released that solves a problem

▸ You need to deploy another client (dual client) if you're using a synchronization strategy

Although this isn't an integration technology per se, it is almost a necessity when attempting an integration project. Two technologies are summarized in Table 4.4 that can facilitate deployment of clients, updates, and applications.

TABLE 4.4 *Tools for Automating Client Update and Application Execution*	TOOL INFORMATION	FEATURES	FOR MORE
	Novell ACU (automatic client update)	Used to automate client install/update for Windows 3.x, Windows 95, and Windows NT clients. It is part of the Client 32 technology.	See Chapter 5
	Z.E.N.works	Allows applications to be executed properly by using information stored in NDS. NAL can also provide detailed software distribution of new clients and applications.	See Chapter 10
	OS Scripting	Various levels of scripting. Microsoft's SMS, as well as NetWare and Windows NT provide login scripting to assist client automation.	See Chapter 11

▸ · ◀

Integrating Application Sharing

One of the biggest challenges in the network is launching applications from the desktop. This success of launching an application depends upon many things being just right for the application to launch properly. Some items, typically managed closely to be successful, include:

- Drive Mappings (or NET USE statements under Windows NT)

- Environment Variables

- Printer Captures (Printer sharing)

- System requirements (Required RAM, hard disk, and so forth)

The way applications are deployed by administrators usually follow a scenario like this:

1. The Admin installs an application once successfully on a particular desktop.

2. The Admin then puts the application files on a shared network applications server.

3. The Admin creates a Login Script and/or batch file that allows it to execute.

4. User messes up drive mappings or some other item that makes it totally impossible to run the newly deployed application properly!

Even though the application is centrally stored, some things must be done for the application to execute. This is what NAL (Novell Application Launcher — part of Z.E.N.works) can accomplish. Some of what NAL tracks for the application includes:

- OLE/ActiveX Controls necessary to run the application (this is accomplished by recording registry and DLL requirements for the application)

- INI file changes

- Drive Mappings (or NET USE statements) that must be in effect

- Registry Settings

- Alternatives if the applications files aren't available (a fault-tolerant option)

NAL can be configured to launch applications stored on an NT Server network (Domain or Workgroup), as well as IntranetWare. In addition, scripting can allow the software deployment and launching of applications via NAL to be totally transparent, no matter which network is being used. See Chapter 10 for more information on using NAL for integration.

The Next Step

Now that you know what kind of integration you're after and potentially which technologies will enable it, you can jump to the chapters that make the most sense. As a summary of what we've described in this chapter, the matrix shown in Table 4.5 should point you in the proper direction for the next step.

TABLE 4.5

Summary of All the
Technolgies Used
for NetWare and
NT Integration

TECHNOLOGY	DESCRIPTION	SERVICES
Duel Client Integration	Used for providing services from two or more dissimilar network services. Provides all the native services, but requires user name and password synch on all services to be the most seamless.	Novell NT client Novell Client 32
Emulation Services	Does not require any client updates. Requires services be routed through a gateway (a potential bottleneck), so not a good solution for heavy I/O. Emulation usually doesn't provide a complete emulation, usually a subset of functionality.	Microsoft FPNW Microsoft Gateway Service
Client Side Management	Near seamless integration of NDS and client OS.	Workstation Manager

TABLE 4.5

*Summary of All the
Technolgies Used
for NetWare and
NT Integration
(continued)*

TECHNOLOGY	DESCRIPTION	SERVICES
Z.E.N.works	Near seamless way to share and execute applications hosted on NT or NetWare networks.	Z.E.N.works
Novell Administrator for NT	Used to synch two dissimilar network OS directories into a Meta-Directory.	(See Chapter 6)
NetVision Synchronicity	Used also to leverage NDS as a Meta-Directory synchronizing to MS NT Domains.	(See Chapter 6)
Novell's NDS for NT	Used to replace the native security engine of NT and use NDS as the single sign-on directory. One of the most seamless ways to integrate fully both services of NT and NetWare networking services.	(See Chapter 7)

► · ◄

Summary

We've covered a lot of ground in this chapter. Hopefully, you have a better sense of what kind of integration can be accomplished and some of the technologies to accomplish them. Most integration projects are actually a mix of several of these technologies. This all depends, as previously stated, on the level of integration you need and on what is available to you. We attempted to show you as much about what's available as possible, but other third-party enablers may also provide further integration.

Integrating NT Workstations

Microsoft's NT Workstation operating system offers some compelling features for organizations that require power and functionality at the workstation level. First, it provides the power of a 32-bit multitasking operating system, but it still renders the ease of use to which Microsoft Window's users have grown accustomed. It also offers desktop security, which means to access resources on an NT Workstation, a user must first log in to it. While this level of security is essential in some environments, it adds complexity to the overall administration of the network.

The Novell NetWare Client for Windows NT simplifies the integration and administration of NT Workstations in a NetWare environment. In addition, it provides NT Workstations with complete access to all NetWare services (file, print, directory, and so on). This chapter discusses the NetWare Client for Windows NT in detail.

When integrating NT Workstations in an environment that consists of *both* NetWare servers and NT Servers, it is necessary to maintain the NetWare client as well as the Microsoft Server Message Block (SMB) client. The SMB client is required for NT Workstations to access file, print, and domain services shared under Windows NT. Just as you need a Novell client to access services under NetWare, you need the Microsoft (SMB) client to access Microsoft services. This chapter will also provide details on the configuration of the Microsoft SMB client.

Novell's Integration Solutions

Novell offers two NT Workstation integration solutions that enable you to integrate NT Workstations seamlessly into your Novell network:

- NetWare Client for Windows NT

- Z.E.N.works workstation management and application distribution

The NetWare Client for Windows NT provides NT Workstations with full support to NetWare services. In addition, it provides NT Workstation users with a single synchronized login to both their NT Workstations, as well as to NDS.

The Z.E.N.works workstation management components of the NetWare Client for Windows NT eliminate the burden of individually administering NT Workstations by storing NT user and desktop configuration information in NDS. By doing this, NT Workstation users use a single user ID for their access to NDS and to their NT Workstation. From the administrative perspective, this means the administrator manages a single account for each user. In addition, once an NT user is attached to the network, individual user security policies and profiles can be downloaded to the workstation. The benefit is users will see exactly the same desktop, despite which physical NT Workstation they use to log in. The Z.E.N.works workstation management is covered in detail in Chapter 10.

NetWare Client for Windows NT

The NetWare Client for Windows NT is 32-bit client software that provides NT Workstations with transparent access to NetWare services and resources. This includes all NetWare services, such as NDS, file, print, security, messaging, management, and so on. Included with the client is support for all Z.E.N.works workstation management and application distribution features, formally known as "Workstation Manager" and "NetWare Application Launcher" (NAL), respectively. These features are covered in detail in Chapter 10.

The NetWare Client for Windows NT and all the included products are available for download free of charge from Novell's Web site at http://www.novell.com.

Choosing the Right Client

When you are evaluating the solutions available to integrate NT Workstations into your Novell network, you may run across client software provided by companies other than Novell. For example, Microsoft offers the Microsoft Client for NetWare free-of-charge, as well. In fact, the product is included with NT Workstation. This always creates the dilemma of whose client you should use.

Our advice to you is, save yourself the grief. Although Microsoft's client offers basic connectivity to your NetWare networks, it neither provides complete support for NDS nor offers the features and functionality of the NetWare client. For example, if you use the Microsoft client, you will not have support for Z.E.N.works, NWAdmin, increased client security through the use of packet signatures, NetWare/IP or Pure IP, and so on.

What this means is that by choosing the Microsoft client for NetWare networks, you can only use a portion of the functionality that NetWare provides. The bottom line is, no one knows NetWare like Novell. Why even consider using a client developed by another company?

NOTE **Microsoft offers several clients providing access to different types of services. The Microsoft Client for NetWare provides access to NetWare file and print services. It should not be confused with the Microsoft SMB client, which provides access to NT Server services (file, print, domain, and so on).**

If you already have Microsoft's Client for NetWare installed on your NT Workstations, we recommend you upgrade to Novell's client for the same reasons previously mentioned. Now, at this point, you probably think we're crazy. This may be especially so if you have quite a few clients already running the Microsoft Client for NetWare. But, before you toss our recommendation (and our book!) out the window, read on.

Normally, changing the client software on a number of machines is a tremendous amount of work. The NetWare Client for Windows NT, however, includes a feature called the Automatic Client Upgrade (ACU) that minimizes this task. ACU enables you to upgrade remotely the client software currently running on your NT Workstations. This can even be done in an unattended mode. For example, ACU could automatically upgrade the client software the next time users log in; you would never physically have to go to each workstation. Although a small amount of effort is involved to setup the ACU upgrade parameters, it will be worth the effort — guaranteed. Using the ACU feature of the NetWare Client to upgrade your NT Workstations will be covered in detail later in this chapter.

Product Features

The NetWare Client for Windows NT includes a number of features that make it the best choice for connecting your NT Workstations to your NetWare networks. Table 5.1 summarizes the major features of the product. The first three features listed are covered in-depth immediately following the table. Installation and the ACU are covered in-depth later in this chapter.

T A B L E 5.1	FEATURE	DESCRIPTION
NetWare Client for Windows NT Features Summary	NetWare Requester	Provides redirection services, auto-reconnection, multiple tree support, packet signing, performance features, and more.
	Protocol Support	Supports both IPX/SPX and TCP/IP. Can coexist with other protocol stacks, such as NetBEUI.
	Extensions to Native Windows NT Interfaces	Extends My Computer, Explorer, and Network Neighborhood to provide access to NetWare resources.
	Customizable Installation	A customizable installation facility that is integrated with Windows NT's native installation process.
	Automatic Client Upgrade	Enables automatic upgrade of client on NT workstations.

NetWare Requester

The NetWare Requester is the main component of the NetWare Client for Windows NT. Its key element is a 32-bit redirector whose purpose is to intercept requests for network services and redirect them to the network for processing. This version of the NetWare Requester provides complete compatibility with earlier versions of Novell's client software. This includes NETX, VLM, and the NetWare 4.1 16-bit Client libraries.

The NetWare requester provides a number of additional features. The major ones are as follows:

▸ Enhanced Performance

▸ Multiple Tree Support

▸ Auto-reconnection

▸ Packet Signing

Enhanced Performance   The NetWare client for Windows NT provides three features that enable you to enhance performance of your network. These features include:

▸ Packet Burst Protocol

▸ Large Internet Packets

▸ Resource Caching

Packet Burst   *Packet Burst* protocol increases performance of large file reads and writes over a wide area network. Without Packet Burst, every read and write made by a workstation must be done one packet at a time. The file server must then respond to each request one packet at a time.

Packet Burst enables the file server to respond to read requests with a burst of packets for every read request received. It also allows the workstation to send a burst of packets when writing to a file server that requires only one response from the server. This increases network performance by reducing the amount of time the workstation spends sending requests and receiving responses from the file server. Packet Burst also reduces network traffic.

Large Internet Packet (LIP)   Another performance feature included with the client is Large Internet Packet (LIP) support. *LIP* increases performance across network routers by allowing a workstation and file server to negotiate the packet size to be used. This negotiation takes place transparently in the background. Without LIP, all packets sent across routers are reduced to 512 bytes.

Large Internet Packets are enabled by default when you install the NetWare Client for Windows NT.

Resource Caching   Performance is also boosted at the NT client through integration with the Windows NT cache manager. *Resource caching* provides network I/O caching of data files and executables where appropriate.

Multiple Tree Support   *Multiple tree support,* a relatively new feature to NetWare, enables an NDS user to authenticate to multiple trees (to which they have security access) with a single login. This enables a user to access resources on multiple trees simultaneously.

Users could previously only be authenticated to one NDS tree at a time. If users needed NDS access to resources on a tree other than the one to which they were currently authenticated, they were logged out of their current tree prior to logging in to the new tree. Previously, the only way to access resources in another tree was to establish a bindery connection to a file server in that tree. This required bindery services be set up on the file server. In addition, the bindery connection did not allow access to NDS resources other than file and print services.

NOTE The *bindery* is a network database used with early versions of NetWare (NetWare 2.*x* and 3.*x*). The bindery is server-centric, meaning each file server maintains its own bindery. If a user needs access to two bindery servers, he or she must have one account on each server. This service is a method used to enable **NDS** to emulate a bindery database.

Auto-Reconnection   *Auto-reconnection* is another useful feature of the NetWare client, which allows the client software to reconnect automatically to the file server if your connection is temporarily lost. Not only does this feature automatically reconnect you to the file server, it also restores the drive mappings and print queue captures of your previous connection.

Packet Signing   *Packet signing* is a security feature that protects NCP communications between server and client. When packet signing is enabled, both the client and server stamp each packet with a digital signature. This prevents unauthorized users from capturing packets on the wire.

The only caveat to using packet signatures is that increasing the signature level value increases security. But at the same time, it decreases network performance.

This is because additional overhead is generated at both the client and server when the digital signatures are created.

The packet signing signature levels are as follows:

- ▸ 0 = Packet signatures disabled

- ▸ 1 = Packet signatures are enabled, but not preferred (only use if required by the file server)

- ▸ 2 = Packet signatures preferred (use if the server requires them, but don't require them if the server doesn't support them)

- ▸ 3 = Packet signatures required. Don't connect to the server unless the server can support packet signing

Protocol Support

With the NetWare Client for Windows NT, you are given the freedom to choose the protocols you wish to use. The software supports both IPX/SPX and TCP/IP and provides full 32-bit support for Novell's Open-Data Link Interface (ODI), as well as Microsoft NDIS.

We will take a closer look at how to choose and configure network protocols in the section "Installing the NetWare Client for Windows NT" later in this chapter.

Extensions to Native Windows NT Interfaces

When you install the NetWare Client for Windows NT, the Native Windows NT 4.0 interfaces such as My Computer, the Window NT Explorer, and the Network Neighborhood are extended to enable access to network resources from the NT Workstation.

With the client software installed, My Computer displays any network drives currently mapped, enabling you to view network directories and files as if they were local. The Windows NT Explorer is extended to enable you to view and browse NDS resources. Figure 5.1 shows the NDS resources of the SDU tree (from our earlier examples) being viewed through the Explorer.

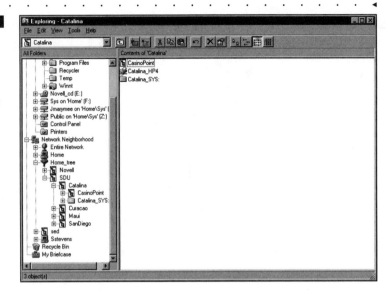

FIGURE 5.1

The NetWare Client for Windows NT extends the Windows NT Explorer to show an NDS tree and its resources. This enables you to browse the resources, as well as to map/unmap network drives and capture printers.

In Figure 5.1, notice the expanded NDS tree in the left portion of the screen under All Folders. On the right, you see the resources available in the NDS container object "Catalina."

If you highlight the printer object and press the right mouse button, you will be given the ability to capture that printer. Double-clicking the printer enables you to view the status of the jobs currently being serviced by the printer. Highlighting the volume and clicking the right mouse button enables you to map a network drive. Double clicking the volume enables you to expand it and view the contents.

Network Neighborhood is expanded in a similar way, as shown in Figure 5.2. When the NetWare Client is installed, the Network Neighborhood displays the NDS tree and enables you to browse and access NDS resources as previously described.

Network Neighborhood provides the same functionality as previously described when mapping network drives or selecting printer or other NDS objects. Another useful available feature is to select an NDS tree while viewing the Network Neighborhood and to press the right mouse button. Doing so presents the menu shown in Figure 5.2, which enables you to log in or log out of the tree, set your current NDS context, or view the current NetWare connection information.

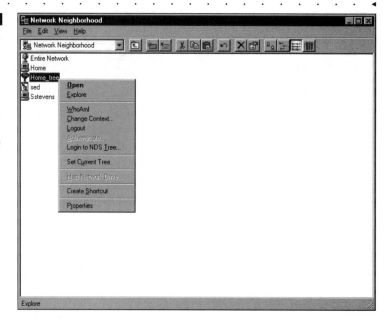

The NetWare Client for Windows NT extends the Network Neighborhood interface to display NDS trees and resources. Expanding the tree enables you to access resources in NDS containers. Selecting a tree and pressing the right mouse button enables you to perform the tasks shown onscreen.

Installing the NetWare Client for Windows NT

Before you install the NetWare Client for Windows NT, you must ensure that your workstations meet the hardware and software requirements of the product. You also need to determine the location (CD-ROM, floppy, network, and so on) from which you will be performing the installation. These are described in the following sections.

Hardware and Software Requirements

Before you install the NetWare Client for Windows NT, be sure the workstation or workstations you are installing or upgrading meet the following hardware and software requirements:

▶ Microsoft Windows NT 3.51 or 4.0 installed (unless you're installing the client at the same time as the Windows NT operating system) on a machine with an Intel based processor

▶ 12MB of RAM, 16MB recommended

▸ 10MB of free hard disk space

▸ A network interface card installed in your workstation

▸ A cable connection to the network

Installation Location Options

You can install the NetWare Client for Windows NT from four different locations:

▸ CD-ROM

▸ Floppy disk

▸ Local hard disk

▸ Network file server

CD-ROM   Installing the NetWare Client for Windows NT is the most basic method of installation. The CD-ROM containing the software can be placed in the local CD-ROM drive of the workstation on which you are performing the installation, or it can be mounted as a volume on a NetWare file server.

Floppy Disk   If you are performing the client installation on a workstation without access to a local or shared CD-ROM drive, or a network directory that contains the installation files, you may need to perform the installation from a floppy disk.

To copy the NetWare Client for Windows NT installation files to floppy disk, run the MAKEDISK.BAT file from the root directory of the NetWare Client for Windows NT CD-ROM. This batch file will copy the necessary installation files to 13 floppy disks (or more, depending on the client version).

Local Hard Disk   You can also perform the installation from a local hard disk. To use this method, simply copy the contents of the NetWare Client for Windows NT to a local hard drive directory.

Network File Server   To install or upgrade the NetWare Client for Windows NT from a network file server, the workstations being installed must be able to log in to the file sever that contains the installation files. This would be the case if, for example, the workstation were already running an older version of the client or Microsoft's Client for NetWare. You should use this method of installation if you wish to install or upgrade multiple workstations simultaneously or if you do not want to be present.

To install from a network file server, you must copy the contents of the NetWare Client for Windows NT CD to a network directory. We recommend you create a directory called NT in the SYS: PUBLIC\CLIENT directory. This way, you can be sure all users will have the proper rights to access the installation files.

Installation Procedures

Installing the NetWare Client for Windows NT is quick and easy, even if you are installing or upgrading a number of workstations. A number of different installation options are available from which to choose. The one you use will primarily depend on whether you are installing one workstation at a time or remotely installing or upgrading a number of stations.

The different options for installing the NetWare Client for Windows NT are listed as follows:

- Install using the SETUPNW.EXE utility

- Install from the Network Control Panel

- Install at the same time as Windows NT

- Install using the Automatic Client upgrade feature

- Install using the Novell Application Launcher (see Chapter 13 for details)

The installation method you use depends on the number of workstations you will be installing and whether the workstation has an earlier version of the client currently installed. Each of these methods is detailed in the following sections. We have categorized the sections based upon common installation requirements, as follows:

▶ Basic installation or upgrade of the NetWare Client on an NT workstation (SETUPNW or Network Control Panel)

▶ Simultaneously install multiple workstations unattended (SETUPNW /U)

▶ Install at the same time as Windows NT (UNATTEND.TXT)

▶ Automatically upgrade client when user logs in (SETUPNW /ACU)

Basic Installation or Upgrade

If you wish to perform a basic installation or upgrade of the NetWare Client for Windows NT on a single workstation or multiple workstations one at a time, you can use one of two methods:

▶ SETUPNW.EXE

▶ Network Control Panel

Using the SETUPNW.EXE utility is the fastest and easiest option. This utility provides a simple graphical interface for the installation, which requires little interaction. Using the Network Control Panel is as easy, but requires a few additional steps.

Using SETUPNW.EXE   To install the NetWare Client for Windows NT using the SETUPNW utility, double-click the SETUPNW.EXE file located in the I386 directory of the NetWare Client for Windows NT CD or other installation location (floppy disk, hard disk, or network directory).

You will be presented with the title screen shown in Figure 5.3.

To install the NetWare Client for Windows NT, you must be logged in to the NT Workstation as Administrator or as a member of the Administrator's group.

NOTE

▶ · ◀

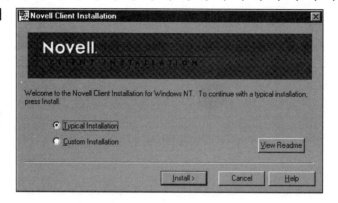

FIGURE 5.3

When you use SETUPNW.EXE to install the NetWare Client for Windows NT, you are presented with this title screen. If you choose Typical, the client will install without any further user intervention.

The default configuration of SETUPNW.EXE is to run the installation with little interaction. By default, the previous screen is the only screen that requires interaction. When you click continue, the installation process will copy the necessary files to your workstation, modify the registry, and automatically attempt to detect your network card, frame type, network protocols, and so on. If you have existing client software installed on the workstation, such as Microsoft's Client for NetWare, the installation process will remove it prior to performing the installation.

If necessary, you can choose the Custom option, which will present you with the screen in Figure 5.4. Each option installs additional client features, such as:

▶ *Novell Distributed Print Services* (NDPS). Novell's latest printing architecture provides bidirectional communication between the user's workstation and network printers, allowing advanced printing features. NDPS is a core feature of NetWare 5.

▶ *Novell IP Gateway.* Provides IPX clients with the capability to share a single IP address for Internet Access. This feature is commonly used if Internet access is required without sufficient IP addresses for every workstation.

▶ *Novell Target Service Agent.* Allows server-based software to back up the local contents of the workstation's hard drive.

- ▸ *Novell Workstation Manager*. Provides management of NT desktop features from within NDS.

- ▸ *Z.E.N.works Application Launcher NT Service*. This feature is commonly used to distribute software via NDS in environments where the NT desktop is secured and the user doesn't have sufficient desktop rights to install software.

- ▸ *Z.E.N.works Remote Control*. Allows this workstation to be remotely controlled through the Z.E.N.works administrator's remote control console.

Many of these features will be covered in detail in Chapter 10.

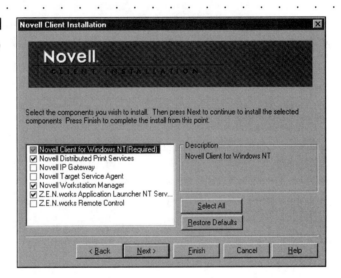

F I G U R E   5 . 4

Choosing the Custom option allows installation of advanced features, such as remote control and server-based workstation backup.

You must also choose the Custom feature if you wish to install Novell's Pure IP support for connecting to NetWare 5 servers via TCP/IP. After choosing the features from Figure 5.4, you'll be presented with protocol choices, as shown in Figure 5.5. Check with your network Administrator to determine the protocol options for connecting to your NetWare servers.

▶ · ◀

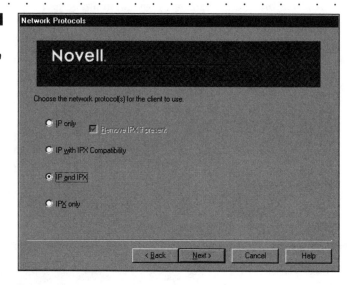

F I G U R E   5.5

If you're connecting to NetWare 5 servers, you can choose either IP or IPX. If your network consists of only NetWare 3.x and NetWare 4.x servers, choose IPX.

Once the installation is complete, you may need to configure the NetWare Client on the workstation. This process is described in the section "Configuring the NetWare Client for Windows NT" later in this chapter.

Using the Network Control Panel   The Network Control Panel can be used to install, update, and remove the NetWare Client for Windows NT. To perform any of these functions, you must be logged in to the NT workstation as Administrator or as a user who is a member of the Administrator's group.

Installing from the Network Control Panel   To install the NetWare Client for Windows NT using the Network Control Panel, from the Windows NT 4.0 Start menu, choose Settings. Then select Control Panel/Network, and choose the Services tab. Then click Add to install the NetWare Client for Windows NT. The Select Network Service dialog box shown in Figure 5.6 will appear.

TIP

Here's a shortcut for accessing the Network Control Panel option: Highlight Network Neighborhood on your Windows NT desktop and press the right mouse button. Then choose Properties and select the Services tab.

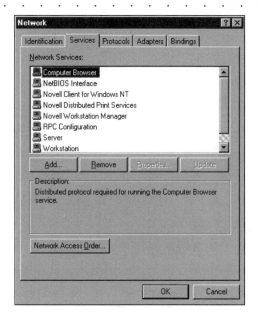

FIGURE 5.6

Installing the NetWare Client for Windows NT through the Network Control Panel is done by choosing Add from the Network Services screen, and then choosing Have Disk in the dialog box shown.

In Figure 5.6, a list of network services available with Windows NT Workstation is shown. To install the NetWare client, choose Have Disk. You will be prompted to enter the path to the Novell NetWare Client for Windows NT files on the CD or network, for example, D:\I386. Then, from the Select OEM Option dialog box, choose Novell NetWare Client for Windows NT and choose OK.

The client software will then be installed on your workstation. When the installation is complete, you must reboot the workstation for the changes to take effect. You may also need to configure the NetWare Client on the workstation. This process is described in the section "Configuring the NetWare Client for Windows NT" later in this chapter.

Upgrading or Removing from the Network Control Panel   To upgrade or remove the NetWare Client for Windows NT using the Network Control Panel, from the Windows NT 4.0 Start menu, choose Settings. Then select Control Panel/ Network, and then choose the Services tab. You will see the NetWare Client for Windows NT in the list of network services, as shown in Figure 5.7.

▸ · ◂

To remove or update the NetWare Client for Windows NT, access the Network Services tab from the Network Control Panel, and then click Remove or Update.

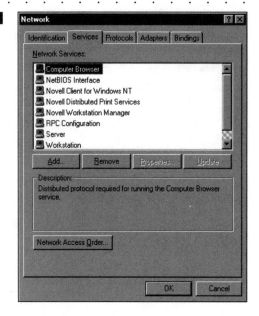

From the Network Services dialog shown in Figure 5.7, the NetWare Client for Windows NT can be removed by simply clicking the Remove button. Once the product has been removed, you must reboot your computer for the changes to take effect.

To update the version of the NetWare client running on your workstation, click the Update button shown in Figure 5.5. Then, when prompted, specify the path to the location to the updated client files. Once the upgrade is complete, you will need to reboot your workstation for the changes to take effect.

Unattended Installation

Upgrading or installing client software is a task most network administrators dread. Generally, this is a process that entails physically going to each workstation and performing the installation. On a large network, client software upgrades often take weeks, or even months, to complete.

To make this task easier, the NetWare Client for Windows NT enables you to perform the installation on several workstations at the same time. You do this by using the unattended install feature of SETUPNW.EXE.

Running SETUPNW /U from a login script

If you are running SETUPNW /U from a login script, make sure you precede the command with a #. This is a standard login script command that enables you to execute an external executable file. For example, the login script to run an unattended installation may look something like this:

```
#SETUPNW /U:\\HOME\SYS\PUBLIC\CLIENT\WINNT\UNATTEND.TXT
```

In addition, users must have administrative access to the NT Workstation before the installation can be performed. To allow this without the chance of a security breach, the /ACU option can be used in conjunction with Workstation Manager. This process is discussed in detail in Chapter 10.

As previously described, SETUPNW.EXE is an installation program that enables you to perform a basic installation of the NetWare Client. Running SETUPNW. EXE with the /U parameter enables you to customize the installation. By running this command from within a login script and installing from a NetWare server, you can configure multiple workstations at once without being physically present.

The syntax for SETUPNW is as follows:

```
SETUPNW /u:path to unattend file
```

The unattended file referenced in the previous syntax is a text file that enables you to customize the SETUPNW installation process. A description of this file follows.

The NetWare Client for Windows NT includes a file called UNATTEND.TXT. This file is actually Novell's version of Microsoft's UNATTEND.TXT included with Windows NT. Novell has modified the file to add Novell NetWare Client Parameters. By setting these parameters, you can control what dialogs appear to the user during the installation and what parameters are configured automatically.

The UNATTEND.TXT file can be found on the NetWare Client for Windows NT CD in the I386\SYSTEM\NLS*Language* (English, French, German, and so forth) directory.

The UNATTEND.TXT file included with the NetWare Client for Windows NT is a self-documented text file. What this means is everything you will possibly want to know about the file, you will find in the file itself. For this reason, we have not repeated all the parameters and options in this book. We recommend you use your favorite text editor to view the file. You may want to think twice before printing it, though, as it's 34 pages long! But don't let the length of the file intimidate you. Only a small portion of it relates to the NetWare client; the defaults of Microsoft's file make up the remainder.

When you modify the UNATTEND.TXT file, save it under a different file name. This way, you still have a copy of Novell's original version of the file. SETUPNW doesn't care what the file name is, as long as you specify the path and file name in the syntax.

TIP

Installing at the Same Time as Windows NT

The UNATTEND.TXT file included with the NetWare Client for Windows NT can be used in conjunction with Microsoft's file to perform an unattended installation of both the Windows NT operating system and the NetWare Client. This can save you tremendous amounts of time if you upgrade the operating system and install the NetWare Client for Windows NT on a number of different machines (for example, if you upgrade from Windows NT 3.51 and the NetWare Client for Windows NT).

If you skipped directly to this section, you may want to turn back a few pages and review the "Unattended Installation" section for an explanation of how to perform an unattended installation of the NetWare Client.

NOTE

To perform an unattended installation of Windows NT and the NetWare client on multiple workstations, those workstations must have an existing network connection. This is because the installation will need to be performed from the network. In addition, to update the system files on the NT Workstation, a user with administrative access must be logged in at each workstation.

Setting up the unattended installation of Windows NT and the NetWare Client consists of a number of steps. These steps are as follows:

1. Copy the Windows NT CD to a file server directory on your existing network.

2. Change to the I386 directory and create a directory called OEM.

3. In the OEM directory, create a directory called NET.

4. In the NET directory, create a directory called NTCLIENT.

5. Open the Windows NT UNATTEND.TXT file located in the I386 directory.

6. In the [Network] section, add the following line:

```
InstallServices = ServicesList
```

7. At the end of the file, add the following lines to the [ServicesList] section:

```
:NWFS = NovellNetWareClientParameters, \$OEM$\NET\NTCLIENT
```

8. Save the UNATTEND.TXT file. (To preserve the original file, you may want to save it under a different name.)

9. Copy the Novell Client CD to the I386\OEM\NET\NTCLIENT directory created in Step 4.

10. Open the Novell NetWare Client for Windows NT UNATTEND.TXT file found in the I386\SYSTEM\NLS*Language* (English, French, German, and so forth) directory of the NetWare Client software. The copy completed in Step 9 placed this directory under the I386\OEM\NET\NTCLIENT directory.

11. Copy the contents of the Novell NetWare Client Parameters section in the Novell UNATTEND.TXT file and paste the contents into the end of the Microsoft file. (Refer to Step 5.)

12. Configure your preferences in both portions of the file and save the file. (Refer to Microsoft's documentation and the section above for details.)

Once you have completed the previous steps, you can begin the installations. To install the products, log each workstation into the network and run WINNT with the following syntax:

```
WINNT /s:sourcepath /b /u:path to unattend file
```

At this point, you may wonder, Why not use Novell's entire UNATTEND.TXT file, rather than copying a portion of it to the Microsoft file? The answer can be found in the beginning of the Novell file. The following is a quote directly from the UNATTEND.TXT file included with the NetWare Client for Windows NT:

> There are sections in this file that belong to the Microsoft Windows NT 4.0 product. It may or may not contain the correct or proper information necessary for the working, valid installation of Windows NT 4.0 on any workstation.

That's reason enough for us!

Automatically Upgrade Client when User Logs In

The final option for installing the NetWare Client for Windows NT is to upgrade the client software automatically running on a workstation when a user logs in. You can do this by using the Automatic Client Upgrade (ACU) feature of the NetWare Client for Windows NT.

The ACU enables you to upgrade multiple workstations automatically running an older version of Novell's client for Windows NT to the most recent version. It is invoked by running SETUPNW.EXE with the /ACU option. When you do this, the ACU checks the version numbers of the Novell client software currently installed at the workstation to determine whether it is outdated. If it is, the latest version is automatically installed.

You can also use this functionality of the ACU if you need to make changes to client configuration when the actual version of the client software hasn't changed. Using the UNATTEND.TXT file included with the NetWare Client for Windows NT, you can set a pair of internal version numbers, which make it appear to ACU that a difference exists in version numbers.

Invoking SETUPNW.EXE from within a login script can enable the client upgrade to take place across the network without requiring you to visit each workstation physically. The login script syntax for running SETUPNW.EXE with the /ACU option is as follows:

```
#\\HOME\SYS\PUBLIC\CLIENT\ACU\SETUPNW.EXE /ACU /U
```

. . . . . .

When invoking SETUPNW.EXE from within a login script, be sure to use UNC paths as shown in the previous example.

NOTE

The previous example login script command assumes the contents of the NetWare Client for Windows NT CD have been copied to the SYS:PUBLIC\CLIENT\ACU directory on a NetWare file server. Although using the directories provided in the example is unnecessary, you will need to copy the NetWare Client installation files to a public location on a NetWare file server.

The ACU is an extremely attractive feature, but one small caveat exists of which you should be aware. Because of Windows NT's Workstation security, an administrator level user is required to update the workstation files. If you are updating multiple workstations when the users log in, not all users have administrative access to their NT Workstation.

To solve this problem, the ACU feature works in conjunction with the Z.E.N.works component of the NetWare Client for Windows NT to create a temporary administrative user to perform the upgrade on a workstation. When it is determined that a workstation requires upgrading, the client creates the temporary administrative user in the NT Workstation's local SAM. It then logs in this user, performs the upgrade, and then automatically logs the user out and deletes the account from the local SAM. This is done in such a way that the user sitting in front of the workstation has no administrative access to the workstation at any point during the process.

Automatically Replacing the Microsoft Client for NetWare

The ACU feature can be used to replace automatically the Microsoft Client for NetWare running on NT Workstations. The process is the same as previously described with one small exception. Because this client is bindery based, SETUPNW.EXE must be run from the user's bindery login script. This login script is located in the SYS:MAIL*userIDnumber* for each user.

Configuring the NetWare Client for Windows NT

After the installation of the NetWare Client for Windows NT is complete, you may need to configure the workstation. In some cases, the default configuration set during installation of the NetWare Client will be sufficient. In addition, some workstation configuration options may have been set in the UNATTEND.TXT file and may not require additional configuration.

The following three areas of the NetWare Client for Windows NT may need configuration:

- ▸ Network adapter driver

- ▸ Advanced workstation parameters

- ▸ NetWare Client Login Preferences

Each of these is described in detail in the following sections.

Network Adapter Drivers

When you install the NetWare client for Windows NT, the installation program will attempt to detect and load the proper driver automatically for the network interface card installed in the workstation. If the Microsoft Client for NetWare was previously installed on the workstation, the installation will continue to use the NDIS driver for the network card in the workstation.

If you prefer to use a Novell ODI driver, you can remove the NDIS driver and install an ODI one. No real advantage exits to making this change, however. In most cases, an NDIS driver will perform as efficiently as an ODI driver. In addition, a limited number of ODI drivers are available with the initial releases of the NetWare Client for Windows NT. If no ODI driver is available for the card in your workstation, you will have no choice but to use an NDIS driver.

Adding a Network Driver   Adding a network driver can be done through the Network Control Panel. To access the Network Control Panel, from the Windows NT 4.0 Start menu, choose Settings. Then select Control Panel/Network, and then choose the Adapters tab. To add a new network adapter, click the Add button. A list of available ODI and NDIS drivers will be displayed as shown in Figure 5.8.

TIP   **Here's a shortcut for accessing the Network Control Panel option: Highlight Network Neighborhood on your Windows NT desktop and press the right mouse button. Then choose Properties and select the Services tab.**

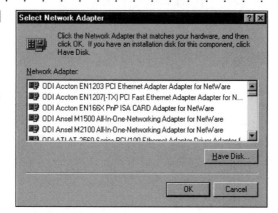

FIGURE 5.8

Adding a new network driver can be done by selecting the Adapters tab from the Network Control Panel, and then choosing the Add button. A driver can be chosen from the list or a different driver can be installed by selecting the Have Disk button.

To install a new driver, choose the appropriate driver for your network from the list shown in Figure 5.8. If the appropriate driver for your card is not shown on the list, it can be installed from a floppy disk or other location by choosing Have Disk.

Configuring a Network Driver   After installing an adapter card, you may need to configure it. In some cases, the card settings and frame type will be automatically detected when the driver is installed and will not require additional configuration. If auto-detection is not possible, you may be prompted to enter the configuration when you select the driver.

To modify the configuration of an existing network driver, access the Network Control Panel by choosing Settings from the Windows NT 4.0 Start Menu. Then select Control Panel/Network, and then choose the Adapters tab. Select the adapter you wish to configure and click Properties. Enter the appropriate configuration information for the network adapter.

If you wish to change the frame type or other protocol information, access the Network Control Panel as previously described and choose the Protocols tab. Then click the Properties button and change the frame type or other protocol information.

Any time you make changes to the network driver or protocol, you will need to reboot your workstation for the changes to take effect.

Configuring Advanced Workstation Parameters

The NetWare Client for Windows NT enables you to configure advanced workstation parameters that control how the client operates in the following categories:

- Environment

- Backward Compatibility

- Performance (Caching)

- Packet Management

- Wide Area Networking

- Contextless Login

- Multiple Protocol Support

A number of advanced workstation parameters exist that you can set under each of these categories, but you should use caution when doing so. Each of the advanced workstation parameters is set to a default that provides optimal performance and functionality in most environments. In some instances, changing these defaults can hurt, rather than help, matters. Only in special circumstances, such as enabling resource caching or increasing the packet signature level (which will decrease performance), should you change these defaults.

If you wish to modify the advance workstation parameters on a workstation, access the Network Control Panel by choosing Settings from the Windows NT 4.0 Start Menu. Then choose the Services tab and then highlight the NetWare Client for Windows NT from the Network Services list. Click the Properties button, and then select the Advanced Settings tab. Figure 5.9 shows the Advanced Settings dialog box.

The advanced settings parameters can be viewed all together as shown in Figure 5.9 or by the different categories previously described. Each parameter provides a brief description and the valid settings available.

Some of the key advanced workstation parameters that affect workstation performance and security are discussed in the following sections.

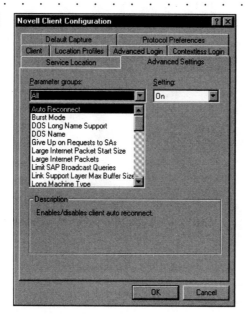

The Advanced Settings tab of the NetWare Client for Windows NT enables you to modify the advanced parameters that control the performance and functionality of the client software on a given workstation. The default parameters provide optimal performance and functionality in most environments.

Packet Burst   *Packet Burst* protocol increases performance of large file reads and writes over a wide area network. Without packet burst, every read and write made by a workstation must be done one packet at a time. The file server must then respond to each request one packet at a time.

Packet burst allows the file server to respond to read requests with a burst of packets for every read request received. It also allows the workstation to send a burst of packets when writing to a file server that requires only one response from the server. This increases network performance by reducing the amount of time the workstation spends sending requests and receiving responses from the file server. It also reduces network traffic.

Packet Burst is automatically enabled when you install the NetWare Client for Windows NT. To modify the default Packet burst parameters, select Settings from the Windows NT 4.0 Start menu. Then select Control Panel/Network/Services/ NetWare Client for Windows NT/Properties. From the NetWare Client Services Configuration screen, choose the Advanced Settings Tab.

This is shown in Figure 5.10.

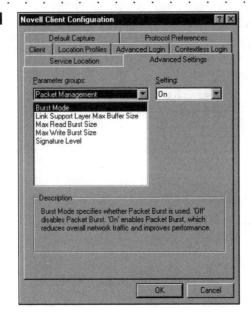

Three parameters affect how packet burst operates: Burst Mode (on/off), Max Read Burst Size, and Max Write Burst Size. These options can be modified by selecting the Advanced Settings tab under the NetWare Client Services Configuration.

TIP

Here's a shortcut for accessing the Network Control Panel option: Highlight Network Neighborhood on your Windows NT desktop and press the right mouse button. Then choose Properties and select the Services tab.

Generally the default settings for Packet Burst are sufficient. If you wish to change the defaults, this can be done through using the following three configuration options shown in Figure 5.10:

- Burst Mode (ON/OFF)

- Max Read Burst Size

- Max Write Burst Size

Large Internet Packets Another performance feature included with the client is Large Internet Packet (LIP) support. LIP increases performance across network routers by allowing a workstation and file server to negotiate the packet size to be used. This negotiation takes place transparently in the background. Without LIP, all packets sent across routers are reduced to 512 bytes.

Large Internet Packets are enabled by default when you install the NetWare Client for Windows NT. The starting size of the LIP packet is dynamically configured based on your environment. To change the defaults, choose Settings from the Windows NT 4.0 Start Menu. Then select Control Panel/Network/ Services/NetWare Client for Windows NT/Properties. From the NetWare Client Services Configuration screen, choose the Advanced Settings Tab.

The LIP settings are shown in Figure 5.11.

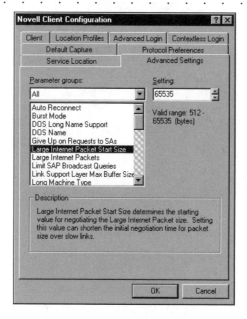

Two LIP configuration options exist: Large Internet Packets (On/Off) and Large Internet Packet Start Size. These options can be modified by selecting the Advanced Settings tab under the NetWare Client Services Configuration.

In Figure 5.11, two options exist that control LIP on your workstation: Large Internet Packets (on/off) and Large Internet Packet Start Size. These options are set dynamically to provide the best possible performance for your network.

Packet Signing   Packet signing is configured by setting packet signing signature levels at the client and at the file server. To change the packet signature levels for a Windows NT workstation, choose Settings from the Windows NT 4.0 Start Menu. Then select Control Panel/Network/Services/NetWare Client for Windows NT/Properties. From the NetWare Client Services Configuration screen, choose the Advanced Settings Tab.

Figure 5.12 shows the packet signature option.

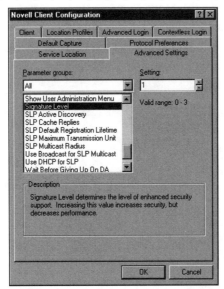

In Figure 5.12, the Signature Level option controls how packet signatures are handled at the client. The only caveat to using packet signatures is that increasing the signature level value increases security but, at the same time, decreases network performance. This is because additional overhead is generated at both the client and server when the digital signatures are created.

The packet signing signature levels are as follows:

▸ 0 = Packet signatures disabled

▸ 1 = Packet signatures enabled but not preferred (only use if required by the file server)

▸ 2 = Packet signatures preferred (use if the server requires them, but don't require them if the server doesn't support them)

▸ 3 = Always require packet signatures

To enable packet signatures at the file server, you will need to use the following set command:

```
SET NCP PACKET SIGNATURE OPTION = n
```

Replace n with the desired packet signature level — 0, 1, 2, or 3.

NOTE

By default, the server is set to 1, which enables clients set to 3 to establish a secure connection. For maximum security, you must set this parameter before DS.NLM loads to ensure that all DS connections use packet signature correctly. Otherwise, a hacker could spoof a server's connection to itself and slip in rogue packets!

Configuring Login Preferences

The NetWare Client for Windows NT enables you to configure the login preferences used when users log in from a particular NT Workstation. Three properties of the NetWare Client control the preferences used during login:

▸ Client Properties

▸ Login Properties

▸ Advanced Login Properties

To modify these properties, access the Network Control Panel, and then select the Services tab. From the list of network services, highlight the NetWare Client for Windows NT and click the Properties button. The previous configuration options appear in the tabbed list and are described in the following sections.

Client Properties   The Client Properties parameters are shown in Figure 5.13.

▶ *The NetWare login screen.* This screen logs the user into NetWare only. This screen is accessed when you right-click Network Neighborhood and select NetWare Login. It can also be accessed by choosing Programs off the Windows NT Start menu, then selecting NetWare (Common), and then NetWare Login.

Some instances may occur where you do not want users to change certain parameters of their login. You can use the Advanced Login parameters of the NetWare Client Services configuration shown in Figure 5.14 to remove initial login choices.

 This information can be controlled on a global basis through NDS by using the Z.E.N.works workstation management features. These features are discussed in Chapter 10.
NOTE

The options in Figure 5.14 also permit configuring a default NT Workstation policy for the NT workstation. If the default policy is not enabled, an alternate policy path and filename can be specified. These policies are created with POLEDIT.EXE and have a .POL extension. The path must be specified in UNC format. For example:

```
\\SDU\SYS\PUBLIC\NTCONFIG.POL.
```

Protocol Preferences

NetWare 5 offers new features not found in earlier versions of NetWare, including Pure IP and Contextless Login Support. Unlike IPX, where *Service Advertisement Protocol* (SAP) broadcasts informed workstations of all available services, NetWare 5's Pure IP doesn't use SAP broadcasts to find network services. The Protocol Preferences options listed in Figure 5.15 enable the administrator to determine how network services will be advertised.

IPX routers store this SAP information in their memory, and respond to workstations on behalf of NetWare servers. Because Pure IP can't rely on broadcasting or routers for service information, a Pure IP network must have alternate mechanisms for advertising and locating services. Clients connecting to NetWare 5 have a choice of service location mechanisms, including *Service Location Protocol* (SLP), NDS, DNS, DHCP, and a host file. Depending on the size and scope of your NetWare 5 network, all of these mechanisms may be used to a certain degree. You'll need special knowledge about your particular network configuration before changing any of these parameters. When in doubt — stick with the defaults.

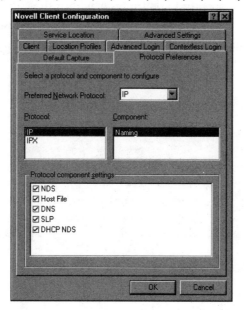

F I G U R E   5.15

If this workstation is connected to a NetWare 5 network, the client can discover network services through a variety of protocols. Be careful — disabling these protocol options may prevent the workstation from finding network resources.

Enabling Contextless Login

In most NDS directory trees, objects such as users, printers, and servers are distributed throughout the NDS directory tree. Rather than a flat view, this directory hierarchy provides a highly scalable design while organizing the users and resources by job function, department, division, or even geographical locations. While the hierarchy greatly increases scalability, it can create some problems for users.

Back in the NetWare 2.x and 3.x days, and even now with NT Server 4.0, users just supply a username/password combination. NetWare 2.x, 3.x, and NT Server 4.0 store the user accounts in a flat file. NDS trees, due to their hierarchical design, may distribute users across multiple containers. As such, a user may need to know information about where they are located within the NDS tree. For example, instead of logging in simply as "Steve," a user must know his or her NDS location, such as ".Steve.Engineers.Provo.Novell". This is awfully confusing to the novice end user!

Enter Contextless Login, a new feature of NetWare 5. When enabled, Contextless Login allows a user to simply enter his or her user name. The workstation client then searches an NDS catalog that contains all users within the NDS tree. The client quickly finds the user within the catalog, and fills out any additional NDS information. Catalog Services, which is only available on NetWare 5, is required to enable Contextless Login. To enable Contextless Login, enter the NDS catalog as shown in Figure 5.16.

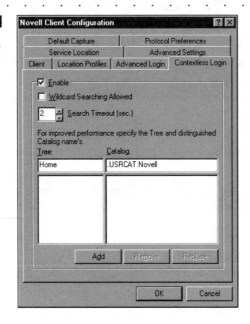

F I G U R E   5 . 1 6

To enable Contextless Login, enter the NDS catalog that holds the contextless login data. Note that you can use multiple catalogs if you log in to more than one NDS tree.

Synchronizing NetWare and Windows NT Logins

As mentioned, after the installation and configuration of the NetWare Client for Windows NT is complete, the workstation or workstations will need to be rebooted before the changes will take effect.

When the NT Workstation comes up after the reboot, the default Windows NT welcome and login screen is replaced with the initial NetWare login screen as previously described. Users can then log in to NDS and their NT Workstation. Selecting the NetWare and Windows NT tabs in the initial login screen sets the parameters of each of these logins.

If the user's Windows NT password is different from his NetWare password, the user is presented with an option to synchronize his NT password with his NetWare password. This option is a checkbox that is displayed when the user enters his current NT password. Once the passwords are synchronized, the user can simply enter one login name and password to log in to both NDS and the user's NT Workstation.

The Microsoft SMB Client

Whenever you're integrating NT Workstations — an environment consisting of both NT Servers as well as NetWare servers — you will need Microsoft's SMB client to access the NT networking aspects of Windows NT. This is in addition to the NetWare client required to access the NetWare resources. The remainder of this chapter covers the details of the Microsoft SMB client, which you must know to implement it in a heterogeneous network.

When Microsoft developed NT, an architecture was created that enabled third-party vendors the ability to add in alternative requesters to access other systems. If NT users wanted to use SMB (NT networking), Banyan, or NCP (Novell) protocols, therefore, NT was made extensible enough to enable a client driver to be created and support these systems.

SMB client is also included with NT (and Windows 95) that enables access to NT networking. You can install two or more clients to access two or more networking services simultaneously. This is what you'll do if you are pursuing a synchronization strategy.

SMB Client Types

The Server Message Block (SMB) has been around for some time. SMB is used to access several types of servers:

> ► *LAN Manager Servers.* These originated with Microsoft and IBM in the late 1980s, when Microsoft and IBM co-designed OS/2. LAN Manager was the networking system running on top of OS/2. To access the LAN Manager server, you needed an SMB client.

▸ *LAN Server.* When IBM broke away from Microsoft, LAN Manager became LAN Server. LAN Server still uses an SMB client to gain access to networking services.

▸ *NT Networking.* When NT was designed, the networking component placed on NT as the N.O.S. was LAN Manager (from the IBM/Microsoft days). As a result, you still need a LAN Manager client today to access NT networking.

Domains and Workgroups

No matter what option you choose, you must supply an NT client with a Domain of which you're a member or a workgroup in which you participate. Here are some considerations when choosing which option:

▸ *Domain option.* You must install the NT Workstation into the Domain as a workstation. This creates a trust relation between the NT Workstation and the server that enables a user to authenticate to an NT Domain and to gain access to her local workstation.

▸ *Workgroup option.* In this option, you participate in a shared workgroup of servers and users who share common peripherals.

No matter which option you choose, if you do not have the station configured to contact a domain or a workgroup, you will be unable to get an NT networking service.

Configuring SMB Client for Integration

Two ways exist to prepare NT for Integration:

▸ As a client to a NetWare system using other network services, such as Oracle or PeopleSoft

▸ As a dual client station, requesting File, Print, and other services from both NT networking services and NetWare

Using NT as a NetWare Client

In this case, after setting up the Novell client per recommendations outlined in this chapter, configure the NT Workstation for Novell's Z.E.N.works workstation management product (Chapter 10).

This will enable the administrator to manage the NT Workstation and enable a single login to the NT Workstation and to NDS.

Using NT as a Dual Requester Station

In this case, you must install two clients: the NetWare client *and* the Microsoft SMB client. Be sure to designate a Domain and login preference when configuring the NT Workstation client.

NOTE

In NT Workstation, an SMB client is automatically installed. You may need to join a Domain to see all other services available under NT networking.

Summary

The NetWare Client for Windows NT enables you to integrate NT Workstations fully into your NetWare networks. NT Workstation users have complete access to all NetWare Services. In this chapter, we looked in-depth at the features and functionality of the NetWare Client. We also examined the various methods of installation and upgrade.

Once the NetWare Client is installed, network administrators face the challenge of maintaining the user account databases on each NT Workstation, in addition to maintaining the NDS database. Chapter 6 explores the Workstation Manager component of the NetWare Client for Windows NT. This utility eases the administrative burden of NT Workstations by allowing them to be managed through NDS.

CHAPTER 6

Synchronizing Network Directories

In Chapter 4, we introduced the concept of a Meta-Directory to you. A Meta-Directory ties all the directories in your network together into a single logical directory. The result is a single point of administration for these directories, which are normally managed individually. Meta-Directories eliminate enormous amounts of redundant administration, thereby saving both administrative time and money.

This chapter discusses the use of NDS as a Meta-Directory. It covers why NDS is the best platform to use as a Meta-Directory in a mixed NetWare and NT environment and the synchronization products available to provide integration of this environment.

The following two synchronization products enable you to use your existing NDS database as a Meta-Directory:

▸ Novell Administrator for Windows NT

▸ NetVision Synchronicity for NT

This chapter provides a comprehensive overview of each product that will help you determine which is best for your environment. In addition, this chapter provides detailed information on the installation and use of both products.

NDS as a Meta-Directory

When you manage a network environment consisting of both NetWare file servers and NT file servers and workstations, probably the biggest challenge you face is the administration of all the different databases. For your NetWare file servers, you manage the NDS database. For your NT servers, you manage the Security Access Manager (SAM) database. If you have NT workstations that are not integrated with NDS or a Domain, you also must manage the individual NT Workstation SAM databases. Then, of course, that still leaves the databases for the add-on services, such as Exchange, SQL Server, GroupWise, or Oracle.

The bottom line is: If you have a mixed NetWare and Windows NT environment, chances are you are creating and managing the same user account over and over again in many different databases.

Using NDS as a Meta-Directory provides a solution. By integrating the NT Server Domains with your existing NDS database, you eliminate redundant administration. NDS becomes the central repository for both your NetWare networks and your NT networks by creating one logical directory managed from a central location.

Any directory used in the capacity of a Meta-Directory must meet the following requirements:

▸ Easy to use and manage

▸ Scalable

▸ Provides a unique object naming scheme

▸ Extensible

▸ Provides a high level of reliability

As described in Chapter 2, NDS provides this functionality and then some. Following are the features that make NDS an ideal Meta-Directory platform:

▸ *Hierarchical directory tree.* The hierarchical nature of NDS makes it easy to locate, use, and manage network resources. As a Meta-Directory, the hierarchical Directory tree provides users with a single point of access to the entire network. In addition, it provides administrators with a central point of administration of all network platforms. As an NDS Directory tree expands into a meta-directory, the hierarchical nature of the tree allows it to scale to support the expanded object requirements of multiple platforms. The hierarchical Directory tree also ensures each object in the tree has a unique name.

▸ *Extensible NDS Schema.* The extensible nature of the NDS database enables new object types to be added to the NDS Meta-Directory to support multiple platforms. When integrating NT Server domains with NDS, new object types are created that provide support for the users and groups of the Domains.

▸ *Distributed, replicated database.* The distributed, replicated nature of NDS makes it a reliable and scalable Meta-Directory. By partitioning and replicating the NDS database, fault tolerance is provided through storing portions of the NDS database on file servers across the network. This process also ensures optimal performance by allowing resources represented in the NDS database to be placed close to the users who use them.

Choosing a Synchronization Product

If you are administering a mixed NDS and Windows NT environment, you essentially have two choices for simplifying management: either domain redirection to NDS with Novell's NDS for NT product (see Chapter 7), or synchronizing NDS and domain data. A *synchronization product* eliminates the need to manage NDS and NT Domains separately, saving tremendous amounts of time. Currently two products are available that provide synchronization: Novell Administrator for Windows NT and NetVision Synchronicity for NT.

Both synchronization products are similar because they used NDS as a central repository for an integrated Windows NT and NetWare environment. In addition, both products use NWAdmin as a central administration utility. The products differ in two areas—how they accomplish integration and price. Although both products integrate NT Server Domains into an existing NDS tree, the components and feature sets differ slightly between the two products. From the price perspective, Novell provides the Novell Administrator for Windows NT free of charge; NetVision charges for Synchronicity.

The following sections provide an overview of the two products, as well as the pros and cons of each. Our intention is to provide you with the relevant facts to assist you in making a decision as to which product is best for your environment.

 To obtain a trial version of NDS for NT, which contains Novell Administrator for Windows NT, visit `www.novell.com/download/`. **For a trial version of Synchronicity from NetVision, check out** `www.netvision.com/download/download.html`.

Novell Administrator for Windows NT

The Novell Administrator for Windows NT (NadminNT) integrates Windows NT Domains and Workgroups with NDS, enabling user and group accounts to be synchronized between NDS and the Windows NT SAM database.

NadminNT provides the ability to synchronize existing NT domains or workgroups with NDS, simplifying the management of existing NT users and groups. In addition, existing NDS users can be given access to Windows NT application server resources. NadminNT will dynamically create users in the NT domain when they are associated with the Domain in NDS. Then, if the user is made a member of an existing NT group that has access to NT applications or other resources, the NDS user automatically receives the rights to those NT resources.

Once synchronized, administration of NT users and groups is done through NWAdmin, eliminating the need to use NT's User Manager. When additions or changes are made to users or groups in NWAdmin, they are automatically synchronized down to the Domain. Although User Manager can still be used, synchronization from the Domain to NDS is not automatic; it must be manually initiated. One disadvantage you will find when synchronizing in this direction is you must synchronize the *entire* Domain; no option exists to synchronize individual objects. Re-synchronizing an entire Domain or Workgroup can take a long time and can generate significant network traffic.

NadminNT Components

Synchronization between NDS and the SAM database is accomplished through the following components:

- NDS Event Monitor (NDSDM.NLM)

- NDS Object Replication Service (ORS)

- NDS Schema Extensions and NWAdmin Snapins

- Integration Utility (IGRATE.EXE)

Figure 6.1 illustrates where each of the components run on the integrated network. Each component is described in greater detail throughout the following sections.

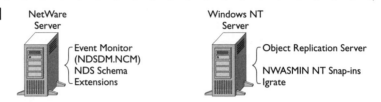

Summary of the components of the Novell Administrator for Windows NT

NDS Event Monitor

The NDS Event Monitor (NDSDM.NLM) runs on NetWare servers and monitors NDS events. It filters the events that relate to the Windows NT systems, such as NT object type creation, deletions, and object moves or attribute value changes. When changes are made to NDS objects that are synchronized with an NT Domain, the NDS Event Monitor notifies the Object Replication Service (ORS) running on the NT system, which, in turn, makes the appropriate change in the Domain's SAM database. If an NT Server participating in the integration is down, the Event Monitor keeps track of the changes and updates the NT Server appropriately when it comes back online.

The NDS Event monitor runs on the server that holds the master replica of the partition synchronized with an NT Domain. For fault-tolerance purposes, it should also be installed on one or more servers that contain Read/Write replicas of the partition.

NOTE **The Event Monitor advertises its availability to the ORS using a Service Advertising Protocol (SAP) type 0x028E (hex value). If SAP filtering is enabled on the servers running the Event Monitor, be sure SAP type 28E is not filtered. Otherwise, the ORS will be unable to locate the Event Monitor.**

NDS Object Replication Service (ORS)

The NDS ORS is a Windows NT service that runs on the Primary Domain Controllers (PDCs) and any workgroup system integrated with and managed through NDS. The ORS receives object changes from the NDS Event Monitor and makes the corresponding changes in the NT SAM database. The service also provides SAM data to the IGRATE utility for upload to NDS.

One benefit to NadminNT is that ORS runs on the NT Servers as a service (as opposed to an application) that is installed with a startup type as *Automatic*. This means when the system is booted (or re-booted), the service automatically starts. Figure 6.2 shows the ORS running on an NT Server. In addition, because ORS runs as a service, it does not require a special user account to be logged in to run.

 For fault tolerance, the ORS is also installed on any Backup Domain Controllers (BDCs). The service remains dormant until a BDC is promoted to PDC. Once this takes place, the service must be manually started through the Services options of the Control Panel.

NOTE

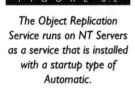

The Object Replication Service runs on NT Servers as a service that is installed with a startup type of Automatic.

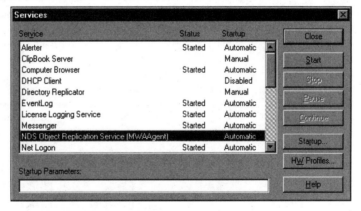

NDS Schema Extensions & NWAdmin Snapin

As discussed in Chapter 2, one of the compelling features of NDS is that it is extensible. What this means is the rules governing the objects that can be stored in NDS (or the *Schema*) can be modified to include new object types. When NadminNT is installed, it extends the Schema, adding new object types to the NDS tree that represent the NT resources. These objects include the following:

▶ *Hybrid Users,* or users who have accounts on both NDS and Windows NT systems

▶ *Windows NT Users,* or users who have only Windows NT accounts

▶ *Windows NT Local Groups,* or Local Groups defined in Windows NT

▶ *Windows NT Global Groups,* or Global Groups defined in Windows NT

▶ *Windows NT Domain and workgroup objects,* or objects that represent the various domains or workgroups that are synchronized with NDS

NadminNT also includes NWAdmin Snapins that allow the new NT objects and their attributes to be displayed and administered from within the utility. Figure 6.3 shows the new NDS objects that represent NT resources in NWAdmin. Table 6.1 describes these icons.

TABLE 6.1	ICON	REPRESENTS	DESCRIPTION
Icon Representation		NT Domain object	Any users and groups that are defined in the NT Domain database but managed through NDS.
		Global groups	Global groups defined in Windows NT.
		Local groups	Local groups defined in Windows NT.
		NT User objects	Users who only have an NT account with no corresponding NDS account.
		Hybrid User object	Users who have an NT account and a corresponding NDS account.

FIGURE 6.3

When the Novell
Administrator for Windows
NT is installed, the NDS
Schema is extended to add
new object types that
represent NT resources.
These object types are
shown under
SDU_DOMAIN in
this figure.

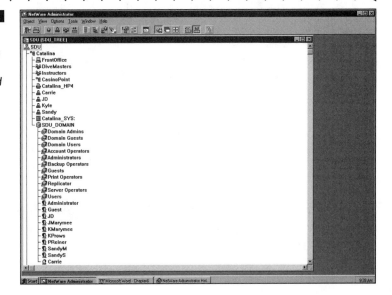

In Figure 6.3, the NT Domain object is called *SDU_DOMAIN*. Under this object are any users and groups defined in the NT SAM database, but managed through NDS. Immediately following the *SDU_DOMAIN* object are the NT Global Group objects and the NT Local Group objects. The last object in this screen shows a Hybrid User object. Hybrid Users are NT users that have a corresponding NDS account. In this example, the Hybrid User Carrie has a corresponding NDS user account (also named Carrie) under the Catalina container.

Integration Utility (IGRATE.EXE)

NadminNT also includes an integration utility (IGRATE.EXE) that allows the integration of users and groups in a mixed Windows NT and NDS environment. After NadminNT is installed, IGRATE is used to perform the initial upload of NT users and groups to NDS. These objects then appear as NT user and group objects under the Domain object in the NDS tree (see Figure 6.3).

After the initial upload to NDS, IGRATE is used to do the following:

▸ Integrate existing NT users into NDS

▸ Integrate existing NDS users into NT

▸ Synchronize existing NT users with existing NDS users

▸ Unintegrate integrated users

Using the IGRATE utility is discussed in greater detail later in this chapter.

Pros and Cons

Our evaluation of the Novell Administrator for Windows NT proved the product to be fairly comprehensive. We did note some limitations, as well, though. Table 6.2 shows some of the pros and cons of the product that we observed.

TABLE 6.2	FEATURE	PROS	CONS
Pros and Cons of Novell Administrator for Windows NT	Administration of NT Users	Allows administration of all NT user properties from within NWAdmin.	Requires an additional user object (Hybrid User) when NDS users are mapped to NT users
	Administration of NT Groups	Allows creation and administration of NT Global and Local Groups from within NWAdmin.	Does not provide synchronization between NDS and NT groups. NT groups and NDS groups must be managed separately.
	Policy Support	Can manage account policies only.	Provides limited NT System Policy support. Does not provide support for administration of audit policies, trust relationships, and user rights. These must be managed through NT's User Manager.

	FEATURE	PROS	CONS
TABLE 6.2 *Pros and Cons of Novell Administrator for Windows NT (continued)*	NDS Event Monitor		Uses SAP to advertise to ORS. Must have SAP enabled on every server running the Event Monitor. Could cause performance problems over a WAN because SAP generates a great deal of broadcast traffic.
	Object Replication Service	Runs as an NT Service. Is not affected by users logged in at the station and is not subject to user rights. Automatically loads when system is booted.	Must have a connection to every server running the Event Monitor NLM. Some connections are unlicensed but uses at least one licensed connection. Only supports PDCs running on an Intel Platform.
	IGRATE		Only runs on NT Workstation or Server. No support for Windows 95.
	Price	Available free of charge from Novell.	

Synchronicity for NT

Synchronicity for NT is a product available from NetVision, Inc. (www.netvision.com). Its product goals are the same as Novell Administrator for Windows NT (to provide a central point of administration for both NDS and NT users and groups). It does this by integrating Windows NT servers with NDS. This integration allows NDS to act as a Meta-Directory, enabling administrators to manage NT users and groups completely through NDS. In addition, it can simplify the management of Windows NT Domains by allowing the synchronization of NDS objects to occur simultaneously with multiple domains.

At a glance, you may think Synchronicity for NT is almost the same product as Novell's Administrator for Windows NT. As you look at Synchronicity for NT in more depth, however, you will see the two products are different.

Synchronicity Product Family

Synchronicity for NT is only one product in NetVision's Synchronicity product family. The goal of Synchronicity is to allow the integration of many dissimilar directory services into a logical whole. Its architectural design allows integration of more than just NT and NDS. Using NDS as the foundation, other Synchronicity products allow integration of many different directory implementations. For example, there are three additional Synchronicity products currently available: Synchronicity for Lotus Notes, Synchronicity for Microsoft Exchange, and Synchronicity for NetWare 3.

Synchronicity for Lotus Notes integrates the Lotus Notes Domino directory with NDS, enabling the Notes users and group accounts to be administered through NDS using NWAdmin. Synchronicity for Microsoft Exchange integrates the Microsoft Exchange messaging directory with NDS, synchronizing NDS user and groups with Exchange mail accounts and group distribution lists. Synchronicity for NetWare 3 integrates the NetWare 3 Bindery with NDS, allowing a central point of administration, as well as a migration path for NetWare 3 customers. In the future, NetVision is releasing Synchronicity products that support such network environments as Microsoft Exchange servers, UNIX servers, and various SQL databases.

All Synchronicity products are designed to be fully interoperable. For example, if Synchronicity for NT and Notes are used in the same environment, the products work together to integrate seamlessly NDS, Windows NT domains, and Lotus Notes Domino Name and Address Book.

Synchronicity for NT Components

Synchronicity for NT accomplishes integration of NT users and groups through the following components:

▸ The Global Event Services NLM

▸ The NT Synchronization Agent

▸ NWAdmin Snapin Modules

Each of these components is described in the following sections.

Global Event Services   One major area of difference between Synchronicity for NT and Novell's NadminNT is the method used to monitor NDS events relevant to NT integration. NadminNT uses an NDS Event Monitor that runs on the NetWare servers and notifies the NDS Object Replication Service on an NT system when an event has occurred. For this design to work, each ORS must have a connection to every Event Monitor running. The Event Monitor advertises its availability using SAP. While functional, this design is not scalable in large network implementations, as shown in Figure 6.4.

FIGURE 6.4

In the NadminNT design, the NDS ORS running on NT systems must have a connection to every NetWare server running the NDS Event Monitor NLM.

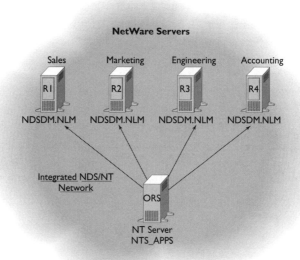

In Figure 6.4, the Domain of the NT Server NTS_APPS is integrated with NDS. For the ORS running on that server to receive notification of NDS events, it must maintain a licensed connection to each NetWare server running the NDS Event Monitor. If multiple domains are synchronized with NDS, every Windows NT PDC running the ORS will have a connection to every server running Event Monitor NLM. (Imagine what a graphic illustrating this would look like!)

In contrast, Synchronicity for NT uses a global event system to monitor NDS events across the entire network. This allows it to detect any change anywhere in a global NDS network and communicate the changes to any Synchronization Agent running on an NT system in real-time. The Synchronization Agent then makes the corresponding changes in the NT Domain.

Synchronicity's global event system is called the Global Event Service (GES). GES is implemented as an NLM (NVGES.NLM) that runs on every NetWare server in the network that holds a Read/Write replica. When an event takes place that affects the NT objects integrated with NDS (such as a user creation), the GES notifies all Synchronization Agents running on NT systems across the network. The Synchronization Agent to which the event applies is the only one that accepts the event; the others ignore the event. Each Synchronization Agent, then, requires only one connection to a server running the GES. This is illustrated in Figure 6.5.

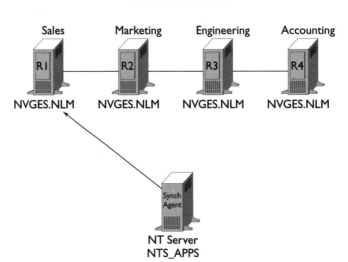

FIGURE 6.5

Each Synchronicity Synchronization Agent requires one connection to the network to receive events from the GES.

In Figure 6.5, the Synchronization Agent running on the NT Server NTS_APPS requires only one connection to the GES. Assume, for example, user Kyle is created on NDS replica 4, which is stored on the Accounting server. Because Synchronicity's event system is global, the Synchronization Agent on the NT server is notified of the event through its connection to the GES running on the Sales file server.

NT Synchronization Agent   The NT Synchronization Agent is an application that runs on one NT server or one NT workstation in a domain integrated with NDS. Its purpose is to receive events from the GES and to make the corresponding changes in the NT domain. Each Synchronization Agent registers with the GES, indicating the type of events in which it is interested (object creates, deletes, modifications, and so on). This way, the GES only forwards events that apply to the domain in which a Synchronization Agent is running. Changes made to users in one NDS organizational unit are sent only to the domains mapped to that organizational unit.

Only one Synchronization Agent is required for each domain. The application can be run on a PDC, BDC, or NT Workstation, and must have administrative access to the domain.

NWAdmin Snapin Modules   The final component to Synchronicity for NT is Snapin modules to NWAdmin that allow the utility to support the functionality added by the product. Snapins are provided for both the Windows 95 and Windows NT versions of NWAdmin.

The Snapins enable you to do the following from within NWAdmin:

▸ Add, delete, or modify NT-only users and groups

▸ Map NDS user and group objects to NT users and groups

▸ Remotely configure Synchronization Agents and NLMs

▸ Modify NT Domain configuration settings

▸ Manage the NetVision GES system

▸ Support NDS Schema extensions added by the product

NDS Schema Extensions   When Synchronicity for NT is installed, the NDS Schema is extended to add objects that support the integration of NT users and groups with NDS. These Schema extensions add the following objects to your NDS tree:

▸ *NT Domain objects*. These container objects represent the NT Domains integrated with NDS.

▸ *NT Global Group objects*. NT Global groups integrated with NDS. These objects can be mapped to NDS group objects.

▸ *NT Local Group objects*. NT Local groups integrated with NDS. These objects can be mapped to NDS group objects.

▸ *NT User objects*. NT user accounts integrated with NDS. These objects represent users that have accounts on NT systems only *and* users that have accounts on both NT systems and NDS. (No separate User object exists for these accounts as with NadminNT.)

▸ *GES Event Container objects*. This object contains all the NDS events for which the GES will notify Synchronization Agents.

▸ *GES Events*. The NDS events used by the GES.

▸ *GES Administrator.* User object used by GES to log in to NDS with full administrative access.

Figure 6.6 shows an NT Domain object called SDU_DOMAIN that contains NT user and group objects.

Figure 6.7 shows a GES Event Container object with all the NDS events for which the GES will notify Synchronization Agents.

▶ . . . . ◀

When Synchronicity for NT is installed, a Domain container object is added to the NDS tree. SDU_DOMAIN is a Domain object that holds the NT users and groups of this Domain that are integrated with NDS.

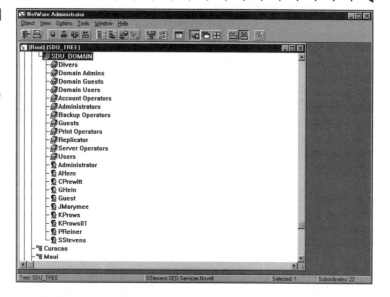

▶ . . . . ◀

The GES Event Container stores all the NDS events for which the GES will notify Synchronization Agents.

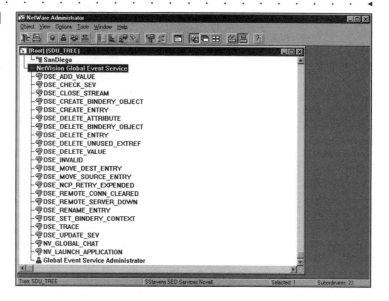

Pros and Cons

Our evaluation of Synchronicity for NT proved the product comprehensive, stable, and easy to use. We did, however, note some minor limitations. Table 6.3 shows the pros and cons we observed.

T A B L E 6.3 *Pros and Cons of Synchronicity for NT*	FEATURE	PROS	CONS
	Administration of NT Users	Allows administration of all NT user properties from within NWAdmin. Provides simple mapping between NDS and NT users with no additional user object required.	None
	Administration of NT Groups	Allows creation and administration of NT Global and Local Groups from within NWAdmin. Provides synchronization between NDS and NT groups.	None
	Policy Support	Can manage account policies only.	Provides limited NT System Policy support. Does not provide support for administration of audit policies, trust relationships, and user rights. These must be managed through NT's User Manager.
	Synchronization Agent	Requires only one connection to the GES.	Runs as an application on an NT system. Is subject to user rights, logouts, and so on.

TABLE 6.3	FEATURE	PROS	CONS
Pros and Cons of Synchronicity for NT (continued)	Global Event System	Global design makes it scalable in large networks.	Does not make journal updates to NDS. If a Synchronization Agent is unavailable when an event occurs, re-synchronization must be manually initiated. This can be scheduled to take place automatically.
	Price		Not free, but worth it!

Evaluating Both Products

The best way for you to make a decision about which product will work best in your environment is to take a close look at the functionality of each product. The following sections provide detailed information on the installation and use of both products. You should read these sections and, if possible, actually install and test each product. Remember that you may obtain trial versions of Novell Administrator for Windows NT and NetVision's Synchronicity for NT from the company's respective Web sites.

Installing and Using NadminNT

The "Choosing a Synchronization Product" section earlier in this chapter provided an overview of the Novell Administrator for Windows NT and its components. This section discusses the installation and use of the product. For an overview of the product and its components, see the "Choosing a Synchronization Product" section.

Installing NadminNT

The installation of the Novell Administrator for Windows NT is a fairly straightforward process. This section takes you step-by-step through the installation of the product. This section assumes you are installing NadminNT for the first time. Remember, though, you may need to run the NadminNT installation program more than once as your environment changes. For example, if a new NT Domain exists that you want to manage through NDS, you must run the installation program to add that Domain to your NDS tree. In this case, during the installation routine you will only select the components needed to install the Domain into your Tree.

What the Installation Does

Before jumping into a discussion on how to install the Novell Administrator for Windows NT, a quick overview of what the installation program does may prove useful. On a first-time installation of NadminNT, the installation process accomplishes the following four main tasks:

▸ *Extends the NDS Schema.* The NDS Schema is extended to add objects and attributes required to support the Novell Administrator for Windows NT. This is done once per NDS tree. (In other words, if you must extend the Schema on more than one tree, you must run the installation program multiple times.)

▸ *Installs the Event Monitor to NetWare Servers.* The Event Monitor (NDSDM. NLM) is installed on one or more NetWare servers. NDSDM.NLM must be installed on the server that contains the Master replica of any partition containing the Domain object. (This is the object that will contain the NT users and groups integrated with NDS.) It should also be loaded on one or more servers that hold Read/Write replicas of the partition.

▸ *Installs the IGRATE and NWAdmin Snapins.* IGRATE is the integration utility used to migrate users from NT to NDS, and vice versa. During installation of NadminNT, IGRATE.EXE is installed in the SYS:\PUBLIC\ WINNT directory. Snapin modules are also added to NWAdmin, which provide support for the new Windows NT objects and attributes that NadminNT uses. MWANT.REG is used to register these components so NWAdmin will recognize them.

▸ *Installs the NDS Object Replication Service (ORS) to the NT Servers.* The ORS is installed to all NT Server PDCs and BDCs of the Domains to be synchronized with NDS.

Before You Install

Before you begin the installation of NadminNT, you must verify you are running the most recent versions of certain parts of your network software. This includes your NetWare servers, as well as your NT systems. In addition, you must ensure each system meets the minimum hardware requirements for the product.

NetWare System Requirements

To install the Novell Administrator for Windows NT on your NetWare servers, you must be authenticated as an administrative user to the Directory tree on which you plan to extend the Schema and in which you have the NT domain object placed. In addition, your NetWare servers require the following:

- NetWare 4.1x (or higher).

- 4MB available hard disk space.

- The most recent version of the DS.NLM (Version 5.96 or higher).

- The NetWare 4.1x CLIB Update Kit (LIBUPx.EXE). This update kit is required on any NetWare server running the Event Monitor (NDSDM.NLM).

- Version 4.11 of the NetWare Administrator utility (which shipped with NetWare).

- The Service Advertising Protocol (SAP) must be turned on at the servers running the Event Monitor (NDSDM.NLM). SAP is on by default. If SAP has been disabled for some reason, at the server console, type **LOAD INETCFG** and then choose Bindings/Select IPX external net/Expert Bind Options/SAP Bind Options. Ensure SAP State is set to ON.

- TCPIP.NLM must be loaded.

Windows NT System Requirements

The installation of the Novell Administrator for Windows NT is performed entirely from the Windows NT side, either from your Windows NT server or from an NT Workstation. To perform the installation, you must be logged into the

Domain as a user with administrative privileges. In addition, NadminNT requires the following on your Windows NT systems:

- ► Windows NT Server Version 3.51 or higher.

- ► NT Workstation Version 3.51 or higher (for any NT workstation workgroups synchronized with NDS).

- ► 2MB of available disk space.

- ► 32MB of RAM on NT servers running the ORS.

- ► 16MB of RAM on NT workstations running the ORS.

- ► The NetWare Client for Windows NT (Version 4.10 or above) must be installed on the NT Systems (Server or Workstation) from which you are installing and administering NadminNT. In addition, it must be installed on any NT Server that is running the ORS (including the PDC of the Domains synchronized with NDS, as well as any BDCs and any Workgroup systems).

- ► Windows NT default shares must be turned on. These are shares created by the system and generally should not be modified. Specifically, NadminNT requires the ADMIN$ be turned on for all Windows NT Systems that are running the ORS. If this share is unavailable, NadminNT cannot install properly.

- ► All PDCs and BDCs of Domains synchronized with NDS must be up during the installation of NadminNT. If any of these systems are missing or down, the installation cannot complete properly.

- ► The internal IPX network number defined on the NT Servers must be set to 0. This parameter is found under the Network Control Panel by choosing the Services tab and then the Protocols tab. Select the IPX protocol and click the Properties button.

Running the Installation Program

The entire installation of NadminNT is performed from a Windows NT system (Workstation or Server). Before beginning the installation, log in to NDS and the Domain as an administrative user (you should have the NetWare Client for Windows NT installed at this point. If so, you can log in to both from a single interface.)

To begin the installation, simply run SETUP.EXE. You are presented with two product overview screens followed by Novell's License Agreement.

As you continue past the introductory screens, you will see a dialog box, which enables you to select the components you want to install, as shown in Figure 6.8.

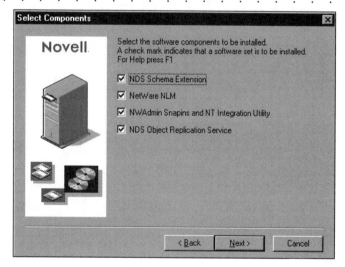

FIGURE 6.8

When installing NadminNT, you are presented with this dialog box that enables you to select the components you want to install. For first-time installations, all components should be selected. For subsequent installations, choose only the components you need.

If this is a first-time installation, all the components shown in Figure 6.8 should be selected. If you are adding to an existing installation, choose only the components you need. For example, if you want to have a new Domain or Workgroup to manage through NDS, choose only the ORS component.

Next, you are presented with a list of NDS trees, as shown in Figure 6.9.

► . . . . ◄

FIGURE 6.9

You must install the Novell Administrator for Windows NT on each tree from which you would like to manage NT users and groups. Only one tree at a time can be selected in this screen. The installation must be repeated if you have more than one tree.

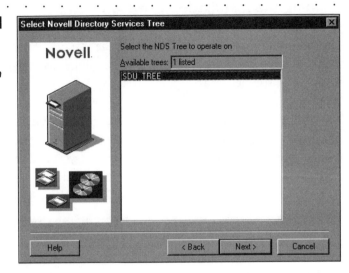

The dialog box shown in Figure 6.9 enables you to select the NDS tree to which you want to have the NadminNT Schema extensions added. This screen only enables you to select one tree at a time, so you must repeat the installation for additional trees from which you would like to manage NT users and groups.

After the tree has been selected, you are asked to select the context in which to begin the search for NetWare servers that are participating in the NetWare/NT synchronization. If you have a small NDS tree, you can select the [Root]. For large trees, you may want to indicate the specific context in which the server that will run the Event Monitor resides. This will minimize the time it takes to search for servers. You will then be presented with a list of NetWare servers as shown in Figure 6.10.

From the list of servers, choose the servers on which you want to install the Event Monitor. You should always first choose the server that holds the Master replica of the partition in which you want to place NT users and groups. It is also recommended you install the Event Monitor on one or more servers with Read/Write replicas of that partition. This provides fault tolerance in the event the server that holds the Master goes down.

Next, you are presented with a list of available NT domains and/or workgroups currently found on your network, as shown in Figure 6.11.

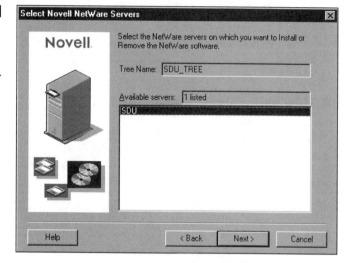

FIGURE 6.10

The NadminNT Event Monitor (NDSDM.NLM) must be installed on the server that holds the Master replica of the partition to contain the NT users and groups. It should also be installed on one or more servers holding Read/Write replicas.

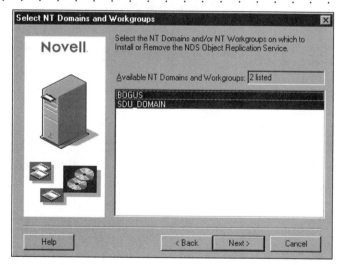

FIGURE 6.11

When you choose a Domain or Workgroup to be managed through NDS, the installation program automatically installs the ORS on the NT systems.

Select the Domains or Workgroups that will be managed through NDS. The installation program then installs the selected Domain and/or Workgroup into the NDS tree and installs the ORS on the necessary servers. When you select a Domain, the installation program automatically finds the PDC and BDCs in the domain, and installs the ORS on them. The ORS automatically is started on the

PDC, but not on the BDC. If the PDC goes down, the service must be manually started on a BDC after it has been promoted to PDC.

Next, you are asked to select the NDS context into which you want to install the Domain or Workgroup object, as shown in Figure 6.12.

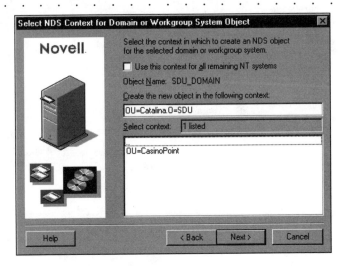

FIGURE 6.12

The NDS context chosen in this dialog box is the context in which the Domain or Workgroup object is created.

This screen is repeated for each Domain or Workgroup chosen earlier in the installation (see Figure 6.11).

The next installation screen enables you to review your installation choices, as shown in Figure 6.13.

If all the parameters shown in this screen are correct, click Next and the installation proceeds. If you want to change some of the installation parameters, click Back to re-select them.

When you proceed with the installation, you are prompted to authenticate to the NDS tree and any NT system chosen earlier in the installation. Be sure to log in as a user with administrative privileges. The installation then begins.

Viewing the Installation Error Log

When the installation is complete, you are presented with a screen that enables you to view the installation error log (if installation errors occurred) and immediately launch the IGRATE utility (see Figure 6.14).

FIGURE 6.13

After all installation parameters have been chosen, you are give the opportunity to review your installation choices.

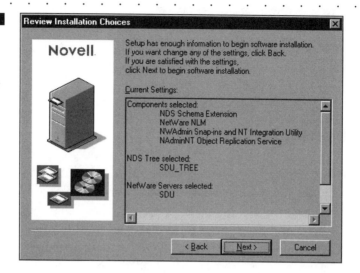

FIGURE 6.14

After the NadminNT components are installed, this screen enables you to view any installation errors encountered and to launch the IGRATE utility.

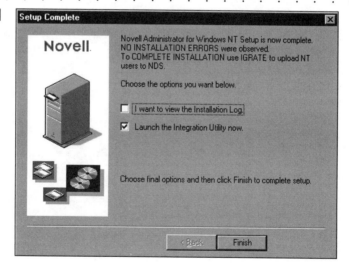

This screen will vary, depending on the results of the installation. For example, if no installation errors are found, the top of the screen will say "NO INSTALLATION ERRORS OCCURRED" and the box to view the installation log will not appear. Also, if fatal installation errors occurred, the box to launch IGRATE does not appear. If this happens, you may need to re-install the product. Refer to the Novell Administrator for Windows NT documentation for further details.

Uploading NT Objects to NDS

Before you can begin managing NT users and groups through NDS, you must upload the Domain or Workgroup databases to your NDS tree. After a successful installation, the IGRATE utility automatically launches to enable you to do this.

To upload the NT users and groups to your NDS tree, select the Domain or Workgroup object you want to upload. This is performed on the right portion of the IGRATE screen (under "Available NT users and groups"). Then, select the NDS context to which you want to upload the objects on the right portion of the IGRATE screen (under "NDS context and users"), as shown in Figure 6.15.

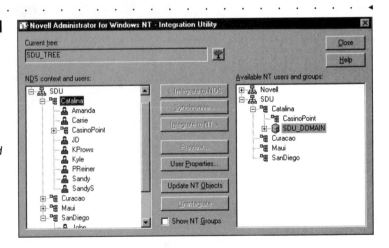

F I G U R E   6.15

After a successful installation of NadminNT, the IGRATE utility is automatically launched to enable the upload of NT users and groups to NDS. This must be done before NT objects can be managed through NDS.

After selecting the Domain or Workgroup object and the NDS context (as shown in Figure 6.15), click the Update NT Objects button in the center of the IGRATE screen. A dialog box appears and asks if you want to update all NT users and groups. Answer Yes to begin the upload.

When the upload is complete, the NT users and groups appear in your NDS tree, as shown in Figure 6.16.

▶ · ◀

FIGURE 6.16

After IGRATE is used to upload NT users and groups, they appear as NT objects in the NDS tree.

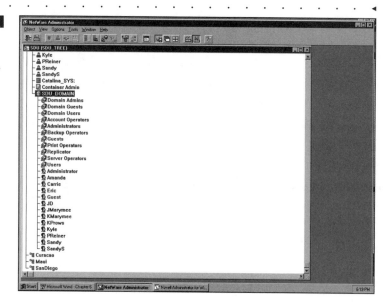

The objects shown in Figure 6.16 include NT Global Group objects, NT Local Group objects, and NT users. These objects can now be managed through NWAdmin. For details on managing NT objects through NWAdmin and additional information on using IGRATE, refer to the following sections.

Using IGRATE

IGRATE is the integration utility included with NadminNT. It enables the integration of users and groups in a mixed Windows NT and NDS environment. In addition, IGRATE launches automatically at the end of the NadminNT installation. This enables you to upload users and groups of an NT Domain to NDS.

IGRATE is used to do the following:

▶ Integrate existing NT users into NDS

▶ Integrate existing NDS users into NT

▶ Synchronize existing NT users with existing NDS users

▶ Unintegrate integrated users

▶ Update NT objects

IGRATE can be run as a standalone utility (IGRATE.EXE is installed in the SYS:\PUBLIC\WINNT directory when the product is installed), or it can be launched from within NWAdmin.

To run IGRATE from within NWAdmin, access the Tools menu from the NWAdmin menu bar and choose NT Integration Utility, as shown in Figure 6.17.

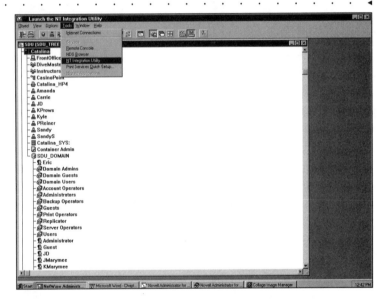

Integrating Existing NT Users into NDS

If you have existing NT users you want to be managed through NDS, you can use IGRATE to integrate them into the Directory tree. When you do this, an NDS user account is created for the NT user in the selected context.

Figure 6.18 shows IGRATE being used to integrate an existing NT user into NDS.

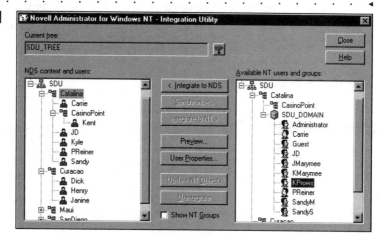

FIGURE 6.18

The IGRATE utility enables you to integrate an existing NT user into NDS. In this example, the NT user KPROWS is integrated into the Catalina container in the NDS tree.

In Figure 6.18, the NT user KProws is being integrated into the NDS context Catalina.SDU. Notice the desired NDS context to integrate to is highlighted on the left portion of the screen under NDS context and users. The NT User to be integrated into this NDS context is highlighted on the right portion of the screen. To complete this integration, click the Integrate to NDS button in the center of the screen.

To integrate multiple NT users into NDS simultaneously, hold down the Ctrl key while selecting the NT users to be integrated.

TIP

Once integrated, the user KProws has a new NDS user account added in the Catalina container. The existing NT User object under the *SDU_DOMAIN* Domain object is changed to a Hybrid User object because KProws now has accounts in both NDS and the NT Domain.

When you integrate NT users to NDS, the NT user properties are used when the NDS accounts are created. (The objects under the NT Domain object contain only the properties supported by Windows NT.) You can, however, apply an NDS User template when the user is integrated to NDS. This creates the NDS user with the properties defined in the template.

To define a template to be applied when NT users are integrated to NDS, click the User Properties button in the center of the IGRATE screen (see Figure 6.18). Two tabs are presented: Passwords and Other Properties. To define a template, click the Other Properties tab and browse the NDS tree for the desired template, as shown in Figure 6.19.

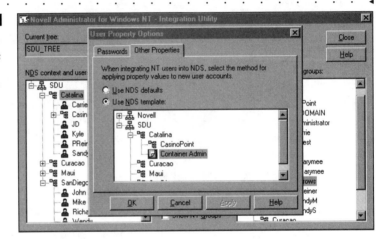

FIGURE 6.19

When integrating NT users to NDS, the User Properties option of IGRATE enables you to define a template to be used when creating the NDS user.

When NT users are integrated into NDS, the Password tab shown in Figure 6.19 can be used to configure the password to be used when the NDS users are created. If no password is defined in this tab, the default setting of No Password with Require Password Change at Next Login is used. Passwords on the existing NT user and the user Hybrid user object in the NDS tree are not changed. When the user logs in, the NetWare Client for Windows NT enables the passwords of the NDS user account and the NT user account (hence, the Hybrid user account) to be synchronized. The NetWare Client for Windows NT is discussed in detail in Chapter 5.

NOTE

Once NT users have been integrated into NDS, those users should be managed through NWAdmin. If Windows NT User Manager is used to change integrated objects, those changes will not be automatically synchronized unless you do a complete upload of NT information into NDS. For large domains, this can take a considerable amount of time and generate excess network traffic.

Integrating Existing NDS Users to NT

If you have existing NDS users you want to use NT resources, you can use IGRATE to integrate the users into the NT Domain or Workgroup. When this is done, an NT user account is created for them in the NT Domain or NT Workgroup selected. Figure 6.20 shows an existing NDS user being integrated into an NT Domain.

F I G U R E   6 . 2 0

IGRATE enables you to integrate existing NDS users into an NT Domain or Workgroup. In this example, NDS user Kyle is being integrated into the SDU Domain.

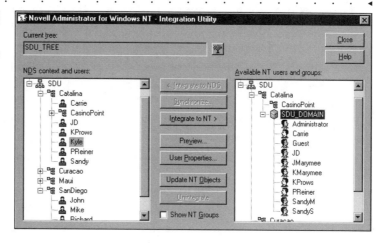

In Figure 6.20, NDS user Kyle is being integrated into the SDU Domain. Notice the NDS user to be integrated with NT is highlighted in the left portion of the screen under NDS context and users. The NT Domain into which this user is to be integrated is highlighted on the right portion of the screen. To complete the integration, click the Integrate to NT button in the center of the IGRATE screen.

To integrate multiple NDS users into NT simultaneously, hold down the Ctrl key while selecting the NDS users to be integrated.

TIP

Once integrated, a user account for Kyle is created in the Windows NT Domain. In addition, a Hybrid User account called Kyle is created under the SDU_DOMAIN Domain object in the NDS tree. This is because the user now has an account in both the NDS database and the NT Domain's SAM database.

When you integrate existing NDS users to NT, the NDS properties of those users are used when the NT accounts are created. Because Windows NT only supports a limited number of user properties, however, only the properties supported by the Domain are used. These properties include User name, Full Name, and Description.

If an NDS User template is used when you perform the integration operation (see Figure 6.19), the template will not overwrite the properties currently set for the user. This is because when the user is created in the NT Domain, the template is applied first and then the NDS user properties are applied.

Passwords on the existing NDS user are not changed. However, the new NT User (and the Hybrid user) are created with the password defined in IGRATE User Properties (see Figure 6.19). If no password is defined in this tab, the default setting of No Password with Require Password Change at Next Login is used. If the passwords on the NDS account and the NT account are different, the NetWare Client for Windows NT allows synchronization of those passwords. The NetWare Client for Windows NT is discussed in detail in Chapter 5.

NOTE

Once NDS users have been integrated into NT, the new NT user objects should be managed through NWAdmin. If Windows NT User Manager is used to change integrated objects, those changes will not be automatically synchronized unless you do a complete upload of NT information into NDS. For large domains this can take considerable time and generate excess network traffic.

Integrating Existing NDS Users to NT Using the Application Servers Page

An optional method of integrating existing NDS users into an NT Domain is to select a user object in NWAdmin, access the User object's Details page, and then select the Application Servers page. From this page, choose Add and then browse the tree to find the NT Domain to which you would like this user to be added, as shown in Figure 6.21.

As with using IGRATE to integrate an existing NDS user to NT, the method shown in Figure 6.21 creates a user account in the NT Domain's SAM database and a Hybrid User account is created in the NDS tree under the Domain object.

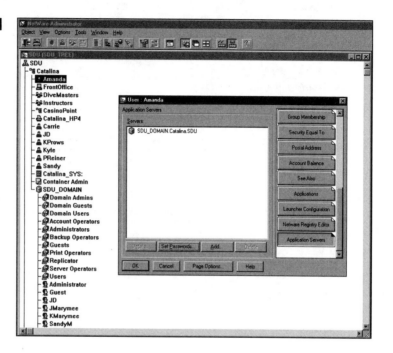

F I G U R E   6.21

Using NWAdmin, as shown in this example, is an optional method of integrating existing NDS users into an NT Domain.

Synchronizing Existing NT Users with Existing NDS Users

If you have users who already have accounts in both NDS and in an NT Server Domain, the IGRATE utility can be used to synchronize the accounts. This enables you to manage the accounts from a single point. When you synchronize the accounts, the NT user objects under the Domain object in the NDS tree are changed to a Hybrid user, which indicates integration with NDS objects.

Figure 6.22 shows an example of using IGRATE to synchronize an existing NT user with an existing NDS user.

In Figure 6.22, the NT user account SandyM is being synchronized with the existing NDS user account Sandy. Notice, the NT user to be synchronized is highlighted in the right portion of the screen under "Available NT users and groups." The NDS user to synchronize with is highlighted in the left portion of the screen under "NDS context and users." To complete the synchronization, click the Synchronize button in the center of the IGRATE screen.

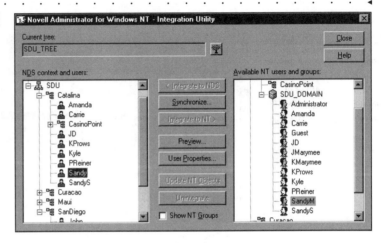

FIGURE 6.22

IGRATE enables
synchronization of existing
NT users with existing NDS
users. In this example, the
user account SandyM in the
SDU Domain is being
synchronized with the NDS
user account Sandy.

Once the synchronization is complete, in the Domain's SAM database the NT user object's name (SandyM) is changed to match the NDS objects name (Sandy). The NT object also assumes the other properties of the NDS object relevant to NT (Full Name and Description).

Passwords on the existing user account do not change as a result of synchronization. The NetWare Client for Windows NT, however, can be used to synchronize passwords between the two systems. The NetWare Client for Windows NT is discussed in detail in Chapter 5.

NOTE

Once NT users have been synchronized with NDS users, the NT user objects should be managed through NWAdmin. If Windows NT User Manager is used to change integrated objects, those changes will not be automatically synchronized unless you do a complete upload of NT information into NDS. For large domains, this can take considerable time and generate excess network traffic.

Unintegrating Integrated Users

After integrating or synchronizing NT users, they can be unintegrated using the IGRATE utility. When an unintegrate operation is performed, the NT user object is no longer synchronized with the corresponding NDS user account. In addition, the Hybrid user object under the Domain object is converted back to a normal NT user account (a user that has an account on NT only). A normal NT user account can be managed through NWAdmin, but is not associated with an NDS user account.

To unintegrate an NT user, highlight the Hybrid user object on the right portion of the IGRATE screen under "Available NT users and groups," as shown in Figure 6.23.

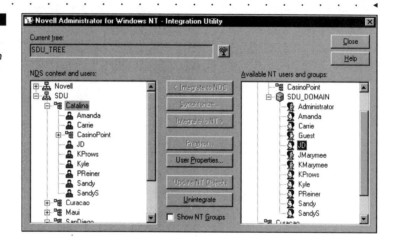

FIGURE 6.23

IGRATE can be used to unintegrate NT users from NDS. In this example, the Hybrid user object JD is being unintegrated from the tree.

In Figure 6.23, NT user JD is being unintegrated from the NDS tree. To begin the unintegrate operation, click the Unintegrate button in the center of the IGRATE screen.

To unintegrate multiple users simultaneously, hold down the Ctrl key while you select the Hybrid user objects.

TIP

Updating NT Objects

Once NT objects have been integrated with NDS, changes made through NT's User Manager will not be automatically synchronized with NDS. IGRATE can be used to resynchronize the Domain with NDS. Unfortunately, no way exists to synchronize NT user objects with NDS on an individual basis; you must resynchronize the entire Domain.

To resynchronize the Domain with NDS, highlight the Domain on the right portion of the IGRATE screen under "Available NT users and groups." Then select the Update NT Objects button in the center of the IGRATE screen, as shown in Figure 6.24.

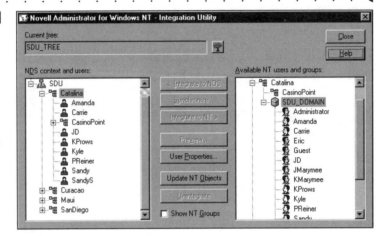

FIGURE 6.24

If NT's User Manager is used to make changes to NT objects that have been synchronized with NDS, IGRATE must be used to synchronize those changes manually. This is done by selecting the Domain object and choosing Update NT Objects.

When you select the Update NT Objects button, a dialog box appears asking if you want to upload all NT users and groups to NDS (see Figure 6.25).

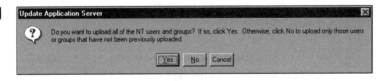

FIGURE 6.25

To upload the entire NT Domain to NDS, select Yes on this screen. To upload only users and groups that have been added using User Manager, select No.

Answering Yes will upload *all* users and groups in the Domain to NDS. If new users or groups have been added with User Manager, answering No will synchronize just the added information.

Managing NT Objects through NWAdmin NT

Once NT objects have been integrated into NDS, they should be managed from within NWAdmin. Although NT's User Manager can still be used, the changes made in User Manager will not be synchronized to NDS automatically; you must initiate the synchronization manually from within IGRATE. And, as mentioned previously in the "Using IGRATE" section, you cannot resynchronize individual objects, but rather only the entire Domain or Workgroup. Refer to the earlier "Using IGRATE" section for details.

NWAdmin Support for NadminNT

To manage NT users and groups, the NadminNT Snapin modules must be added to NWAdmin for Windows NT (NWAdmin NT) that allows the new NT objects to be viewed and managed from within the utility. The Windows NT registry of the station from which NadminNT was installed is modified during the installation to support these Snapins. If other administrative stations or users exist that will manage Windows NT users and groups from NWAdmin, however, those registries must be modified manually. To do this, run the MWANT.REG file in the SYS:\PUBLIC\WINNT directory.

Once the registry has been modified to support NadminNT, NWAdmin NT can be used to manage the new NT objects as described in the following sections.

Managing the Domain or Workgroup Object

Domain and Workgroup Objects are container objects that represent the Windows NT systems integrated with NDS. When an upload of NT Objects is performed, the NT users and groups are placed in the Directory tree under this object, as shown in Figure 6.26.

In Figure 6.26, SDU_DOMAIN is the Domain object created when NadminNT was installed. The objects contained in SDU_DOMAIN are the NT users and groups that have been integrated with NDS using the IGRATE utility.

Domain and Workgroup objects can only be created through the NadminNT installation program. If you have new Domains or Workgroups you want to integrate with NDS, you must re-run the installation program. When you are prompted for the components to install, check the NDS Object Replication Service box only. This option installs the Domain or Workgroup specified into the tree and installs the ORS software on the appropriate Windows NT systems. (For more details on this, see the "Installing NadminNT" section earlier in this chapter.)

▶ · ◀

The Domain object is a container object used to store the NT users and groups managed through NDS.

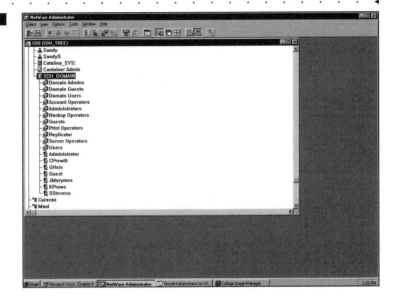

Managing Domain or Workgroup objects consists of the following two primary tasks:

▶ Managing System Modals

▶ Managing Network Settings

To access these options, from within NWAdmin NT, access the Domain or Workgroup object's Detail Page by highlighting the object in the tree, clicking the right mouse button, and then choosing Details (or from the NWAdmin menu bar, choose Object/Details).

System Modals   The System Modals page of the Domain or Workgroup object defines how passwords are used by the NT systems, as shown in Figure 6.27.

The System Modals page in Figure 6.27 corresponds directly with the Account policies defined in Windows NT User Manager. The Account policies can be viewed on the NT system by choosing Policies from the User Manager menu bar, and then choosing Account.

Figure 6.28 shows the Account Policy definitions in User Manager.

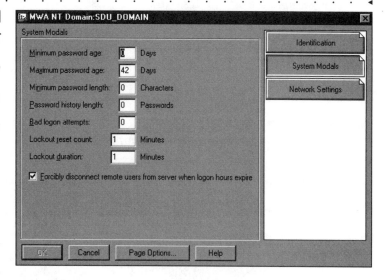

The System Modals page of the Domain or Workgroup object controls passwords on the Windows NT system. This NDS page corresponds directly to the Account policies in Windows NT user Manager.

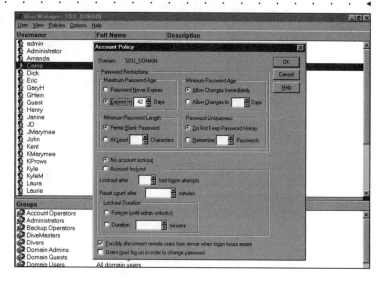

The Account Policy definitions in the Windows NT User Manager correspond directly to the System Modals page of the Domain or Workgroup object.

Although the presentation of the options on this screen and the screen shown in Figure 6.27 are different, you will notice the parameters are basically the same. Once a Domain or Workgroup is synchronized with NDS, the Account policies should be managed through NWAdmin and not through User Manager.

One exception exists to this. Notice the "Users must log on in order to change password" option at the bottom of Figure 6.28. This option is unavailable under NWAdmin and must be managed through User Manager.

Account policies are the only Windows NT policies that can be managed from NWAdmin. No option exists to manage User Rights, Audit Policies, or Trust Relationships. These must be managed under NT's User Manager.

Network Settings   The Network Settings page of the Domain or Workgroup object enables you to control how NadminNT operates, as shown in Figure 6.29.

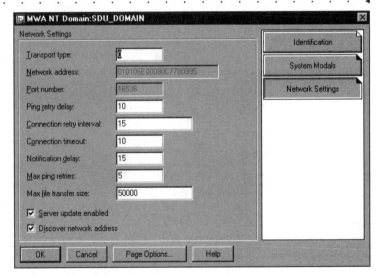

F I G U R E   6 . 2 9

The Network Settings page of the Domain or Workgroup object controls how NadminNT operates.

In most cases, the default settings on this screen are sufficient, although some instances occur where you may want to fine-tune these parameters. Table 6.4 provides a brief definition of these parameters and their usage.

The two types of NT User objects managed through NadminNT are

▶ *NT User objects.* These are NT users with an account on NT systems only, but their accounts are managed through NDS.

▶ *Hybrid User objects.* These users have accounts on both NT and NDS.

TABLE 6.4	PARAMETER	DESCRIPTION
Network Settings Parameters	Transport type	The number representing the transport you are using (IPX or IP).
	Network address	The network address of the NT system running the ORS for this Domain or Workgroup. This number is normally automatically detected. If you have more than one network adapter in the NT system running the ORS, however, you must manually enter the correct network address. To do this, uncheck the Discover network address box at the bottom of the screen. If this box is checked, the Network Address field is grayed out, as shown in Figure 6.29.
	Port number	The specified IPX or IP port used by the network address. This number is dynamically assigned.
	Ping retry delay	The number of seconds the Event Monitor will wait before it reattempts to send an event ping to the ORS.
	Connection retry interval	If an NT Server running the ORS does not receive an event ping from an Event Monitor in the number of minutes defined in this field, it attempts to establish communication with the NetWare server running the Event Monitor.
	Connection timeout	The number of minutes the NT Server running the ORS will keep an inactive connection to a NetWare server.
	Notification delay	The number of seconds the Event Monitor waits before it notifies the ORS of a change in an NT object integrated with NDS. When the ORS is notified, the corresponding change is made in the SAM database on the NT system. Increasing this number reduces the frequency of pings the Event Monitor sends to the ORS. Decreasing this number decreases the amount of time required for changes to be reflected in the SAM database.

Continued

TABLE 6.4	PARAMETER	DESCRIPTION
Network Settings Parameters (continued)	Max ping retries	The number of times the Event Monitor attempts to notify the ORS of a change in NDS. If the NT server running the ORS does not respond within the number of pings set in this option, the Event Monitor continues to ping the ORS, but doubles the Ping retry delay with each unacknowledged ping.
	Max file transfer size	The maximum packet size the ORS can receive from the Event Monitor. The default of 50,000 bytes is sufficient for most networks.
	Server update enabled	This option should be set only by the integration utility. If an update of NT objects to NDS did not complete properly, this option is cleared. If it is, the next time the Update NT objects option is run in IGRATE, a complete upload of the domain or workgroup is performed. This ensures the correct NT user and group information.
	Discover network address	If this box is checked, the network address of the NT server running the ORS is discovered automatically. If you have multiple cards in your NT server, the first network address in the list is discovered. If this is not the correct address, deselect this box and specify the correct network address in the Network Address field.

Figure 6.30 shows these two types of NT objects in the Directory tree.

You can distinguish the two NT user object types by their icons. Regular NT User object icons face to the right, Hybrid User icons face left. In Figure 6.30, GHEIN and PREINER located under the SDU_DOMAIN are Hybrid users; all other user objects in this container are NT Users.

NT User Objects   When you access the Details page of an NT User object within NWAdmin, you will notice the property pages are identical to the properties you would find if you were looking at the user under NT's User Manager. The only difference is the presentation. To enable you to compare these properties, Figure 6.31 shows the properties of the NDS NT User object in NWAdmin NT. Figure 6.32 shows the same user being viewed under NT's User Manager.

Two types of NT objects exist that are managed through NWAdmin NT: NT Users and Hybrid Users. This tree shows both types of users. The Hybrid users are the last two user objects shown under SDU_DOMAIN; the remaining user objects are regular NT Users.

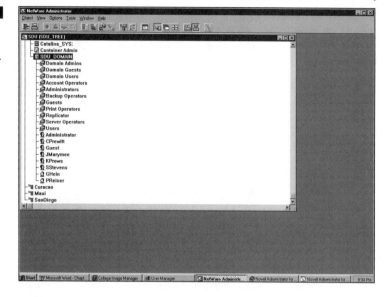

An NT User's properties being viewed with NWAdmin.

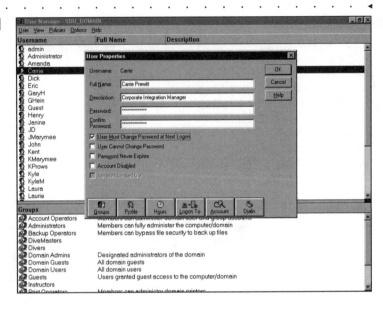

FIGURE 6.32

An NT User's properties being viewed with NT User Manager.

The benefit to this is you now have a single point of administration for both NDS and NT users. Any changes made to the NT User object in NWAdmin automatically are synchronized to the SAM database on the NT system (the reverse is not true, though), so you are no longer required to use multiple administration utilities.

Creating an NT User Object   Creating an NT User object in the NDS tree (which, in turn, will create an NT user in the SAM database on the NT system) is done a little differently than creating a standard NDS user.

To create an NT User object, highlight the Domain or Workgroup object representing the Domain or Workgroup where you want to create the new user, and click the right mouse button. (You cannot use the Object/Create function to create NT Users.) When you select Create from the menu, the New Object dialog box shown in Figure 6.33 appears. This dialog box enables you to create new NT objects.

To create a new NT user, select MWA NT User from the list and click OK. You will then be presented with a dialog box similar to the dialog box presented when you create a regular NDS user, as shown in Figure 6.34.

FIGURE 6.33

Creating a new NT object in NDS is done by highlighting the Domain or Workgroup object in the NDS tree, clicking the right mouse button, and selecting Create. The new object you want to create can be chosen from this dialog box.

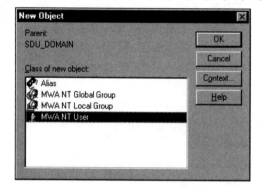

FIGURE 6.34

Creating an NT user object in NWAdmin

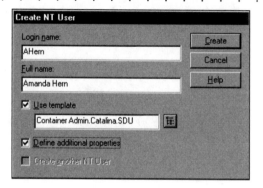

When you Click create at this point, the user object is created under the Domain or Workgroup container selected (in this case, *SDU_DOMAIN*) and the user is also created in the SAM database on the NT system. Once the user object is created, it should be managed through NWAdmin. The user object's properties correspond directly to the properties found in NT's User Manager.

Hybrid User Objects   When an NT User object is integrated with NDS or synchronized with an existing NDS user, the object under the Domain or Workgroup container is changed from an NT User to a Hybrid User. In addition, when an NDS user is integrated with NT, a Hybrid User object (in addition to the regular NDS object) is created under the Domain or Workgroup container. Integrating NT users to NDS and NDS users to NT is covered in depth in the "Using IGRATE" section earlier in this chapter.

When you use NWAdmin to access the Details page of a Hybrid user account (see Figure 6.35), notice the properties of the object do not correspond directly to the properties in NT User Manager. This is because Hybrid Users have a corresponding NDS user account and any NDS properties that overlap with NT properties must be set at the NDS user level.

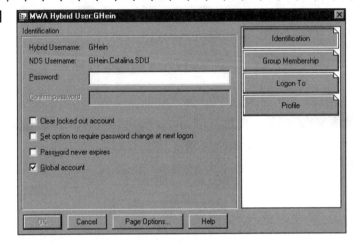

In Figure 6.35, notice the only properties available are those relating specifically to NT. The other properties normally found in an NT User object (such as Full Name, Description, Password, Logon Hours, and Account) are managed through this user's regular NDS user account.

The benefit to Hybrid Users is, not only are you managing with a single administration utility (NWAdmin), you are now managing one user account instead of two.

Creating a Hybrid User   The two ways to create a Hybrid User account are:

▶ Through IGRATE (see the "Using IGRATE" section earlier in this chapter for details)

▶ Using the Application Server page of an NDS User object

When you create a new NDS user, you can automatically create a corresponding NT User account (hence, a Hybrid User account) through the user's Application Server page. In fact, this page of an existing NDS user can be used at any time to create a corresponding NT account.

For a new user, select the Define Additional Properties box during the creation process. Then choose the Application Servers page. For existing NDS users, simply access the User objects Details page and then choose Application Servers page. From this page, choose Add and then browse the tree to find the NT Domain to which you would like this user to be added, as shown in Figure 6.36.

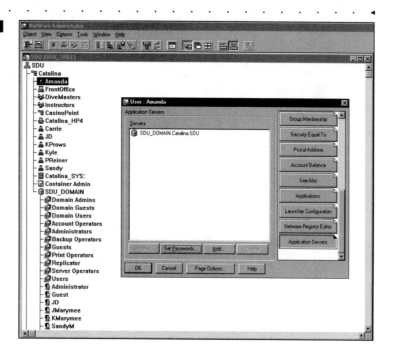

F I G U R E   6.36

Using NWAdmin as shown in this example is an optional method of integrating existing NDS users into an NT Domain.

As with using IGRATE to integrate an existing NDS user to NT, the method shown in Figure 6.36 creates a user account in the NT Domain's SAM database and a Hybrid User account is created in the NDS tree under the Domain object.

Managing NT Groups

Managing NT groups under NWAdmin is a bit different from managing users because no way exists to map an NT group to an NDS group. What this means is, even though NT groups can be managed through NDS (which eliminates the need to use two administration utilities), you still must manage NT and NDS groups separately.

NadminNT supports both NT group types (Global Groups and Local Groups). Figure 6.37 shows the NT Group objects in an NDS tree.

▶ . . . . ◀

FIGURE 6.37

NadminNT supports NT Global and Local Groups. In this figure, under the SDU_DOMAIN container object, Global Group icons have a globe in the background; Local Group icons have a computer in the background.

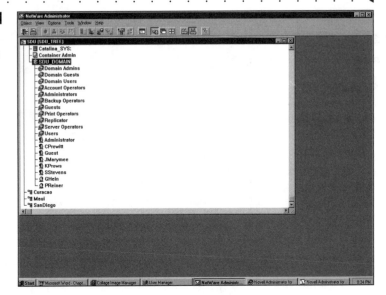

In Figure 6.37, the first three objects under the SDU_DOMAIN container are NT Global Groups (distinguished by the icon with a globe in the background). The group objects following the Global Groups are Local Groups (distinguished by the icon with a single computer in the background).

Managing group objects consists simply of adding members to the group. When you access the Details page of an NT group object from within NWAdmin, you are presented with the two options: Identification (which enables you to enter a description for the group) and Members.

When adding members to an NT group, you can select both NT-only users and Hybrid Users, as shown in Figure 6.38.

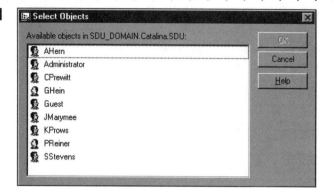

FIGURE 6.38

When managing NT group memberships through NWAdmin, both NT Users and Hybrid Users can be made group members.

Any user who is made a member of an NT group in NWAdmin is made a member of the actual NT group in the SAM database on the NT system. The users will then inherit the group's rights to NT resources. (NT group rights cannot be managed through NadminNT; they must be managed from the NT side.) In the case of a Hybrid user (which is an NDS user with a corresponding NT account), when you make him or her a member of an NT group, you are essentially giving an NDS user transparent access to NT Application and other resources.

Creating NT Groups

Creating NT groups in the NDS tree (which, in turn, creates an NT group in the SAM database on the NT system) is done a little differently than creating a standard NDS group.

To create the group, highlight the Domain or Workgroup object that represents the Domain or Workgroup where you want to create the new group and click the right mouse button. (You cannot use the Object/Create function to create NT Groups.) When you select Create from the menu, the New Object dialog box shown in Figure 6.39 appears. This dialog box enables you to create new NT objects.

To create a new NT group, select group type (global or local) from the list and click OK. You will then be prompted for the name of the new group.

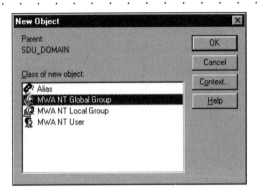

F I G U R E   6.39

Creating a new NT object in NDS is done by highlighting the Domain or Workgroup object in the NDS tree, clicking the right mouse button, and selecting Create. The new object you want to create can be chosen from this dialog box.

When you click Create, the group object is created under the Domain or Workgroup container selected (in this case, the SDU_DOMAIN) and the group is also created in the SAM database on the NT system. Once the group object is created, it should be managed through NWAdmin. The NT Global and Local group object properties correspond directly to the properties found in NT's User Manager.

Installing and Using Synchronicity

The "Choosing a Synchronization Product" section earlier in this chapter provided an overview of Synchronicity for NT and its components. This section discusses the installation and use of the product. For an overview of the product and its components, please see the "Choosing a Synchronization Product" section.

Installing Synchronicity for NT

The installation of Synchronicity for NT is a fairly straightforward process. This section takes you step-by-step through the installation of the product. This section assumes you are installing Synchronicity for NT for the first time.

What the Installation Does

Before we jump into a discussion on how to install Synchronicity for NT, let's quickly review what happens during the installation:

- ▸ The NDS Schema is modified to support GES and Synchronicity for NT.

- ▸ The NWAdmin Snapin for GES and Synchronicity for NT are installed. The registry of the NT system used to install the product is modified to support the NWAdmin Snapins.

- ▸ The Synchronicity for NT Synchronization Agent application is installed on one NT server or NT workstation in each NT domain to be synchronized. Each NT workgroup server to be synchronized also must be running the Synchronization Agent.

- ▸ If the installation program detects that certain NetWare system files must be updated for the product to run, it automatically updates those files.

- ▸ The NVGES.NLM and related files are installed on all NetWare servers. After the file is installed, the NLM is loaded on each server.

- ▸ The synchronization application is loaded on each NT machine on which it was installed and an initial configuration is performed.

- ▸ The NDS user account(s) to be used by the NT Synchronization Agent applications are created and configured.

- ▸ The synchronization process is started on each Synchronization Agent.

Before You Install

Before you begin the installation of Synchronicity for NT, you must verify your system meets the minimum requirements of the product. These requirements are as follows:

- ▸ File servers running GES must be NetWare 4.1 or greater.

▸ Windows NT Servers or Workstations running the Synchronization Agent must be Windows NT 3.51 or greater.

▸ Windows NT Servers or Workstations used to administer Synchronicity for NT must be running the most recent version of Novell's NetWare Client for Windows NT or Windows 95/98.

Running the Installation Program

Before you begin the installation of Synchronicity for NT, be sure you have the latest version of the NetWare Client installed on the station from which you are installing. Otherwise, the installation will not complete properly. Also, make certain you are logged in to both NDS and NT as a user with administrative privileges.

The installation program for Synchronicity for NT can be started in one of two ways:

▸ By manually running the install program.

▸ If you are installing from the Synchronicity CD-ROM, an option to begin the installation appears when the CD is inserted.

Whichever method of starting the installation you choose, the first screen you see is the Synchronicity Welcome screen. Next, you are asked which components you want to install, as shown in Figure 6.40.

If you choose All Possible Components as the installation type, all components of the product are installed. If this is a first-time installation, selecting this option provides you with everything you need. If this isn't a first-time installation, you may want to choose a different option, which enables you to select the components you want to install.

After you choose the installation type, you are asked where (on the station from which you are installing) you would like to add the program icons for the Synchronicity applications. This includes the Synchronization Agent and the password utilities. Choose the Program Folder in which you would like these applications to appear and click Next to continue.

Choosing the Installation Synchronicity for NT Installation type. Selecting All Possible Components will install all the components necessary for a first-time installation.

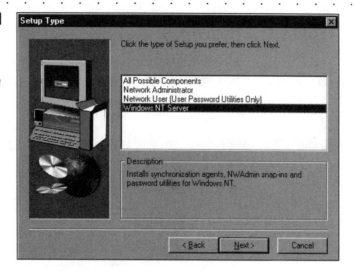

At this point in the installation, you have the opportunity to review your installation choices and make any necessary changes, as shown in Figure 6.41.

Reviewing the installation choices.

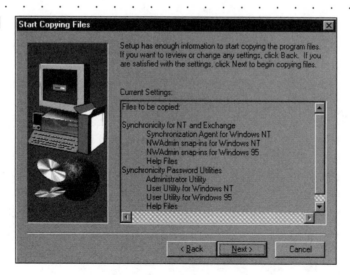

If the installation choices on this screen are correct, click Next to continue; otherwise click Back to re-enter your selections. The file copy to the station you are installing from then begins. This process copies the applications and the required DLLs and makes the appropriate registry changes on your station.

After the file copy to the local machine, you are then prompted for the NDS tree to which you want to add the Schema extensions, as shown in Figure 6.42.

FIGURE 6.42

Selecting the NDS tree and Schema extensions you want to add.

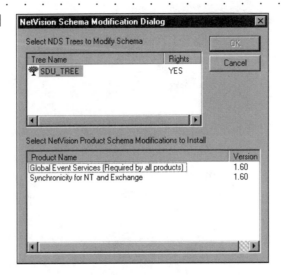

If this is a first-time installation, you must add the Schema extensions for both the GES and Synchronicity for NT. These Schema extensions are necessary for the product to function properly. When the Schema modification is complete, you receive a message indicating the modification was successful.

You are then prompted to enter your license files. If you are evaluating Synchronicity and do not have a license file, leave this blank. However, if you choose to use Synchronicity, you must add a valid license file as shown in Figure 6.43. Otherwise, the product will expire in 30 days (which might upset your users!).

You are then prompted for the Novell file servers on which you want to install GES, as shown in Figure 6.44.

In this screen, select the Novell servers on which to have the GES NLM (NVGES.NLM) installed. You should select every file server in the tree that stores a writeable replica. Also on this screen, be sure the two check boxes at the top are selected. This ensures the GES is started when the installation is complete and each time the file servers come up. When you continue, the necessary NLMs are copied and loaded at the servers automatically.

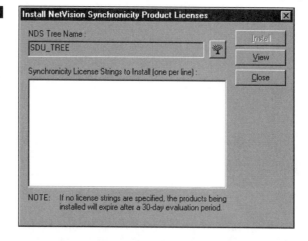

FIGURE 6.43

You must enter a valid license file before continuing, or leave the license blank for a 30-day trial evaluation.

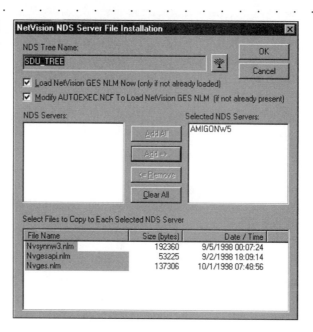

FIGURE 6.44

Selecting the Novell file servers on which to install and load GES. GES should be installed on every file server in the tree that stores a writeable replica.

The installation of Synchronicity for NT is now complete. You are asked if you would like to read the ReadMe file. Answer Yes and review the file contents.

You will then receive a message saying the setup is complete and you are instructed to run the Synchronicity application. Double-click the Synchronicity for NT application in the Program Folder selected during the installation (it should already be open on your screen).

When you start the application for the first time, you receive the following message:

> The NDS object representing this Domain or Workgroup does not exist. Create the NDS object and import the NT objects?

When you answer Yes to this question, the Domain or Workgroup object is created in your NDS tree and all the NT users and groups are uploaded to NDS.

Once the upload is complete, you can use NWAdmin to complete the necessary integration.

NOTE   **If you're using the latest version of the NetWare Administrator utility (NWADMN32.EXE), it may be necessary to copy the Synchronicity snap-ins into the SYS:\PUBLIC\WIN32\SNAPINS directory. The Synchronicity snap-ins are found in the Synchronicity directory on the NT Server where Synchronicity was installed.**

Using Synchronicity

You can set many options to optimize your particular environment. In fact, Synchronicity tends to take less time to configure and manage than Novell Administrator for NT does because of the following reasons:

▶ During install, Synchronicity automatically detects if the Windows NT Domain has been installed into NDS. If it hasn't, then the Synchronicity Agent migrates the Domain information to NDS.

▶ Synchronicity uses the GES from NetVision to forward user creations, deletions, and so on. This allows a "rules-based" type of administration. Snapins are unnecessary in NWAdmin for Synchronicity to work.

▶ Synchronicity allows scheduled synchronization updates (manual dredge) from NDS to a Domain and vice versa.

As a result, you have less items to manage daily.

Creating Synchronized Users (NDS to Domains)

With the GES and Synchronicity Agent running, you can create a user under NDS and have it appear under the Windows NT Domain. In our example, we'll create user MarieF (see Figure 6.45). She is a user under the context Catalina.SDU. When we created MarieF, an event was generated and sent to the Synchronicity Agent running on the Windows NT Server. The Synchronicity Agent received the event and created her under the Domain Object *SDU_DOMAIN* in the context Catalina.SDU (see Figure 6.46).

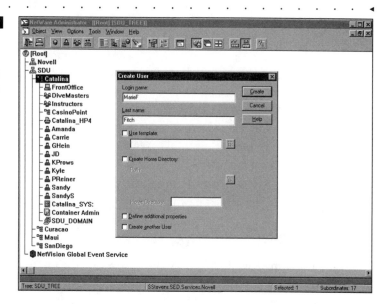

FIGURE 6.45

Creating a user under NWAdmin creates a corresponding user in each Windows NT Domain that is integrated by default.

Likewise, if we create a group, it will also be synchronized to one or more Windows NT Domains, depending on the configuration. How does Synchronicity know which objects to synchronize and which ones to ignore? The answer to this lies in the configuration of the Synchronicity Agent and its *scope*.

▶ · ◀

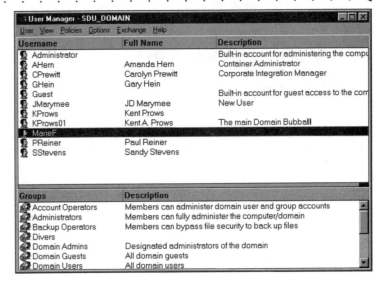

The user that has been synchronized to a Windows NT Domain quickly appears under Windows NT User Manager console.

Configuring the Synchronicity Agent and Its Scope

When an event is generated (such as user create, delete, move, and so on), the GES notifies one or many Synchronization Agents that the event happened. The Agent decides whether the event is pertinent to the Agent's interest. For example, the Agent may be interested in all user creations under the context Sales.Novell. This is known as the *scope*.

In addition, we, as administrators, may not *want* to synchronize all user and group creations. Perhaps we only want to synchronize user information and not groups. The way to do this is under the Synchronicity Agent itself, *or* you can use the Domain Object under NWAdmin. First, let's look at using the Agent.

Using the Agent for Configuration — Network   In Figure 6.47, you can see the Synchronicity Agent (which is normally minimized). To make any configuration changes, you must first stop synchronization temporarily. Clicking the red button off the toolbar does this.

Once this has been done, you can then change some of the parameters that control how the agent on this domain synchronizes. To show this screen, choose Configure/File from the menu bar.

F I G U R E   6.47

Before configuration changes can be made, synchronization must temporarily be stopped using the Synchronicity Agent.

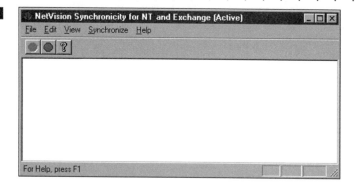

At this point, you can also change configuration by right-clicking the Domain object (such as SDU_DOMAIN in our example) and selecting details. See Figure 6.48 for an example. If synchronization has *not* been disabled, all configuration options are grayed out. This also applies to the Synchronicity Agent.

NOTE

F I G U R E   6.48

Once Synchronization Agent has been disabled, you can also change synchronization parameters using NWAdmin. These options are grayed out if synchronization is still in effect.

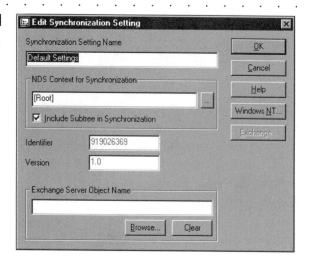

Now that you have the configuration screen up and editable (see Figure 6.49), you can change synchronization options. The first tab represents the Network configuration option. The options for this tab include the following:

▸ *NDS Tree Name.* This option tells the Synchronicity Agent to which NDS tree to synchronize.

▸ *Enable Synchronization with Exchange.* If your NT domain hosts Microsoft Exchange, you can configure Synchronicity to automatically synchronize NDS user and group information to Exchange mailboxes and distribution lists.

▸ *Windows NT Domain or Workgroup Name.* This option tells the Agent to which Domain to synchronize changes. This is usually the same domain as the server where the Synchronicity Agent is running. Note that you cannot change this parameter from the administration console on the Synchronicity NT Server. These parameters can only be modified from within NWAdmin.

▸ *Windows NT Workgroup Server Name.* This option is only used if synchronizing to a workgroup and *not* a Domain. If a workgroup is used, this field is used to specify to which Windows NT Server name to synchronize.

 In a Windows NT workgroup, each server can be synchronized because each server contributes to the user pool. In a Domain, only PDCs and BDCs host user accounts that are used globally.

NOTE

Using the Agent for Configuration—Application   Under the Applications tab are the following two options:

▸ *Start Synchronization When Application Starts.* This means when the application is launched, begin synchronization immediately. If this option is unchecked, the administrator must manually initiate synchronization. Note that you must have the NetVision Synchronicity agent added to the Startup folder.

F I G U R E   6.49

Most configuration options are available under the Synchronicity Agent after synchronization has been disabled.

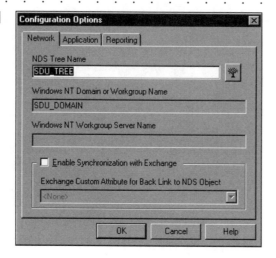

▶ *Start Application Minimized.* This allows the application immediately to minimize itself to the Start Bar. This is useful if you want synchronization to begin automatically. If unchecked, the application begins like a regular application. This is useful if you are tweaking options for the best configuration (see Figure 6.50).

▶ *NT Container Update Interval.* This parameter determines how often the NDS domain object is updated when certain NT domain configurations change, such as trust relationships, account policy, and audit policy.

▶ *Resynchronization Action Interval.* This parameter determines how often selected resynchronization events will occur. Resynchronization events can be configured on the domain object within NDS.

NOTE

Ideally, the Synchronicity application should be dropped into the Startup folder off the Start button. When configured to begin minimized, the Windows NT Server will start, then the Synchronicity application will start and the program window will be minimized automatically. It then appears as a minimized application next to the Start button.

The Synchronicity Agent allows configuration of the application startup.

Using the Agent for Configuration — Reporting   Some reporting options are available for the Synchronicity Agent under the Reporting tab. Windows NT has an Event Logging system to which many services under Windows NT already report. By default, the Synchronicity Agent reports all *Warning* level alerts and higher to the Windows NT Event System Log (see Figure 6.51).

Reporting of the Synchronicity Agent can also be configured to report either to the Windows NT Event System Log, to a specific file, or to both.

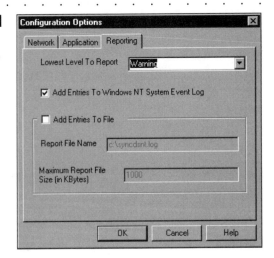

If you want any logged output to go to a file of your choice (either in addition to, or instead of the Windows NT System Event Log), you can select Add Entries To File. This sends all selected errors to that file.

Configuring the Synchronicity Agent via NWAdmin

One of the best features of NDS is the ability to manage resources via NDS using a tool such as NWAdmin. The Synchronicity Agent actually configures itself out of the Domain object that it creates to represent the Domain. Similar to configuring the Agent from the Synchronicity application, you must first stop synchronization at the Agent you're about to configure. Once you have done this, the options to configure the Agent under NWAdmin will no longer be grayed out.

To begin, right mouse-click the domain object you want to configure. (Remember, each Domain object corresponds to an Agent running on a PDC and one or more BDCs. All Agents use the configuration you're about to change.) Then select the Details option. You are presented with a list of options you can configure (see Figure 6.52).

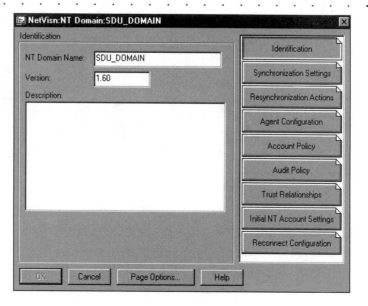

FIGURE 6.52

The NWAdmin tool enables administrators to change the characteristics of the Synchronicity Agent.

Remember, some of these options can also be configured by the Synchronicity application. NWAdmin merely provides you with another way to do this and a way to do it remotely, as well.

Configuring Synchronization Settings via NWAdmin   By selecting the detail page for Synchronization Settings, you can set user, group, and password options for synchronization. By default, all objects below [ROOT] are automatically synchronized to the domain. However, if you wish to change any of the default settings, or create new synchronization settings, simply choose the ADD or EDIT buttons (see Figure 6.53).

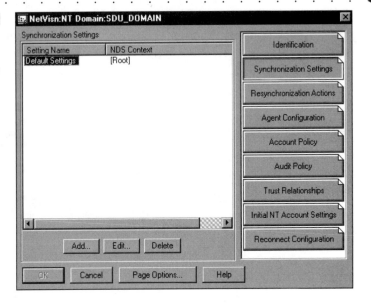

F I G U R E   6 . 5 3

Multiple synchronization policy settings that can be configured under NWAdmin

By default, the entire NDS tree will be synchronized to the domain. If desired, a smaller portion of the NDS tree can be selected. Edit the NDS Context for Synchronization and pick the portion of the NDS tree where synchronization is desired (see Figure 6.54). If multiple NDS contexts are required, you must create multiple synchronization policies.

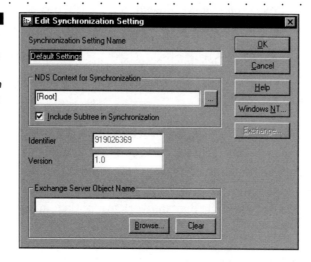

By default, the entire NDS tree is synchronized to the NT domain. Use the NDS Context for Synchronization setting to customize which NDS contexts are synchronized to the NT domain.

Additional synchronization policies for user accounts, group memberships, and passwords can be configured on every domain synchronization setting. To modify user, group, and password policies, select the Windows NT button shown in Figure 6.54.

Windows NT Synchronization Settings: Users   Unlike NDS for NT, which uses a single user account for both NDS and NT Domain access, Synchronicity must intelligently synchronize two user accounts — one in NDS and one in the NT domain. Synchronizing multiple accounts, especially across disparate systems, introduces a few "special case" scenarios. Fortunately, Synchronicity allows the administrator to customize NDS and NT domain synchronization, as seen in Figure 6.55.

▶ *Synchronize User Creation.* This option allows the creation of users in the domain or workgroup if the event is within the desired NDS context scope.

▶ *Attempt to Create Unique Name on Name Collision.* Sometimes, a user will already exist in the domain or workgroup. Because domain/workgroup name lists are flat (no hierarchy involved), only one JesseF can exist, for example. The attempt to create another JesseF if one already exists in the domain will fail, *unless* this option is checked. When this option is checked, Synchronicity creates a similar name (such as JessF01) to avoid a name collision.

> ▸ *Do not Process on Name Collision.* If this option is checked, Synchronicity will not create a domain account if a name collision is detected.

> ▸ *Synchronize User Deletion.* Self-explanatory. If a user is created and the event is within scope, the user account is deleted from the domain or workgroup.

> ▸ *Synchronize User Modification.* This option deals with changes to user information. This includes those common attributes between NDS and the NT domain, including Full Name, Description, and so forth. Windows NT doesn't store much information regarding a user. If the user data is similar between NDS and the domain/workgroup, then it is synchronized (as in Full Name (NDS) ⇨ Full Name (domain)).

> ▸ *Synchronize Modification of NT User with NDS User.* These options determine how modifications from NT domain administration utilities (specifically, User manager) are handled within NDS. By default, modifications are not synchronized, but can be enabled as needed.

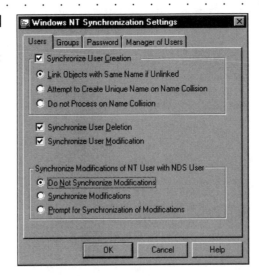

F I G U R E   6.55

The Windows NT Synchronization Settings set policies for NDS and domain user object synchronization

Synchronization policies can also be configured for Groups (see Figure 6.56) and passwords (see Figure 6.57). While the default group and password configurations are fine for most environments, Synchronicity permits changing these settings on every synchronization policy.

FIGURE 6.56

Synchronicity allows customization of Group synchronization settings. These settings determine how NDS and Domain groups interact.

FIGURE 6.57

When a new domain user is created, its password is set to its name. Synchronicity also permits leaving the password empty or setting the domain password to a default value.

Configuring Other Options under NWAdmin   Some other settings can be configured under NWAdmin, which include the following:

▸ *Account Policy.* This option enables management of global account policies for the Domain. Note, these settings apply to *all* users created in the domain.

▸ *Audit Policy.* This option sets Audit Policies within the Domain. This tracks logins, logouts, system restarts, and so on. The only other way to configure this is with User Manager under Windows NT.

▸ *Trust Relationships.* This option enables the administrator to view any Trust Relationships between this domain and another domain. This is especially useful if Resource Domains depend on this domain for user storage.

▸ *Resynchronization Actions.* This option enables an administrator to schedule resynchronization from NDS to this Domain. This is especially useful to ensure NDS objects are linked to valid NT objects, and they are current. One or more options can be scheduled on an Hourly, Daily, Weekly, Monthly, or Immediate basis.

Working with Synchronized Objects

Once an object has been created using NDS and the Synchronicity Agent, any changes that can be synchronized between the two will be synchronized. When a new NDS object is created, the Synchronicity Agent must keep track of the NDS object *and* the Windows NT object to which it is mapped.

A good example is the user MarieF created earlier (see Figure 6.58). Here we see MarieF is a member of the Domain *SDU_DOMAIN*. We have the ability to synchronize passwords if we want and even to view her NT account details. This includes adding or removing her from other groups, settings allowed for login times under Windows NT, and disabling her account, among other things. Likewise, we can also view the corresponding Windows NT Object under NWAdmin, and manipulate many of the same details we see under Details in Figure 6.57.

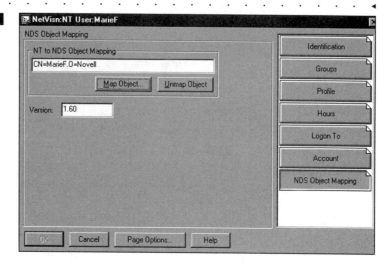

FIGURE 6.58

An object created using Synchronicity has a name mapping to its corresponding Windows NT object.

Mapping and Unmapping Objects

When a new NDS object is created, a *mapping* is created that tells Synchronicity which NDS objects maps to which Windows NT object. By default, Synchronicity attempts to create identical names (when it creates a new NT user) and map them together (as shown in Figure 6.59).

If you no longer want to have these two objects synchronized with each other, you can select Unmap Object and the two will no longer synchronize.

Another scenario might appear when you have an *existing* NDS object that you want to synchronize to an existing Windows NT Domain object. As shown in Figure 6.60, we have an NDS user named LLewis who must be synchronized to an existing Windows NT User named LindaL. To do this, we can select either the NT object, *or* the NDS object and select the mapping option. (Under the NDS object, it's called *NT User Name Mapping*; under the NT object, it's called *NDS Object Mapping*.) In this figure, we've chosen to map the two under the Windows NT object. User LLewis is now synchronized to the NT user LindaL.

NOTE

Synchronicity also has the facility to recognize existing names when creating new NT objects. For example, if an NDS user is created that has the name Ghein, the Synchronicity Agent sees if a Ghein already exists in the Windows NT Domain. If the name already exists and is unmapped to an existing NDS user, the Agent maps the new NDS user to the existing NT user name.

FIGURE 6.59

Object names in NDS and
NT are mapped with like
names when possible.

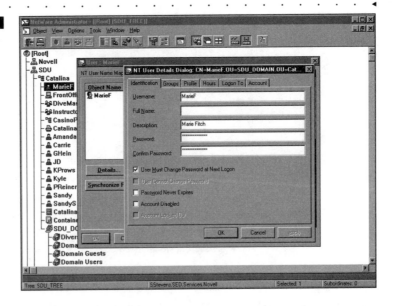

FIGURE 6.60

Objects of the same or
different names can be
mapped either under details
on the Windows NT
object or details on the
NDS object.

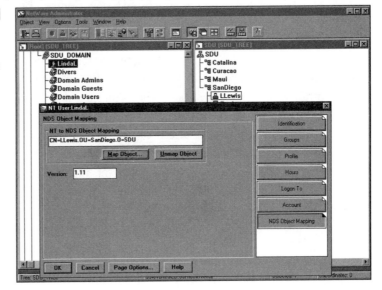

TIP

When dragging-and-dropping NDS objects within NWAdmin, user mappings are maintained to the Windows NT objects (such as User and Group objects). If an administrator moves an NDS user within the tree, synchronization continues to work. When the object is moved to a new location, the mapping information is updated in the Windows NT object detail page labeled NDS Object Mapping.

Synchronizing Passwords with Mapped Objects

One of the challenges of using a synchronization product is keeping the object information in synch! Synchronicity does an excellent job, but whenever you have two separate databases, synchronization is always an issue.

One of the largest issues is keeping passwords in synchronization. This is primarily because users are the ones who may be changing and maintaining passwords. If you, the administrator, are setting and handing out passwords, the world is your oyster. If your users are setting passwords, then a little more effort may be involved.

You have four ways to synchronize passwords effectively using the Synchronicity product.

Synchronizing Passwords under NWAdmin   Using the option shown in Figure 6.61, you can set passwords for both the NDS and the Windows NT user account from one window.

NOTE

If you are attempting to keep passwords in synchronization, do *not* use the standard password-change options under NWAdmin and/or User Manager. These are hard-coded and do not know about each other. If you have used one or the other by mistake, you can use the Admin Synch Tool to resynchronize the passwords.

Synchronizing Passwords under the Client   When using the Novell Windows NT client, an option exists to synchronize passwords between the NT Server and NetWare systems. This puts control of the password into the hands of the user, who may unwittingly change one password while not changing the other. This usually results in a Help Desk call.

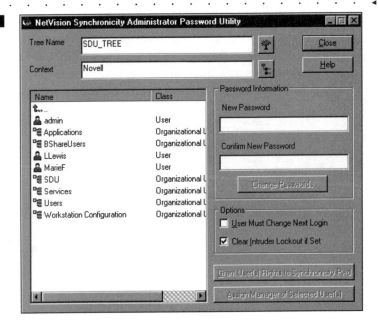

F I G U R E   6.61

Using NWAdmin, you can keep passwords in synchronization between NDS and Windows NT users.

Synchronizing Passwords Using the Synchronicity Admin Password Tool Knowing how tough it is to keep passwords in synch, NetVision has included two new tools with Synchronicity: Admin Password Synch Tool and User Password Synch Tool.

The scenario best describing where the Admin Password Synch Tool (the Admin tool) could be used is in a Help Desk situation. Users may have changed one password but not the other, *or*, through some other accident of fate, now cannot perform a login with one user name and password. This tool enables a Help Desk person with proper rights to change one user's or groups of users' passwords with a few mouse clicks. As shown in Figure 6.62, the Help Desk person chooses a new password and to which user, or groups of users (by container), to apply the new passwords.

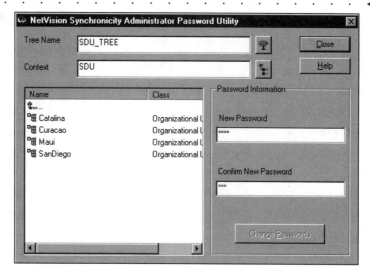

FIGURE 6.62

Using the Admin Password Synch Tool by NetVision, administrators or Help Desk personnel can synchronize one user's or groups of users' passwords with a few mouse clicks.

Synchronizing Passwords Using the User Password Utility   Another option for the user, instead of simply relying on the client to aid in password synchronization, is the ability to change passwords on both systems (NDS and Windows NT Domain/ Workgroup) using a NetVision Synchronicity utility called *User Password Utility* (see Figure 6.63). Using the User Password Utility, a user can change a password and synchronize it to both NDS and Windows NT. A user must know the existing password to use this utility (if one already existed). If the user does not know the old password, then he or she probably should call the administrator or Help Desk to help resynchronize it.

NOTE

This utility not only works with Synchronicity for NT, but also for all other NetVision products. If you support Lotus Notes servers in addition to Windows NT Servers, this utility will synchronize passwords among all three systems (NDS, Notes, and Windows NT).

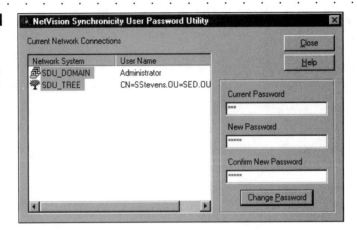

F I G U R E   6.63

The user can use the User Password Synch Utility to assist in keeping passwords in synchronization between multiple systems (such as NDS, Windows NT, and Notes).

Summary

This chapter discussed the use of NDS as a Meta-Directory. It covered why NDS is the best platform to use as a Meta-Directory in a mixed NetWare and NT environment and the synchronization products available to provide integration of this environment. A synchronization product eliminates the need to manage NDS and NT Domains separately, saving tremendous amounts of time.

The two synchronization products available (Novell's Administrator for Windows NT and NetVision's Synchronicity for NT) are similar because they use NDS as a central repository for an integrated Windows NT and NetWare environment. In addition, both products use NWAdmin as a central administration utility. Although both products integrate NT Server Domains into an existing NDS tree, the components and feature sets differ slightly between the two products.

A look at these two products reveals that both accomplish the goal of integrating NT Domains and Workgroups with NDS nicely. Synchronicity for NT is easy to use and scales quite nicely for all sizes of networks. Even though NetVision charges for the product, it is well worth the price. NadminNT is a bit more complicated to use, and is best suited for smaller network implementations. You can't beat the price though; it's free.

CHAPTER 7

Integrating with Novell's NDS for NT

This is perhaps the most exciting chapter in this entire book! In fact, many people could argue the *only* way to truly integrate Windows NT and NDS is by providing native security replacement of the Windows NT Domain. Many customers over the past two years have repeatedly requested this capability, only to be told Novell was working on the solution.

Well, the time has come for this solution to be made available at last.

This chapter discusses replacing the native security system inherent to Windows NT with another security and naming system, namely NDS. We'll discuss what NDS will and won't do, as well as a bit on how it is architected. Understanding what Windows NT Domains and NDS do to provide security and naming in the enterprise is important (this means you need to do your homework and *read* some of the earlier chapters). Only then will you fully appreciate and understand why this is such awesome technology!

NDS for NT is part of an overall Novell strategy to integrate services running on Windows NT into the enterprise by using NDS as a central directory. Small and large deployments of Windows NT can benefit from simplifying Domain management with NDS for NT.

The Purpose of NDS for NT

So, why replace native security at all? Replacing something inherent to the operating system must have significant value; otherwise, why go through the hassle?

NDS in the Enterprise — Naming and Authentication

As discussed in earlier chapters, the primary reasons for using a Directory are naming (finding resources) and authentication (ensuring you are who you *say* you are). NDS is designed for just such a purpose.

To be effective, a directory should be able to provide this service network-wide, not only to a specific operating system. For example, NDS has traditionally been used as an authentication/naming system for NetWare services, such as file and print. Extending single sign-on to other operating system services (such as Windows NT services) is a natural progression in the NDS evolution as a directory.

Consuming Services

Chapter 4 also discussed consuming network services. This might mean a database, a mail server, a workflow service, and so on. How we consume this service (what protocol or client) is usually separate from how naming and authentication was used to get access to it.

As an example, we may use NDS to find a Lotus Notes server, background-authenticate to it (an NDS function perhaps), and then use the Notes server using a Notes client. Why this is important has to do with a client's interaction with the Directory. A client may not care what directory is used, as long as a user has been authenticated. If the network service allows access (because the user has been validated), the client provides its function to consume the service, regardless of the directory service used. The more invisible this process is to the user, the better used a service will be, hence, better productivity.

By replacing the native security system in Windows NT, network services residing on Windows NT are not affected. In fact, the client (be it a SQL, Notes, or Exchange client) won't even be aware a change has occurred. People using the services *will not* notice a change in the system. The administrator will, because only a single user name and password set must be maintained (more on the password set later in this chapter).

Single Sign-On with Existing Security Architectures

Many naming and authentication architectures are being offered today, including (to name a few):

▸ Novell's Bindery Service (NetWare 3.*x*)

▸ Novell's Directory Service (NDS)

▸ Windows NT Domain Directory

▸ IBM's Mainframe login

▸ UNIX Login (NIS and such)

▸ Various client/server applications (Notes, SAP, Oracle, and so on)

Each one has a provision for finding out about a particular item (such as User or a database), authenticating to the service, and then consuming it (such as reading your e-mail). Once authenticated, an object (such as user) must have a client available to consume the service (such as an e-mail client).

The challenge comes when attempting to put all these together into a coherent usable network. Multiple passwords and user names become a real administration challenge.

The idea of integrating these directories via a Meta-Directory (see Figure 7.1) addresses the following integration issues:

▶ One Directory can be used to locate resources existing in several other Directories.

▶ Resource creation (such as users or groups) can be created from a single Meta-Directory and synchronized down to subdirectories.

▶ Keeping user names and passwords in synchronization can create a semblance of single sign-on.

▶ Multiple architectures can be made to work together without re-engineering existing technologies.

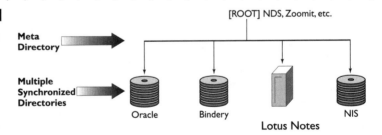

FIGURE 7.1

A Meta-Directory can serve as a single Directory focal point to other existing directories. This provides a single place to create resources (users, for example) and to find them.

Meta Directory

Multiple Synchronized Directories

[ROOT] NDS, Zoomit, etc.

Oracle   Bindery   NIS

Lotus Notes

The downside to using a Meta-Directory is using one doesn't provide true single sign-on, merely the semblance of one. As a few directories become the predominate foundation on corporate enterprises, true single sign-on can be achieved. This is because, rather than creating a new directory (naming and authentication scheme) for each new network service that comes along, software companies can write to one or two standard directories (such as NDS APIs and/or LDAP) that provide naming and authentication. Novell is attempting to make NDS one of these standards through its strategy of licensing NDS to all the major platform providers (see Chapter 8) and porting it to platforms where the vendor chooses not to license NDS (such as on Windows NT).

Integrating Existing Directories while Providing a Single Sign-On Platform

Today, NDS for NT attempts to solve this challenge while providing a platform for future NDS-enabled single sign-on network services. By using NDS for NT, networks gain several major benefits:

- A single Directory can be used *today* (NDS) while supporting existing network services (such as Exchange and Notes) that use another naming/authentication service (the Windows NT Domain).

- Truly only *one* user account exists. There is no need to synchronize multiple user accounts because only one real Directory is being used.

- Management can still be accomplished using existing tools (such as USER MANAGER on Windows NT and NWAdmin for NDS). No re-training is required.

- NDS for NT provides a foundation on Windows NT for future network services to use NDS natively or by way of a certificate system for network authentication and naming.

Using NDS for NT, existing Domains become part of an NDS tree. This could mean just one Master Domain or multiple Domains, all joining into one NDS tree containing all users, groups, and other resources. Resource Domains remain untouched when a Master Domain or Multiple Masters are migrated to an NDS tree.

Figure 7.2 shows an NDS tree with several Domains now integrated into the tree. Each Domain supports users and groups and has a trust relationship to one or more resource Domains.

▶ · ◀

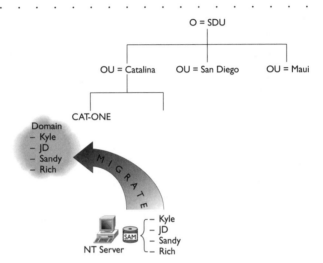

With NDS for NT, Novell is providing the ultimate best of both worlds for integrating Windows NT services and NetWare services under one Directory — NDS.

▶ · ◀

The Design of NDS for NT

Whether replacing the Windows NT native security system was even possible was hotly contested even within Novell. Several attempts were made to create this product early on, only to be stymied by the lack of APIs on Windows NT to accomplish such a feat. In the end, it was a savvy team of engineers who figured out a way to supplant the security system elegantly using Microsoft APIs.

This section discusses the security components of the Domain and how Windows NT uses it, as well as how NDS maintains these components to support a single security system.

Maintaining Domain Support

One of the main problems with redirecting the NT security database was providing a set of functionality that allowed current applications to exist. A base set of compatibility providing seamless integration had to be created to make security redirection successful, such as:

- A Domain had to appear present, *even though* none existed.

- Existing tools had to continue to work (such as Exchange Administrator and User Manager).

- The product had to use as many published APIs as possible to maintain future compatibility.

- Users needed to be able to join more than one Domain.

- NDS for NT had to use and provide as much of the Domain security components as possible.

- Fault tolerance had to be present to keep services running (using the PDC/BDC servers that already existed).

In fact, with NDS for NT, BackOffice applications think a Domain is still present. NDS for NT creates the appearance of a Domain.

To understand better how NDS for NT works, it helps to understand the way Windows NT performs user validation.

Validating Security in a Domain

Every copy of Windows NT that ships has a security database as part of the operating system. If you recall from Chapter 3, this database is called the *Security Accounts Manager* and is stored as part of the Registry (in a secure area of the Registry). The only way you can access this data is by either:

- Reading and writing it using the Windows NT APIs

- Accessing the domain portion of the Registry files (brute force), as some backup packages do

When an application reads and writes to the SAM database using the Win32 APIs, a process occurs to allow this function, whether you are accessing the SAM in a local machine or one on a remote Domain Controller. This process makes use of two library DLLs: SAMSRV.DLL and SAMLIB.DLL.

The process that takes place when an application talks to SAM goes something like this:

1. The client application makes an API call to create/change/delete/ update a SAM object (User, Group, Server, or Workstation).

2. Windows NT internally calls the SAMLIB.DLL to carry out the request.

3. SAMLIB.DLL sends Remote Procedure Calls (RPCs) to SAMSRV.DLL. If the application running is on the Primary Domain Controller (see Chapter 3), this process still occurs.

4. SAMSRV.DLL communicates to the SAM database to make the requested changes or lookup.

Note, the only item that reads and writes to the SAM database is the SAMSRV.DLL library. That library (in a Domain implementation) is only located on the Primary and Backup Domain Controllers in a "pure" Windows NT network.

The Role of SAMSRV.DLL in a Domain Implementation

When using Windows NT in a Domain configuration, every Windows NT operating system (Workstation and Server) will have a SAMSRV.DLL and a SAMLIB.DLL. The only SAMSRV.DLL that *matters* is the one on the Primary Domain Controller (PDC) and Backup Domain Controllers (BDCs). Each client that authenticates to the Domain (using SAMLIB.DLL or the equivalent under Windows 95/98 and 3.*x*) will RPC to the SAMSRV.DLL running on the PDC or a BDC. If a user attempts to manage the Domain, the SAMLIB.DLL *must* be able to contact a PDC or else no management can be done (User Manager will shut down).

The Role of SAMSRV.DLL in a Workgroup

When using NT Server or Workstation in a workgroup configuration, whichever machine is the designated machine to be used for authenticating users is the one SAMLIB.DLL will attempt to contact when performing management or authentication requests.

SAMSRV.DLL in a Standalone Workstation or Server

If you are a totally standalone workstation, then your local SAM database is where your user account information is stored. Even though this is the case, your local SAMLIB.DLL will RPC to your local SAMSRV.DLL to authenticate or enable you to perform management of your local objects. The reason to do it this way is you *may* someday be part of a larger network. Therefore, this mechanism enables you to authenticate to a remote database (SAM) if necessary.

NDS for NT and SAMSRV.DLL

You may see where this is going. Because the only software that communicates to the SAM database is SAMSRV.DLL, the only item that must be changed to have Windows NT use a different database is SAMSRV.DLL! With a different SAMSRV.DLL, which uses NDS instead of the Registry-based SAM database, all authentication and management requests can be redirected to NDS, instead of to the SAM database! This is, in fact, exactly what NDS for NT replaces to accomplish the level of integration it does. See Figure 7.3 for an overall architecture of how NDS for NT replaces the SAMSRV.DLL.

Now that we have described the way the SAM database is redirected, let's look at the way Windows NT supports user IDs and enables granting users rights under the Windows NT system.

Validating User Accounts Using NDS for NT

Once NDS is used as the database for user information in a Domain, there comes the issue of user authentication. This is particularly true where passwords are involved.

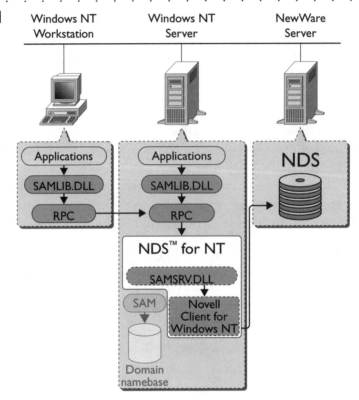

FIGURE 7.3

NDS for NT works by simply replacing the NT Server SAMSRV.DLL with one that uses NDS instead of the SAM database. All requests for authentication and management are re-directed to NDS instead of the SAM database.

Passwords and Windows NT   When Windows NT authenticates a user, it uses a hash algorithm to encrypt the user's password at the client before sending it to the server. The server will receive the hashed password and compare it to a stored hash it has at the server to see if it's valid. If it is, the user is logged on. If not, authentication is rejected. Note, no way exists to reverse-encrypt the password once it has been hashed. The server merely compares one hash to another to verify the authenticating user entered the right password.

Passwords and NDS   In the NDS world, a user enters in a password just like in Windows NT. The difference is NDS will use a hashed version of the password to verify the user and then to download the user's *private key* to complete the login. Once the private key is down, a *credential set* is created to complete the login. This credential is used to log a user transparently into more servers, as he needs access.

This prevents a user from having to enter a user name and password every time she needs access to another server.

NOTE **NDS uses the RSA security algorithm for authentication. RSA uses a Private/Public Key pair to create a user credential. To do this, the private key must be retrieved from NDS and brought to the client workstation. This is the purpose of the password hash. It verifies the user identity before the private key is downloaded.**

Password Maintenance and NDS for NT   Even though NDS for NT provides the capability of creating only one account for both Windows NT and NetWare access (through NDS), two passwords are required: one for Windows NT user authentication and one for "pure" NDS logins.

Because each password type is unique (they use different hash algorithms), therefore, two passwords must be stored on *one* NDS User object *if* that user needs to log in both to NDS and Windows NT. Normally, it's a challenge to keep two passwords for different systems in sync, especially if users routinely move between workstations or change their passwords while disconnected from the network.

However, this situation is alleviated somewhat by four things:

1. If a client workstation is running a Novell NDS client and a Microsoft client, and then changes the password, it is synchronized.

2. If the client workstation is only running a Microsoft client and the user changes his or her password, NDS for NT intercepts the clear-text new password at the PDC, hashes the password with the respective NT and NDS password hashing algorithms, and enters the new passwords for both NDS and the domain. As a result, the two passwords remain synchronized.

3. If the client workstation is only running Novell's Client for NDS and the user changes his or her password, the client will determine whether the user is a member of any NT domains. If the user is a member of an NDS for NT domain, the client software hashes the password with the respective NT and NDS password hashing algorithms and enters the new passwords for both the domain and NDS. As a result, the two passwords remain synchronized.

4. If all else fails, Novell provides the capability (with NDS for NT) to change/synch both passwords for a user using the NWAdmin tool. This is particularly useful if users forget their passwords. However, the administrator must change the password within by selecting the "Domain Access" tab on the user account, not the standard "Change Password" button.

An important thing to remember is that even though a user may need two passwords (one for NDS, one for Windows NT), if that user is a member of 10, 20, or 1,000 Domains, he or she will only have *one* Windows NT password to access all those domains when using NDS for NT to manage the domains. This is because, no matter how many Domains a user is a member of, that user only has *one* account in NDS!

What's this, you say? How did NDS for NT get the "clear-text" password? Aren't passwords sent across the wire in an irreversible format? Well, the answer is: yes and no. During normal authentications, the NT password is encrypted (hashed) with an irreversible algorithm and sent to the PDC or BDC for authentication. The PDC or BDC can't decrypt the hashed password — it just compares the hashed password value with the value stored in the domains. However, due to backward-compatibility issues, changing the domain password requires that the new password be sent to the PDC in such a manner that the PDC and BDC reverse the hash and determine the "clear-text" password. NDS for NT simply intercepts this "clear-text" password, hashes it according to the NDS password hashing rules, and stores this as the new NDS password. The result? It is practically impossible for the NT Domain and NDS password to differ. And that means fewer help desk calls in a mixed environment!

Security IDs and Tokens Under Domains

Windows NT security uses the concept of a Security ID (SID) and Resource ID (RID) to identify users and resources that need access to the system. NetWare uses a similar scheme in the form of an *Object ID* to identify users and other objects. Table 7.1 describes the IDs and how they are used in Windows NT.

TABLE 7.1	SECURITY ID	USE
Security IDs	The Domain ID	When a Domain is created, an ID is created that uniquely identifies this Domain from all others in the network. When a trust is formed with another Domain, each Domain must have a unique way to identify itself. This ID is guaranteed as unique by Microsoft.
	Resource ID	This ID is created when a new object (such as a User) is created. It uniquely identifies the object within a particular Domain. When combined with the Domain ID, it is called a SID (Security Identifier) and uniquely identifies an object system-wide.
	Security ID	SIDs provide a Domain and Multi-Domain unique object ID. It is the combination of the DID and the RID. This is important to remember when we discuss the way NDS for NT v1.0 stores and generates IDs.

NT Security ID and Access Control

When an object is given rights to a service (such as files) under Windows NT, the SID/RID is used to identify the object. We'll assume in this example that User RMarymee will be given access to a file directory on a Windows NT server.

Each file directory under Windows NT has a list of objects that have access to the file system directory. This list is composed of SIDs. This is because storing a SID in the list, instead of a full user name, is far less costly (from a system perspective). When a user RMarymee attempts access to this directory, the NT security system checks to see if RMarymee's SID is in the Access Control List (ACL) for that directory. If it isn't, RMarymee will not have proper permission and access will be denied.

Knowing this, it is *critical* that NDS for NT retain the user IDs when migrating from the SAM database to NDS. Otherwise, all the existing rights mappings will be lost. NDS for NT preserves user IDs for just this reason.

NOTE

Under the Windows NT file system, there is no inheritance model as under NetWare. In NetWare, the operating system looks at the next-higher file directory to see if the user has access rights granted there. This will continue up to the root of the volume. In Windows NT, if the user does not have access rights, permission is denied.

Security Tokens and BackOffice Services

Another area where security IDs are used is authorization to use network services. When a user accesses a BackOffice service running on Windows NT, the service can check with the Domain and see if the user has already been authenticated to the Domain. This is done through a set of APIs called the *Security Support Provider Interface (SSPI)*. When a service checks authentication, a token is handed back to the service, indicating the user *has* been authenticated properly. Once this has been verified, the service must check its own authorizations of what services that user can successfully request from the network service. Figure 7.4 shows an example of a user (MikeH) accessing a SQL Server on Windows NT Server MARS.

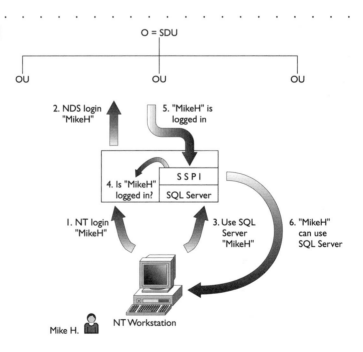

FIGURE 7.4

Windows NT BackOffice services use Domain security to provide a single sign-on to a BackOffice service. This is done through the SSPI.

In this example, SQL Server is running on a Windows NT Server. User MikeH is logged into the Domain SOLAR_SYS. MikeH will now attempt to query the SQL Server database residing on server MARS within the Domain SOLAR_SYS. The sequence of events would be as follows:

1. MikeH loads the SQL client and attempts to connect to the SQL Server on MARS via the MS-RPC (Remote Procedure Call protocol). The SQL client uses MS-RCP to communicate to the SQL Server.

2. The SQL Server receives the request and queries the Windows security system about MikeH via the SSPI. At this point, the Domain query is redirected out to NDS via the SAMSRV.DLL file.

3. The SSPI hands back a token indicating MikeH has been authenticated.

4. The SQL Server looks at its own internal management tables and sees what access to SQL tables that MikeH has.

5. The SQL Server responds to the SQL client to indicate whether access was accepted.

6. MikeH performs his queries or other database accesses based on what he's allowed to perform.

Supporting IDs with NDS for NT and NDS

When NDS for NT displaces the SAM database in lieu of NDS, the SIDs and RIDs must still be (and still are) supported to support already deployed BackOffice and Windows NT services seamlessly. In addition, because the SAM database no longer exists, NDS must be used to store the SIDs and RIDs for the Domains now maintained by NDS. When a service requests to see if a user has been authenticated to the Domain (which *appears* to exist for this sake), NDS can look up the user's SID and generate a token the service can then use to check against its own security tables.

Installation of NDS for NT

Installing NDS for NT is simple. In fact, only three main steps exist in the entire installation:

1. Install NDS for NT on the NT Server (mostly a special Novell client for Windows NT).

2. Run the Domain Object Wizard (SAMMIG.EXE).

3. Install the NDS for NT administration utilities (NWADMN32.EXE, NDSMGR32, and the NWAdmin Snapin).

Each of these steps is summarized in the following sections.

Installing NDS for NT on an NT Server

Installing NDS for NT on an NT Server is quite straightforward. Simply run WINSETUP.EXE from the root directory of the NDS for NT CD or insert the NDS for NT CD into the CD-ROM drive (and the auto-start will bring up the INSTALL screen) and select Install NDS for NT.

During this step all the NDS for NT files (including the SAMSRV.DLL) are copied to the NT Server. In addition, a special NetWare Client for Windows NT is installed, which allows the SAM redirection component to communicate with NDS.

After the file copy is complete, a dialog box appears indicating the server must be rebooted for the changes to take effect. After the server is rebooted, the Domain Object Wizard (SAMMIG.EXE) is automatically launched.

NOTE

NDS for NT must be installed on the Primary Domain Controller (PDC) and all Backup Domain Controllers (BDCs). Install NDS for NT on the PDC first, then on the BDCs.

Running the Domain Object Wizard

After the NT server is rebooted (as described previously), you must log in to your NT Server as Administrator and log in to NDS as Admin or another user with Write access to the [Root] of the NDS tree. The reason is NDS for NT must extend the NDS schema to support the NDS for NT objects. If the schema has already been extended, you'll need to log in as an account that has object creation rights in the part of the tree into which you will be migrating Domain objects. Once this step has been completed (or skipped automatically if the schema has already been extended), the Domain Object Wizard will automatically run, as shown in Figure 7.5.

▶ • ◀

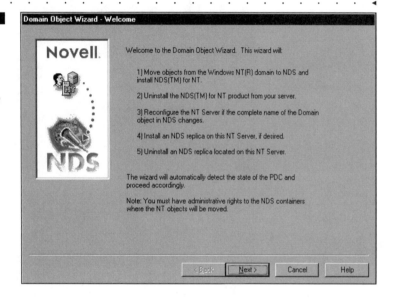

F I G U R E 7.5

Use the Domain Object Wizard for domain migration or removal, domain renames, and for placing an NDS replica on the NT Server.

Next you will be prompted to select the NDS tree to which you want to move the Domain users, groups, and workstations. When you select the tree, the Object Wizard will check to see if the NDS for NT Schema extensions have been made. If they have not, you will be prompted to extend the Schema before you can move the NT Domain to NDS.

Once the Schema has been extended, you will be asked to specify the context in which you want the Domain Object created. Note that if the Schema has been previously extended, the Schema extension question will not appear.

You will then be given the option to search the NDS tree for existing User objects with the same name, as shown in Figure 7.6.

FIGURE 7.6

Searching the NDS tree for NT users who already exist enables you to map NT users being moved to existing NDS users.

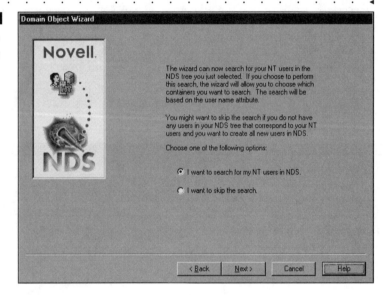

If the users of the NT Domain already have accounts in NDS, you can choose the option to search for NT users in NDS. This enables you to map the NT User objects being moved with existing NDS User objects. In addition, if you are migrating multiple Domains into NDS, you can take a redundant user account and map that account into one NDS account, simplifying management. Figure 7.7 illustrates this scenario.

If you chose to search the tree, you will be asked to indicate the container where you wish to begin the search. When the search is complete, a summary of the information gathered by the wizard will appear. This summary is shown in Figure 7.8.

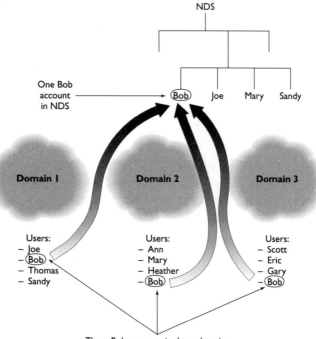

FIGURE 7.7

Searching for NT users in NDS

The screen in Figure 7.8 enables you to tell the Domain Object Wizard how you want to handle each NT object being moved to NDS. This is done using the three buttons in the center-left portion of the screen. These buttons enable you to do the following:

▶ *Create as.* This enables you to create an NT user being moved as a new NDS User object.

▶ *Associate with.* This enables you to associate the NT user being moved with an existing NDS User object.

▶ *Don't Move.* This enables you to specify you don't want a particular NT user moved to NDS.

FIGURE 7.8

The Domain Object Wizard enables you to determine how you want to handle each NT user in the move.

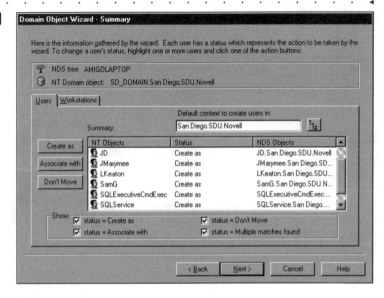

Once the objects have been moved, the move statistics will then appear, indicating how many objects were moved and if any errors occurred.

At this point, you are given the option to view the move log. This log will provide you with a summary of the objects moved and the NDS context to which they were moved.

NDS for NT requires access to NDS to resolve domain users and groups. NDS for NT can use NDS replicas on remote servers, or a local NDS replica of the domain can be placed directly on the NT Server. To place an NDS replica during the NDS for NT install, simply click the box shown in Figure 7.9. You'll need to choose where to store the NDS files on the NT Server, and choose a name that will represent the NT Server within the NDS Tree.

TIP

When should you place an NDS replica on the NT Server? If the NT Server is in close proximity to other NDS servers, it's probably unnecessary to place an NDS replica on the NT Server. However, if the NT Server is separated from all other NDS servers by WAN links, it's a good idea to place a local NDS replica on the NT Server. This ensures that NDS for NT will function when the WAN is down.

To maintain security of the **NDS** database files, **NDS for NT** will only install a replica on **NTFS** formatted partitions. Be sure to use the standard **NT** file system utilities (such as Explorer) to limit access to the **NDS** database files. This happens automatically when an **NDS** replica is initially placed on an **NT Server**.

▶ • ◀

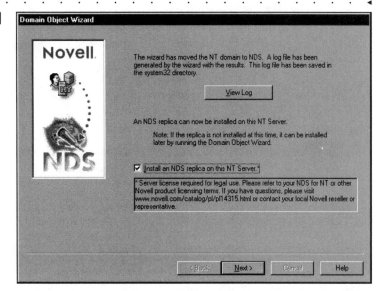

Installing the NDS for NT Administration Utilities

After you install NDS for NT and run the Domain Object Wizard, you will need to install the NDS for NT Administration Utilities. This step installs NWAdmin for NT (NWADMN32.EXE), as well as the necessary Domain object Snapins on your workstation. If NWADMN32.EXE has previously been installed, you can elect to install only the Snapin for Domain management and register it (automatically) with your local workstation.

To install the administration utilities, simply run ADMNSETUP.EXE from the I386 directory of the NDS for NT CD and follow the prompts. If you insert the CD-ROM into your CD-ROM drive, the installation menu will reappear. You can also choose to install the administration options from this screen.

NOTE

For die-hards who like to edit their registry entries directly, the registry value is placed under **HKEY_CURRENT_USER/Software/ NetWare/Parameters/NetWare Administrator/Snapin Object DLLs Win32.** A new string value can be created (usually named after the **IWSAM.DLL** file), and the value is a path to the **IWSAM.DLL** file. The same **IWSAM.DLL** can be used with Windows 95/98 or Windows **NT.** In NetWare 5, you can set up support for the Snapin merely by copying the **IWSAM.DLL** file into the sys:public\win32\snapins directory. NWADMN32 looks for snapins in that directory and will automatically attempt to load all snapins residing there.

Running the NDS Console

On NT servers with NDS replicas, the NDSCONS.EXE utility (found in the same directory as the NDS database files) allows an administrator to view NDS connections, set NDS parameters, and monitor NDS replication information (also known as DSTRACE). Any replication trace parameter can be enabled by selecting the appropriate option, as shown in Figure 7.10. The actual NDS replication information is displayed in the DSTRACE windows, as shown in Figure 7.11.

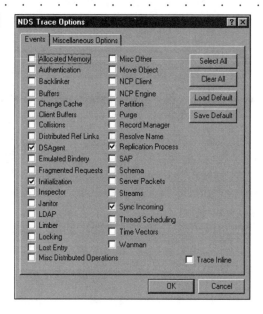

FIGURE 7.10

Details about NDS replication can be enabled or disabled by selecting the appropriate option(s).

▶ · ◀

F I G U R E   7 . 1 1

*NDS replication information
is viewed in the DSTRACE
window.*

After the Migration

To accomplish management tasks, here are a few guidelines:

▶ When creating, deleting, or managing Users and Groups, you can use either User Manager (a Windows NT tool) or NWAdmin (an NDS tool).

▶ When assigning rights to printers or files hosted on NetWare, use NWAdmin, Filer (DOS), or command-line tools included with NetWare.

▶ When assigning rights to printers or files hosted under Windows NT, use the Explorer icon (Windows NT 4.0), File Manager (Windows NT 3.51), or the NTTOOLS found on the domain object within NWAdmin32.

▶ When managing services (such as Exchange or SQL Server), use the appropriate managers to create Users needed for those services. If you use the existing User Manager with Exchange, for example, User Manager creates a User (into NDS transparently) and then invokes Exchange Manager.

NOTE

Novell has also included a utility to manage Exchange Servers and Exchange Mailboxes. This utility is part of the **NDS for NT** product. It is officially called *Administrator for Exchange* and is typically found in the **/i386/mm4x** directory of the **NDS for NT CD-ROM.**

Implementation Considerations

If you have decided to use the NDS for NT technology, you should be aware of a few caveats:

▶ You can run NDS for NT in an IPX, Pure IP, or mixed IPX/IP environment. In mixed IPX/IP environments, it may be necessary to deploy Novell's Pure-IP Compatibility Mode gateways, which are part of the NetWare 5 operating system. See the NDS for NT README file for more information on support in a Pure-IP environment.

▶ Even though NDS for NT can host an NDS replica on the NT Server, you'll need at least one NetWare server somewhere in your network, because many of the NDS-related server-based utilities (DSREPAIR, DSMERGE, DSMAINT) are not yet available for the NT Server platform. If you don't have NetWare deployed today, you can get a three-user version of NetWare 5 (with a full version of NDS!) free from Novell's Web site, or from your local Novell office.

▶ If you decide to remove NDS for NT, the Migration tool (SAMMIG.EXE) allows the NDS hosted Domain information to be downwardly synched to the Domain database. NDS for NT also maintains the old SAMSRV.DLL. After the migration tool has moved the Domain information back into the local SAM, the old SAMSRV.DLL is once again made the current function (after a standard Windows NT reboot).

▶ For maximum NT domain performance, use NDS replicas hosted on NetWare 5 servers. NDS for NT supports up to 1,000 users per domain for NetWare 4.10, up to 20,000 users per domain for NetWare 4.11, and over 45,000 users per domain on NetWare 5.

Many questions surround NDS for NT. For your benefit, we have included several white papers, as well as Q&A papers to answer the most commonly asked questions. For the most updated information, contact Novell's Web site at www.novell.com.

Management of an NDS/ Windows NT Network

Managing a network with a common directory becomes a much easier task than dealing with multiple directories. Object management (such as User or Group objects) becomes a much easier task, especially when users only have to remember *one* password and user name.

You can leverage a network using NDS for NT including redeployment options to make a Windows NT Domain/NDS network more efficient. For example, if the data-store (NDS) can be replicated to any server (and any server can contain multiple replicas), then more deployment options are open to the network designer. This allows a more out-of-the-box kind of network design, rather than being stuck with the typical deployment limitations.

The task of managing the integrated network can be split into two areas:

- Management of objects (Users and such) for single sign-on

- Management of network services

This is because when a user logs in, products such as NDS for NT enable the administrator to create and manage only *one* User object. Because the one object is the only thing managed by many tools (for example, NWAdmin and User Manager in this strategy *both* deal with the same exact User object), synchronization of two or more directories is unnecessary. When you deal with *service* administration (such as Exchange, Notes, or SQL Server), you may still need a form of synchronization on the network to manage the service itself.

Management of Users

Now that we have all the Domains comfortably moved into NDS, how do we go about managing aspects of those Domains objects under NDS? Although management can still be done from the standard user tools under Windows NT (such as USER MANAGER and Explorer), the idea is we can create, delete, and manage objects such as Users using NDS for NT.

Today with NDS for NT, the majority of this management takes place using the standard NDS Administration console, NWAdmin. The Snap-in that comes with NDS for NT will work with either the Windows 95 version of NWAdmin or the NT version (installed separately). In either case, the Snap-in will look the same to the administrator.

NOTE

One exception exists to NDS for NT domain management between Windows 95/98 and Windows NT. You cannot set the NDS and NT passwords under Windows 95/98. Only changing the NDS password is possible under Windows 95/98 in this release. When changing passwords for NDS and the Domain under NWAdmin, ensure the change is made under *Domain Access* under the User account or under the Domain object. If you use the standard *Change Password* option under the User object, only the NDS password will be changed.

Adding and Removing Users from Domains with NWAdmin

The most basic of administration objectives is to grant user access to a resource, such as a Domain. You can do this in several ways using NWAdmin:

▸ Domain-centric

▸ User-centric

In either approach, we assume the User is already created in NDS. In fact, the User account could be *anywhere* in the NDS tree. In our example (Figure 7.12), the user Sam has been created under our container SDU.

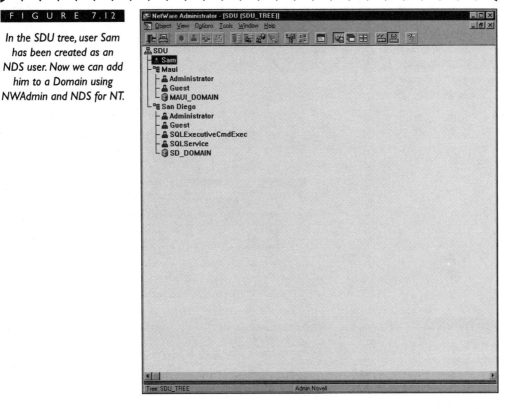

FIGURE 7.12

In the SDU tree, user Sam has been created as an NDS user. Now we can add him to a Domain using NWAdmin and NDS for NT.

Domain Centric User Creations and Deletions   If we look at our current Domain (Figure 7.13), only a few default users exist, such as Administrator and Guest. In addition, we see two accounts that were migrated, which are necessary for SQL Server to run. These are the *service accounts*. SQL Server processes will login as these accounts to have access to the Windows NT system for their functions.

To add Sam as a Domain member, we need to modify the Domain object in NDS (Domain-centric). To do this, we select the Domain object *SD_DOMAIN* and choose *Details*. Then we can choose the *Members* list and perform an add operation (Figure 7.14).

▶ . . . . ◀

Default user accounts were migrated when NDS for NT was installed. At this point, user Sam isn't a Domain member yet.

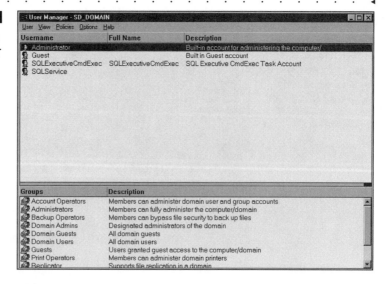

▶ . . . . ◀

One way to add a user to a Domain under NDS is to select the preferred Domain object and choose to add to the members list.

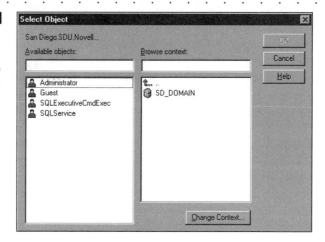

Once the user has been added to the Domain member list, anyone running USER MANAGER can see the user has been added. If USER MANAGER is already running, you may need to press the Refresh key (F5). Figure 7.15 illustrates the new user after the add operation.

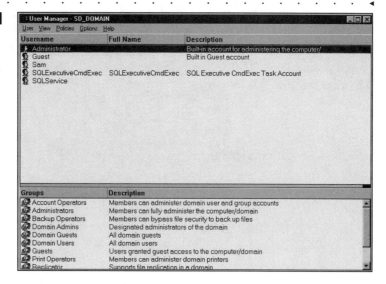

After the user has been added under NDS, the change can immediately be seen under USER MANAGER.

Domain-centric management is useful when you need to add one or multiple Users to a Domain at one time. To do this, select the Domain object, and choose *Details* on it. Then select the *Domain Members* detail page to see an existing list. To add multiple Users, select the *Add* button, and then select as many users (from the browser) as you like. After completing this, choose the *OK* button. Now you can look at the USER MANAGER utility to verify the Users have been created.

Deleting a User is even easier under NWAdmin. Just as you can add one or more Users under the Domain object, you can also delete one or more Users. Simply select one or more Users under the Domain object and choose Delete.

One important thing to note is when we delete a User from NDS, we will also effectively remove that User from *all* Domain memberships and groups. If that User object was a member of 5,000 Domains, an Exchange User, a SQL Server User, and had access to File and Print Shares, as well as NetWare resources, a single User object delete will effectively remove the User from the *entire* system! This is a comprehensive way to manage the entire system, as opposed to the traditional way of removing the User from multiple Domains and NDS as a separate action.

User Centric Creations and Deletions   To add a User to one or more Domains under NWAdmin, you first select the User or create the new user. In our example, we have an NDS User named Dick who will be added to Domain SD_DOMAIN (Figure 7.16).

F I G U R E 7.16

You can also add a User to a Domain by selecting an NDS User and choosing Details on that User under NWAdmin.

We'll now choose *Details* for user *Dick* under NWAdmin and select the *Domain Access* detail page (Figure 7.17). Any current Domain memberships can be seen.

Viewing a User's membership in multiple Domains, as well as all of their group memberships, is impossible using USER MANAGER. Under NWAdmin, you can see *all* Domain and group memberships at one time.

NOTE

Now to add user *Dick* to the SD_DOMAIN, you need to browse the NDS tree looking for the desired Domain objects. In our case, we're looking for SD_DOMAIN. After selecting the Domain object, it will be added to the Domain membership list for the User. By default, *Dick* is added to the *Domain Users* group for that Domain. Figure 7.18 depicts this.

FIGURE 7.17

To add a User to a Domain,
you can select the Domain
Access detail page for
the User.

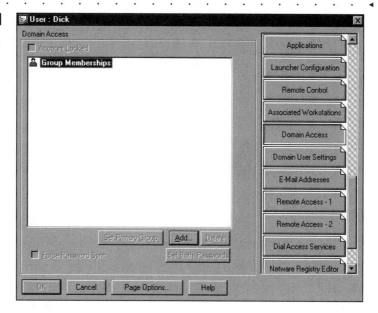

FIGURE 7.17

To add a User to a Domain,
you can select the Domain
Access detail page for
the User.

Once user *Dick* has been added to the SD_DOMAIN, you can grant him membership to other groups supported by the SD_DOMAIN. To do this, select the SD_DOMAIN object and choose *Add.* Instead of bringing up a list of Domain objects, NWAdmin will show the groups available for SD_DOMAIN (Figure 7.19). You can then choose another group, such as *Print Operators,* and select OK. The view for this user will now reflect the new group membership (Figure 7.20).

Deleting a user from a Domain or Domain groups is just as simple. In the same place where you can add a Domain or Group membership, you can also delete membership. The procedure is as follows:

▶ To delete a user from a Domain Group, select the group name and click the *Delete* key.

▶ To remove a user *entirely* from a Domain (the Domain and all group memberships), select the Domain itself and click *Delete.*

▶ . . . . ◀

F I G U R E   7.18

Once SD_DOMAIN has
been selected, you can see it
added to the Domain object
list, as well as to group
memberships. By default,
user Dick is added to the
Domain Users group in
SD_DOMAIN.

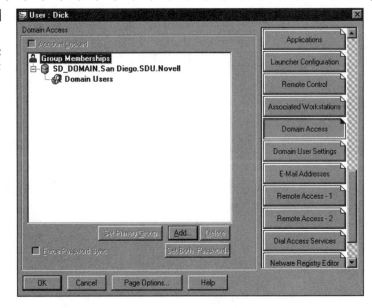

▶ . . . . ◀

F I G U R E   7.19

If a Domain object of which
a user is a member is
selected, a list of Domain
groups will appear. You can
then add the user to one or
more Domain Groups.

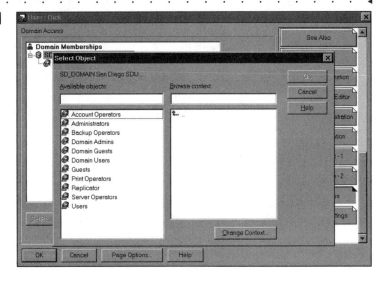

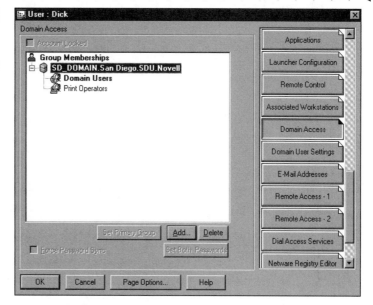

F I G U R E 7.20

A complete listing of the Domain and Groups a user belongs to can be seen from the User/Details screen under NWAdmin.

Once you have completed this, the changes will be reflected immediately under USER MANAGER.

Adding and Removing Users Using USER MANAGER

When administration is performed using the existing Microsoft tools, the user is unaware the Domain has been redirected to NDS. The tools currently used to manage Windows NT include:

- ▸ User Manager

- ▸ Server Manager

- ▸ Explorer (for assigning NTFS Permissions)

- ▸ Printer Administration (Permissions to Printer Shares)

- ▸ Tools that perform User creation/deletion, such as Exchange Administrator

- ▸ Third-party tools, such as Enterprise Administrator

When using these tools, the person using them won't know the Domain has been redirected.

Be aware of some things, though, when you use these tools. We'll use USER MANAGER as an example of what to expect.

When creating a user under USER MANAGER, you cannot specify where in the NDS hierarchy the user will be created. You *can* specify a general area where USER MANAGER-created users are placed. For example, we'll create a user, *Mike*, under USER MANAGER (Figure 7.21).

▶ · ◀

F I G U R E   7.21

When creating a user under USER MANAGER, no way exists to specify where the User object should be created in the NDS hierarchy.

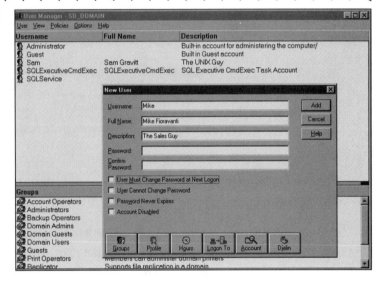

Because Mike was created in the San Diego Domain (SD_DOMAIN), the NDS object representing Mike will automatically be placed adjacent to the SD_DOMAIN object in NDS (Figure 7.22).

One provision that enables the administrator to control this is an option set during install time that specifies where USER MANAGER-created objects should be placed in the NDS tree. After installation, this value can also be set on the Domain object using NWAdmin. If no location is chosen, the default will be the same NDS container as the Domain object.

FIGURE 7.22

When a user is created under USER MANAGER, the User object will be placed adjacent to the Domain object. In this example, this means user Mike will be placed in the same container as SD_DOMAIN.

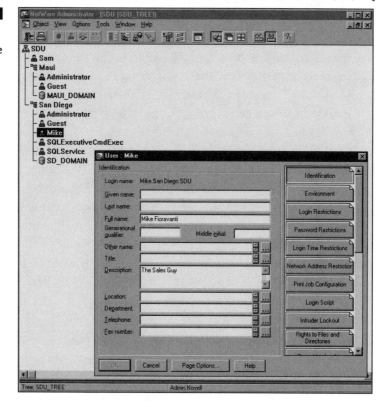

As you can see, the information for Mike is reflected also under NWAdmin when we view the User. This is because USER MANAGER and NWAdmin are looking at the *same* object in NDS! The information for user *Mike* is stored in only one place, and that's NDS.

Deleting a user using a tool like USER MANAGER also has different ramifications than removing the user from NDS (NWAdmin). When you delete an NDS user, that user is wiped from the system! When using USER MANAGER, if a user is deleted, the NDS object and all other Domain memberships the user has will remain. If user *Mike* is a Member of Domain SD_DOMAIN, MAUI_DOMAIN, and LA_DOMAIN, and a Domain Admin deletes Mike from Domain LA_DOMAIN, Mike will still be a member of Domains SD_DOMAIN and MAUI_DOMAIN.

Moving Users Between Domains

A common complaint from Domain administrators has to do with moving users from one Domain to another. In a "pure" Windows NT Domain system, the Master Domain is used to host the User objects for the network. As you recall from Chapter 3, a Master Domain consists of a Primary Domain Controller NT Server and perhaps one or more Backup Domain Controller servers. One-way trusts connect the Resource Domains to the Master Domain(s). Each Resource Domain consists of a PDC and maybe a BDC, as well.

Let's take an example where we have two Master Domains: One in LAX and one in NYC. Those are the corporate offices for the SDU Company, so this is where the Master Domains should reside. In addition, LAX and NYC have a bidirectional trust to each other. This way, the administrators can manage either Domain.

User *Bobby* has been created in the LAX Domain because he's based in San Diego. In the San Diego office, there is a resource Domain (SD_DOMAIN) and a BDC of the LAX Domain, so Bobby can locally authenticate. As long as the BDC of LAX_DOMAIN is up, Bobby can log in. If the BDC is down, Bobby can authenticate over the WAN link (although this is not preferable). Bobby also has been given some access to the Resource Domain PARAMUS because he occasionally travels to New Jersey (see Figure 7.23).

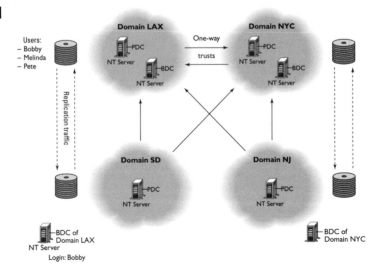

F I G U R E   7.23

A typical Domain design based on two regional offices and local office sites with resource domains.

As it turns out, Bobby gets relocated to the Paramus, New Jersey, office. Bobby now needs to login, but he's permanently based in New Jersey. The administrator of the system must do one of two things:

▶ Install another NT Server in New Jersey as a BDC of the LAX_DOMAIN (so Bobby can still locally authenticate).

▶ Move Bobby's user information to the NYC_DOMAIN because the New Jersey office already has a BDC of the NYC_DOMAIN.

Usually, the administrator will choose the latter because adding new hardware for a user move usually doesn't make much sense. The downside to this is a simple way doesn't exist to move Bobby's account information from one Domain to another. This usually entails several steps:

▶ Find out all the File and Print Shares to which Bobby has access.

▶ Document which groups Bobby is a member of, in case he needs them at his new location.

▶ Delete Bobby's account on the LAX_DOMAIN.

▶ Create a new BOBBY account on the NYC_DOMAIN.

▶ Give the new Bobby account a new password (because the old one will be lost).

▶ Add Bobby to the groups he needs.

▶ Re-assign Bobby the File and Print Shares he needs.

All this is because the user information for Bobby is hosted in the Domain (SAM) database. Once the user information is hosted in NDS, the scenario becomes much simpler.

Figure 7.24 depicts the same system implemented as an NDS tree.

F I G U R E   7.24

The same system implemented as an NDS tree simplifies relocation of network users by enabling the administrator to perform a simple drag-and-drop operation to move the user from one location to another.

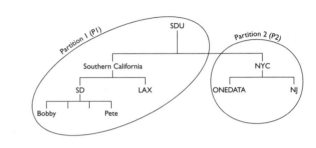

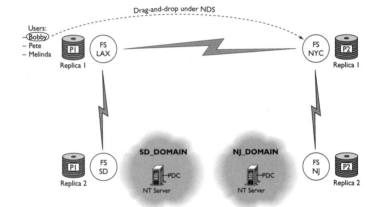

The Domains SD_DOMAIN and NJ_DOMAIN have been redirected to NDS so the user information is now hosted solely in NDS. In LAX, an NDS server (FS_LAX) hosts partition 1 (all the West Coast NDS info). In San Diego, an NDS server (FS_SD) contains a replica of Partition 1. An NT Server in San Diego still represents the SD_DOMAIN resource Domain.

In New York, a similar deployment is represented, except it's specific to the East Coast region.

Now, if Bobby is relocated to the New Jersey office, the administrator can perform a simple drag-and-drop operation using NWAdmin. By selecting Bobby's account, pushing the *control* key, and dropping the Bobby object on the new location, a move can be accomplished. Bobby will be represented in the NJ container under NYC in the SDU organization. In the background, Bobby's user information will be moved to Partition 2, which is hosted in NYC and replicated to NJ. Bobby will now have location authentication when he logs in at the New Jersey office. Note, the administrator didn't have to document *anything* about Bobby's user account. The administrator merely performed a user move under NDS!

At this point, the administrator could grant Bobby Domain membership to the NJ_DOMAIN, and then assign permissions to Bobby for any File/Print Shares he needs. This feature of NDS for NT alone can save hundreds of hours in administration when user moves are a common occurrence.

Managing Passwords

When running mixed systems (such as Windows NT and NetWare), password maintenance becomes another item that must be managed carefully. Both NDS and Windows NT (Domains and Workgroups) have separate ways to manage passwords. In NDS, a Public/Private key system is used, whereas Windows NT uses a DES (Data Encryption Standard) method.

Passwords are stored and used differently in both systems. Here is the difference:

▸ With NDS, the user provides a password. Once the password is validated, the *Private* key is retrieved from NDS. The private key is then used to authenticate to NDS. After this is complete, the private key is removed from memory.

▸ With Windows NT, the password is hashed using an MD4 (Message Digest) algorithm then sent to the server. The server will compare the hashed password with the hashed version stored on the server. If they compare equal, the user is authenticated.

Because the authentication methods are different between the two systems, NDS for NT needs to store two values if one NDS account will use both NDS and Domains. One value is used to retrieve the private key from NDS; the other is the hashed password value Windows NT needs for authentication (see Figure 7.25).

▶ . . . . ◀

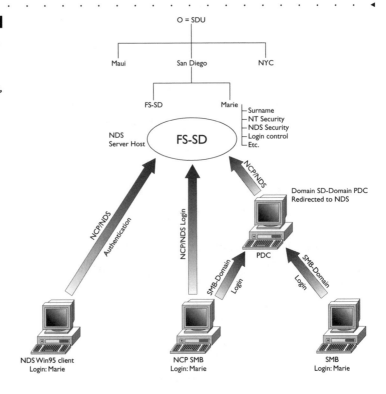

FIGURE 7.25

NDS and Windows NT use
passwords differently for
authentication. A system
using NDS for NT, therefore,
will store two values for
each User object.

Several things are happening in Figure 7.25. Three workstations are all logging in using the user account *Marie*. The Marie account only exists once in NDS, but it is a member of the SD_DOMAIN. Therefore, two values exist on the Marie NDS account depicted in Figure 7.25 as *NT Security* and *NDS Security* (this isn't literally what the attributes are called, but it's workable for our explanation). Table 7.2 describes what each workstation login will entail.

NOTE

The NCP client (NetWare Core Protocol) and SMB (Server Message Block) refer to the Novell and Microsoft client-to-server protocols, respectively. These protocols are also used in the authentication process to each server type. NCP is used for NDS authentication and SMB is used for Domain authentication. A workstation may have either protocol or both protocols, depending on what services he or she needs to access.

TABLE 7.2	CLIENT TYPE	LOGIN PROCESS
Login Process When Clients Log In from NDS, SMB, or Combined-Client Workstations	NCP-Only client	Marie logs in with her user name and password.
		The password provided during login is used to retrieve the NDS private key needed to complete the authentication. The password hash is compared using the *NDS Security* value depicted in Figure 7.25.
	SMB-Only client	Marie logs in with her user name and password.
		The password is hashed and sent to the Primary Domain Controller (PDC).
		The re-redirected Domain (using NDS for NT) will retrieve Marie's hashed password value from NDS, stored in the *NT Security* value depicted in Figure 7.25.
		The PDC will compare the two values.
		If they are equal, the user login is approved.
	NCP and SMB client	Marie logs in with her user name and password.
		The NCP client will obtain the NDS private key to complete the authentication if the password is correct.
		The SMB client will hash the password and complete the sequence the same as an SMB-only client.
		If the password provided both systems is correct, Marie will be logged into both systems.

As depicted in Table 7.2, the login process will access a different value for the user depending on the client used. But how did the values get set in NDS?

▶ When a user or administrator changes a password using an older NCP-only client, only the *NDS Security* value will get updated.

When a user or administrator changes a password using a new NCP-only client, the client determines whether the user is a member of any domains. If so, the NCP-only client changes both the NDS Security and NT Security values. Therefore, the passwords remain in synch!

▶ If an SMB-only client is used to change the password, NDS for NT intercepts the password change at the PDC and changes both the NDS Security and NT Security values. Therefore, the passwords remain in synch!

▶ If both clients are in use, and the password is changed, then both credentials (*NDS Security* and *NT Security*) used to log in will be in sync!

As you can deduce, it is practically impossible for the NDS and domain passwords to get out of sync. However, if they do, NDS for NT provides the capability for an administrator to match the passwords again using NWAdmin.

So, why hassle with all of this password management? Consider the alternatives:

▶ If you have NDS and Domains in your network without NDS for NT, you will have *two* user accounts *and* two passwords to keep in synch.

▶ The Windows NT password stored in NDS is used for the user, whether they are a member of one Domain or a thousand.

▶ If you use a synchronization product, such as Novell Administrator for Windows NT or NetVision's Synchronicity, then for every Domain you have, you must keep the passwords in synch. Five synchronized Domains means *six* passwords to keep in synch (one for NDS and five for the Domains).

Figure 7.26 depicts a system using a synch solution with three synched Domains and NDS for NT with three redirected Domains. Note, user *Sam* only needs one NDS password and one Windows NT password, even though he's a member of all three Domains! With the Synch solution, Sam has four user names and four passwords that must be kept in synch.

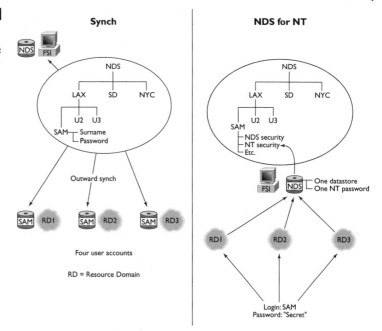

An NDS user with NDS for NT only needs one Windows NT password to access any number of Domains. Here, Sam is a member of three Domains and only needs one password.

Granting File Share and Printer Share Permissions   As mentioned previously, NDS for NT still allows the use of Microsoft tools to administrate the Domain. One of these tools is the Explorer, which allows granting of permissions to shares and NTFS volumes. In addition, the Printer permissions work exactly as before. The difference is the Domain User information is being serviced from NDS using NDS for NT.

Granting File Share and NTFS Permissions   For those of you who already have used Windows NT Access Control, this will appear exactly the same. For those of you who haven't, this is designed to give you an inkling of what is involved when setting access controls in Windows NT.

Figure 7.27 depicts granting user Sam access to the file system share called CDrive. To do this, select the drive or subdirectory where you wish to grant access. Right mouse-click the directory or drive and choose Sharing. Then choose Permissions. At this point, you can choose to show users enabling you to grant a selected user rights to the file system. The users you will see (when using NDS for NT) are the NDS User objects that are members of the selected Domain. That's all there is to it!

F I G U R E   7.27

When using NDS for NT, administrators can continue to use the same tools to grant access to file system shares and NTFS permissions.

Granting Printer Share Permissions   Similar to the file system, you can also grant access to shared printers in the Windows NT network when using NDS for NT. The way to accomplish this is in the control panel/printers options *or* select the share and right mouse-click. Choose Permissions. You can then select a Domain and show users in that Domain you wish to grant access. Again, when you are using NDS for NT, you will see NDS users who have been made members of one or more Domains. Figure 7.28 depicts the screens you will see when granting this access.

Managing NT File and Print from NWAdmin   NDS for NT also provides the NTTOOLS tab on the domain object, which launches several of the most common NT Server tools from within NWAdmin32. Figure 7.29 depicts the various tools that are included within NWAdmin32 for managing NT Server services, including NT Server file system management.

You can also grant shared printer access to NDS for NT Domain members using the current Microsoft Windows NT tools.

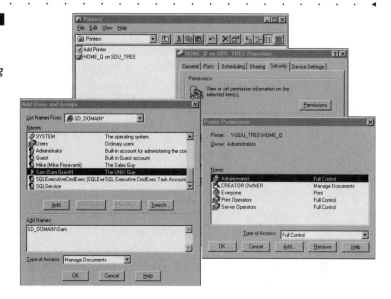

The NTTOOLS option on the Domain object starts additional Microsoft tools for common NT Server management.

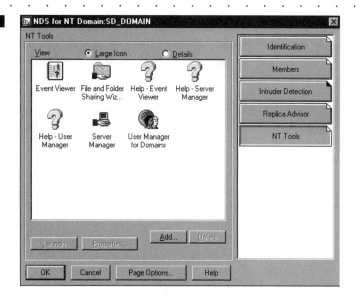

NDS Partitioning and Replication with NDS for NT

Some NDS for NT installations, such as remote offices with a single NT Server, will use NDS for NT's capability to store an NDS replica on the NT Server. The NDS engine is *exactly the same* as found on other platforms (see Chapter 8 for more details on cross-platform NDS). With NDS for NT, the NT Server is a full "NDS Citizen," meaning that it can fully participate in NDS partitioning and replication.

Managing the NDS database on the NT Server can be accomplished through two utilities. NDSMGR32.EXE, which is installed with the NT Management Utilities, is the standard tool for all NDS replica and partition operations (create, delete, merge, and so on), whether the partition or replica is on the local NT Server or on a remote server. NDS replicas on the local NT Server can also be added or removed through the SAMMIG.EXE utility.

NDS for NT also includes a Replica Advisor within NWADMN32. The Replica Advisor graphically displays where the NT Domain objects reside within the NDS tree structure (Figure 7.30). This gives the administrator the capability to quickly determine which replicas are required on a particular NT Server to ensure that NDS for NT functions even when remote NDS servers are unavailable.

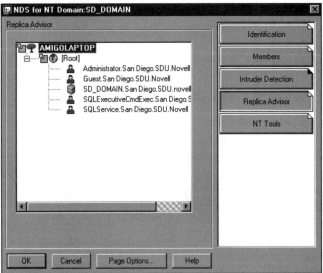

FIGURE 7.30

The Replica Advisor lists the location of all domain objects within NDS. This allows the Administrator to quickly determine which replicas are necessary on the NT Server.

Extending the Domain with Groups, Workstations, and Trusts

As you manage the Domain using NDS for NT, common things typically are done with a Domain that can also be accomplished with NDS and NWAdmin, such as creating and managing groups (global and local). Other things, such as Trust Relationships, are supported by NDS for NT, not manageable by NDS and NWAdmin.

Creating New Global and Local Groups

As you deploy and manage Domains, you may need to create more groups to support the Domain. To create new groups, you can use one of two tools:

- *User Manager.* Create a new global or local group under File options.

- *NWAdmin.* Select the Domain object where the new group will be created. Then choose Create from the Object menu option. You can also right-click the Domain object, choose create, and then select the type of group desired (global or local).

Deciding when to create a local or global group depends on your system deployment.

Adding Workstation Accounts

After a Domain is created, NT Workstations (or other servers) can join it. Typically, these stations are seen in SERVER MANAGER after the workstation has joined the Domain. To view which workstations and servers are a member of a Domain, run SERVER MANAGER from an NT Server and select the Domain in question.

When a Domain has been redirected, you'll see the workstations that are part of the Domain show up in the Domain object list (Figure 7.31). There isn't any configuration you can affect with NWAdmin. The workstation objects must be stored in NDS objects to support the workstation login.

Workstation objects appear as special NDS objects within a Domain. They are not specifically manageable under NWAdmin.

But What About Trusts?

Trust relationships are by far the most unmanageable part of Domains. The idea of Trusts in and of itself is a good idea. Trusts allow several things in Windows NT networking:

- A single user can be managed instead of several.

- If a single user account is all you need, then you only need one password as well (if the *entire* network is NT-based).

- Any trusted user can be given access to resources outside their Domain.

By using a trust, the administrator gains management of only one user name/password pair, while enabling that user account to be granted access control to any resources available by a Trust Relationship.

Many downsides exist to Trusts, which can outweigh their benefits:

▸ There is no easy way to manage Trusts. (Which Domain trusts which Domain?)

▸ If a Domain is renamed, all Trusts to it are broken.

▸ If a server is renamed, all Trusts to it are broken.

▸ Trusts must be manually constructed and managed.

▸ If a Trust is removed, users that obtained access control rights through the Trust will lose them.

NDS for NT still supports Trusts when using a re-directed Domain. In fact, one Domain may be redirected and trusting another Domain that is NOT redirected.

Trusts to another Domain show up as workstation objects within the NDS for NT Domain object under NWAdmin.

NOTE **Any object typically hidden under the Domain is suffixed by a $. When you see an object such as NTS_JD$, therefore, it means the object NTS_JD (a workstation) usually cannot be seen by a USER MANAGER administrator. Trusts will be seen suffixed by a $.**

Elimination of Trust Relationships with NDS for NT   Consider Figure 7.32. The user Ann is granted access because her home Domain (SD_DOMAIN) is trusted by Domain LAX_DOMAIN. If we didn't have a Trust, we might have a situation like Figure 7.33. This entails two user accounts and two passwords, but no Trust Relationships.

F I G U R E   7.32

In a typical Domain deployment, Trusts are used to grant access to a user from one Domain to another. In this case, user Ann can be given access to resources in the LAX_DOMAIN because of the Trust.

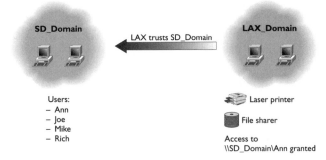

F I G U R E   7.33

A method of eliminating Trusts without NDS for NT entails creating a separate user account on each Domain. This is a messy solution because each user name and password must be kept in synch.

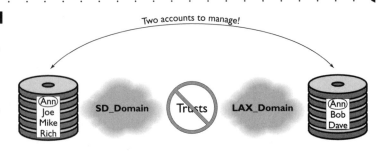

Using NDS for NT, we get the best of both worlds. Figure 7.34 depicts both Domains (SD_DOMAIN and LAX_DOMAIN) redirected to NDS using NDS for NT. The user account Ann has been given Domain membership to both Domains. Ann only has one user account and password that must be managed because the NDS account is the only account referenced by either Domain. She can be given access controls to any resource in either Domain (just like having a Trust!).

If she no longer needs access to either Domain, the administrator merely needs to remove her membership in either Domain. In a "pure" Windows NT network, we could remove Ann from "Trusting" Domain, but not from her "home" Domain. To do this, we would have to delete her account entirely!

With NDS for NT

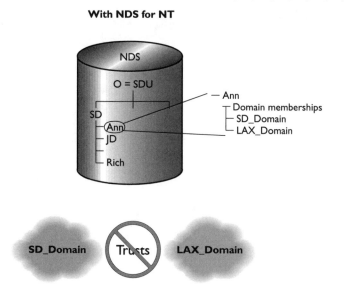

FIGURE 7.34

Using NDS for NT, you get the best of both worlds: One user account and password to maintain, ability to grant user access controls to any Domain of which the user is a member, and no Trusts to maintain.

When Trusts Must Be Maintained   When performing a migration from Domains to NDS for NT, there will be times when a Trust will remain in place, either temporarily or indefinitely. Such may be the case with an existing deployment of Windows NT.

In Figure 7.35, a Single Master Domain (SLC_MASTER) has been deployed to house the user accounts. A resource Domain (SD_DOMAIN) in San Diego contains resources for the San Diego office. Because the existing user account DNelson has access to San Diego resources because of the Trust, breaking the Trust after migrating SLC_MASTER and/or SD_DOMAIN to NDS for NT will cause DNelson to lose his access rights. The reason is, when DNelson was created (before or after NDS for NT migration), he was assigned a unique ID with respect to the Domain in which he is "homed." This ID is stored in the resource Domain access control list for the Share to which he has access.

If the Trust is removed, his account number will become an Unknown. In cases like this, a Trust can be left in place indefinitely.

F I G U R E   7.35

*Existing Domain
deployments may need to
leave some Trusts in place to
maintain access control
rights from users in
a Master Domain
to resources in a
Resource Domain.*

Management of Users versus Network Services

When it comes to managing a network *service*, more considerations may exist than just the Domain. A good example is Exchange Server, which requires a Domain be present to operate. In addition, Exchange has its own database of user information, which it maintains for mailbox information. When a user is created, a mailbox is created as well (or should be). Exchange, in a pure Windows NT system, would only use the Domain to validate a user authentication. The flow for each under a "pure" Windows NT system would be as follows:

1. User CPREWITT is created using User Manager.

2. User Manager invokes Exchange Manager and passes some of CPREWITT's user information to Exchange Manager.

3. The administrator completes the required Exchange Manager information for CPREWITT.

4. CPREWITT can now log in and use mail.

This accomplishes the creation process. Note, User Manager handles the Domain information and a separate utility (Exchange Manager) handles the Exchange Directory information.

NOTE   As Microsoft moves forward with Active Directory Services (ADS), one of the committed actions for Exchange is to have Exchange use ADS for *all* its directory information. Today (and probably until one or two more releases of Exchange), Exchange maintains all this information in its own directory database.

To use Exchange now, the flow would be similar to this:

1. CPREWITT logs into the Domain.

2. CPREWITT invokes an Exchange (or MAPI) client to use mail services.

3. The Exchange Server gets a request to receive new mail for CPREWITT.

4. Exchange Server checks with the Domain database (through the SSPI).

5. SSPI returns that CPREWITT is authenticated.

6. CPREWITT uses her mailbox.

Managing User Accounts and Exchange

Novell has elegantly provided a way to manage Domains centrally using either Novell or Microsoft tools with NDS for NT. This isn't where the Novell strategy stops, however. Novell customers have also asked Novell to allow other services to be managed from NDS. The first one of these tools that manages a third-party service is the Novell Administrator for Exchange.

> **Novell already allows management of Novell-created services, such as GroupWise and BorderManager from NDS. These add-ons enable customers to manage services that are not Novell-created network applications.**
> **NOTE**

The Novell Administrator for Exchange uses a synchronization philosophy to keep user accounts hosted in NDS (and Domains) synchronized to Exchange Mailboxes. It accomplishes this via a snap-in running under NWAdmin for NT.

> **Microsoft Exchange Server does *not* keep user information in the Domain. It uses its own database to keep track of user mailboxes and other user information.**
> **NOTE**

When an administrator creates an NDS user and adds that user to a Domain, he or she has the option to have a mailbox on Exchange created for that user. The user *must* be a member of at least one Domain that is part of the Exchange *Site*. A *Site* is a collection of one or more NT Servers where Exchange is hosted.

Once the user has been created as an Exchange user, the administrator can manage that user's information using NWAdmin and NDS. Changes (such as a phone number) can be synchronized to the Exchange user attribute data.

The Novell Administrator for Exchange comes with NDS for NT (included with the CD-ROM that comes with this book) and is reliant on NDS for NT to operate.

Managing User Accounts and Other BackOffice Services

As noted, other services exist for which Novell has indicated it will provide support. To other BackOffice services, NDS for NT is transparent. Although they may benefit from NDS for NT, NWAdmin and NDS cannot necessarily manage them. Table 7.3 summarizes the BackOffice services today and the functionality provided when using NDS for NT.

Additional NDS/Network Management Tools for Mixed Systems

Novell has committed to creating enhanced tools for integrated management. This includes the Java-based Console One utility that will support a snap-in architecture (just like NWAdmin). Co-management utilities that manage a single user account and all its related services will continue to become available, both under NWAdmin, and Novell's Java-based Console One.

TABLE 7.3	BACKOFFICE SERVICE	NDS FOR NT SUPPORT
BackOffice Services and NDS for NT Support	Exchange Server	Management can be accomplished using the Exchange Administrator tool or the Novell Administrator for Exchange.
	SQL Server	Can use an NDS for NT redirected Domain to authenticate Domain users requesting SQL access. SQL Server must be administered using the SQL Admin tool provided by Microsoft.
	Internet Information Server (IIS)	Uses the redirected NDS for NT Domain to check access privileges before allowing access via Active Server Pages (ASP). By managing the Domain, you can manage part of IIS.
	SNA Server	Uses the redirected NT Domain to check access privileges.
	System Management Server (SMS)	Uses SQL Server for part of its database storage. NDS for NT with NWAdmin has no provision for creating software distribution packages or remote management. This functionality will be more comprehensive with the Novell Workstation Manager product in a new release.

Novell also includes with NDS for NT a version of its *Novell Administrator for Exchange* tool. This enables an administrator to manage, create, and delete Exchange mailboxes for users as part of NDS for NT redirection. As an added benefit, you can actually manage the Exchange Site, as well as use NDS and NWAdmin.

In addition, Microsoft has announced and previewed a common console tool called *Microsoft Management Console* (MMC). MMC uses an ActiveX component architecture to extend management of services with ActiveX Snap-in components (similar to NWAdmin today).

Summary

Novell has created a tool that allows a single Directory service to be used under NetWare and Windows NT seamlessly. NDS for NT allows the creation of a single user and enables that user to have access to services under Windows NT (such as file, print, and BackOffice services), as well as NetWare services (such as file, print, and GroupWise).

The next release of NDS for NT continues that evolution, allowing NDS replicas to be fully hosted in either a mixed network (NetWare, Windows NT, and/or UNIX) or in an all-Windows NT network solution.

CHAPTER 8

NDS Cross-Platform

This chapter discusses the architecture, purpose, and use of NDS on multiple platforms. You should have a clear understanding of *what* NDS Cross-Platform provides and what it doesn't provide. We won't necessarily discuss specific implementation case studies. We will discuss the entire NDS cross-platform strategy, however, of which NDS for NT is a part. This strategy allows NDS to run on Windows NT, IBM MVS, IBM AIX, Sun Solaris, Fujitsu, SCO UnixWare, and, of course, NetWare, to name a few platforms.

If you've read Chapter 7, you will already have a good understanding of NDS on NT and the general idea of the product. You will also know what to expect on the other operating system platforms. Integration of NDS is not solely limited to Windows NT, but it is (or will be) available for the majority of operating systems available today. With this in mind, this chapter will be beneficial for administrators who must support different operating systems on a daily basis.

NDS Naming and Authentication

As discussed in earlier chapters (such as Chapter 2), NDS is really a naming and authentication service. It provides the capability to find resources in a large distributed system. The key to remember, especially when designing or deploying a directory service, is that a directory is designed to help locate and use *resources*. A directory is not just another way to define an organizational chart for the company!

Naming under NDS

NDS provides several core features that make it extremely useful as the enterprise directory:

- ▸ NDS acts as a central repository for network resources.

- ▸ NDS is extensible, allowing custom objects to be added to the network directory.

▸ As a central repository, NDS provides an unambiguous place for network resource searches (for example, "find all printers that support Postscript for me").

▸ NDS provides a central point for management.

Central Repository of Data

NDS was designed to provide a flexible way to name and locate resources. As a central repository, NDS reduces the number of databases that must be maintained on the network. This extends to services and applications running on Windows NT that take advantage of the Directory. Any service proxied through to the NDS will also eliminate a database dependency.

NOTE

The NDS for NT product does just this (proxy). It makes User Manager and other NT security-dependent products, such as Exchange, *think* a Domain is present, while all the data is being stored in NDS instead. The net result ends up the same: one database (NDS) that supports multiple applications (Exchange, SQL Server, User Manager, and so on).

Extensibility for New Applications

NDS provides the capability to create new naming types (objects) by way of an extensible Schema (rules for creating objects in a Directory). As NDS is deployed on non-NetWare platforms, therefore, custom objects and object information (attributes) can be created to accommodate the new host system. As an example, Figure 8.1 shows a Windows NT Domain represented in the NDS tree. This Domain object is not part of the basic Schema (rules) for NDS. It was added (by way of Schema extensions) to accommodate Windows NT Domains in the Novell Administrator for Windows NT product or by installing NDS for NT.

A good example of where extensibility would come in useful is the case of running a SQL database (such as Oracle) on a Windows NT Server. The Windows NT security system (SAM and Domain) is unable to create a custom object type for the instance of an Oracle server running on a Windows NT Server. NDS, as a directory service, can. Therefore, an NDS object called *Oracle Server* can be created and managed from the Directory.

▶ . . . . ◀

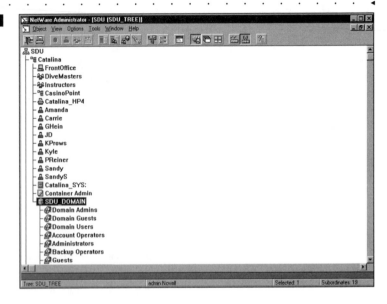

Custom objects and attributes can be created to represent any type of resource or user type in NDS.

Unambiguous Reference for Network Searches

A heterogeneous network contains many different resources. Half the battle of using network resources is *finding* them. As a central repository, NDS provides an unambiguous place for network-wide resource searches.

If you are looking for a printer and NDS contains objects representing all the UNIX, Windows NT, and NetWare printers, one query can encompass *all* the network printers!

Central Point for Network Management

If all the resources are in one place, *and* if they use the Directory to store management information, one point of contact (the Directory) can be used to manage all the participating network resources.

For example, if the routers store and read their configuration information in the Directory, a central management tool (such as NWAdmin or the Java Common Console) can manage the router infrastructure.

Not all of these options are available today. Cross-Platform NDS merely opens the way for this to occur by making access to the Directory ubiquitous on all the places where these network services are hosted.

Authentication

The ability to provide a single user name and password is highly desirable, especially in a large network of resources. This type of environment has typically been called *single sign-on*. For this to be possible, something must provide a core authentication for the network.

Another service of the Directory is core authentication. As NDS (or at least *some* directory!) becomes more ubiquitous, a single login environment becomes more possible. If a directory (such as NDS) is available on all the major platforms (operating systems), then the directory can function as an authentication agent on those platforms. As you can see in Figure 8.2, with NDS hosted on MVS (the mainframe), Sun Solaris, and Windows NT, a user can log in with a single name and password, gain access to resources on *each* of these systems, and begin to use services on them. Services would include database, e-mail, and so on.

▶   •   ◀

F I G U R E   8.2

NDS hosted on each system acts as an authentication agent. After a user logs in, his or her credentials are automatically forwarded to each operating system as he or she the user requests services hosted on that operating system.

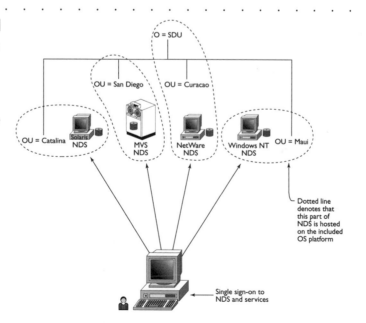

Creating a Single Login Environment

As discussed in earlier chapters, a single login network is an administrator's dream. This means one user name and password for every user receiving access to all network resources. The following are three ways this is approached with NDS:

▸ *Single sign on.* Resources recognize and use NDS authentication hosted on an O/S platform.

▸ *Proxy single login.* A service *thinks* it is using the native authentication, yet it is *really* using the Directory. This is the case when NDS for NT and a BackOffice service is used (such as SQL Server or Exchange). Chapter 7 discusses this in detail.

▸ *Synchronization strategy.* NDS information is synchronized to another security database. When a user logs in, his or her user name and password are the same. The client transparently logs in to both systems after the user has supplied one name and password. This is the Novell Administrator for Windows NT discussed in Chapter 6 or the Synchronicity product from NetVision.

Supporting Extensible Authentication

As an evolution of NDS authentication, Novell is also pursuing a strategy of additional authentication options such as Certificates and Kerberos.

NOTE The default authentication option in NDS today (whether NetWare or other platforms, such as Windows NT) is Rivest, Shamir, Adleman (RSA) Public/Private Key authentication. Although this is extremely secure, customer demand warrants the inclusion of other authentication schemes, such as Kerberos for flexibility.

Discussing other authentication schemes in detail is beyond the scope of this book. In short, the only choice in Novell's initial NDS Cross-Platform technology will be RSA Public/Private key (the one currently in NDS on NetWare today) with others to follow.

Caveat of Single Sign-on

The key to making single sign-on work is the cooperation of the services people need and the operating systems upon which they are hosted. If the services either do not use the Directory authentication or they cannot be proxied, no benefit is realized. For example, if you're using a database service that runs on UNIX, this database service must accept the NDS login as valid for authentication. Otherwise, two logins will be necessary. Figure 8.3 illustrates this sort of example.

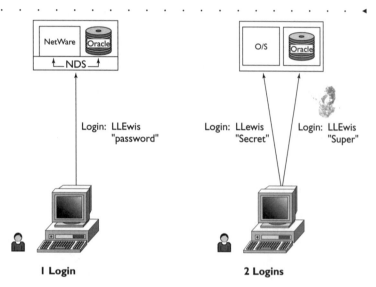

The Purpose of Cross-Platform NDS

NDS is one of the few available true X.500-based Directory services available today. As discussed, it provides two of the most fundamental services needed to tie the enterprise network together: naming and authentication.

As a result of being successful with creating a true X.500-based Directory service (the culmination of seven years of work!), NDS is the *de facto* Directory service in use today. The drawback has been that NDS was only available on NetWare. Services such as an Oracle database could not take advantage of NDS naming and authentication on a UNIX platform, for example. As a result, limited leveraging of NDS has occurred on any platform other than NetWare.

NOTE **Client access has not been the primary problem to date. In fact, NDS clients are available today from Novell, Microsoft, Caldera (a LINUX port), and SCO UnixWare. In addition, access through Lightweight Directory Access Protocol (LDAP) has been available free from Novell's Web site for several months and is now a core component of NetWare 5!**

Enter Cross-Platform NDS. With NDS on the majority of operating systems, enabling services to use the features of NDS becomes a much more attainable objective. In addition, Novell is providing NDS in a standalone environment to anyone who wants it.

Availability of Cross-Platform NDS

When Novell decided to create Cross-Platform NDS, the two major ways to develop versions for the different operating system platforms were as follows:

▶ Provide free access to NDS source code to an operating system vendor and assist them in porting it.

▶ Create the specific operating system versions at Novell if vendors did not wish to port it themselves (for example, Microsoft).

Novell has licensed NDS source code to several major operating system. They have ported (or are porting) NDS to run natively on their respective platforms.

Novell, with a bit of assistance from Sun Microsystems, has developed NDS for Solaris, which includes not only the core NDS functionality, but authentication redirection that allows standard Solaris access mechanisms (ftp, telnet, and so on) to authenticate using NDS credentials. NDS for Solaris differs a bit from NDS on other Unix platforms (AIX, HPUX) as it focuses primarily on NDS access, while the other Unix versions include file, print, and directory support.

Because Microsoft did not want to port NDS to the Windows NT operating system, Novell has done it by using published APIs in Microsoft's Software Developer Kit (SDK). A standalone version of NDS on NT is included with the CD-ROM included with this book. To obtain an updated copy of NDS for NT, you can access the Novell Web site at www.novell.com.

When to Use Cross-Platform NDS

As mentioned previously, Cross-Platform NDS, in and of itself, isn't necessarily a solution. Usually something that leverages NDS will be used (such as NDS for NT) to form a complete solution. This section discusses a few places using NDS for NT as an example where cross-platform NDS might be used.

Using NDS as a Platform for Integration NT Server Services

This would include using NDS as the directory for providing an integrated solution for NT Server:

- *Novell Administrator for NT.* This product could use NDS locally running on Windows NT to synchronize locally.

- *NDS for NT Version.* This allows NDS running locally to be the complete local database for all services that use the NT SAM.

NDS Cross-Platform Used by Network Services

In this scenario, NDS is leveraged by services that already use NDS as an authentication method. A prime example is the Oracle database. With Oracle running on HP/UX, Sun Solaris, Linux, or NetWare, a user can log in once to NDS and use the Oracle database without having to provide another user name and password.

 NOTE

As noted previously, this option has been available for Oracle on NetWare for some time. Using Cross-Platform NDS allows this to be possible on all the other platforms where NDS and Oracle run.

NDS Cross-Platform as a Directory Development Option

With NDS distributed with certain major operating system platforms, developers can develop to a ubiquitous directory that can run in a fully distributed state. Much the way Network Information Service (NIS) comes with versions of UNIX, NDS will also be available. This ensures a common directory on which developers can rely that is included with all major operating system platforms.

Cross-Platform NDS and Services Integration

What NDS Cross-Platform is and what it is not must be clear. By itself, NDS does *not* provide a solution. NDS *must* be combined with another service to make it useful. NDS Cross-Platform is NDS running on a host operating system— nothing more, nothing less.

Another value for running NDS is provided by Novell and other directory developers in the form of additional services. These services include:

▶ The NDS/LDAP responder for NT, which enables Windows NT to act as an LDAP server using NDS as the Directory database.

▶ NWAdmin (Win32) and Console One (Java) management consoles for NDS.

▶ NDS Manager for graphical NDS database manipulation.

▶ NDS for NT, which is the product that actually provides native services integration (discussed in detail in Chapter 7).

The latter product (NDS for NT) provides immediate value in the form of Windows NT services integration. With this product, a single login provides access to NetWare resources, as well as Windows NT file, print, and BackOffice services.

For other services (such as databases or other network services), NDS on NT does not provide any integration unless that service (such as Oracle) uses NDS.

For other operating systems (such as UNIX), the level of services integration depends on the platform owner.

▶ · ◀

Cross-Platform NDS Architecture

From an integration perspective, it helps to understand how Cross-Platform NDS is architected.

Abstraction of NDS Dependencies

When NDS was designed, no one knew (although we like to think we did) that directories would be important over the next few years. Remember, NDS design started circa 1989 for a 1993 ship date and was based on X.500 Directory recommendations. As a result, NDS only ran on NetWare and made native calls to the NetWare file system.

To create a cross-platform Directory, Novell needed to abstract NDS native calls so those dependencies wouldn't be impossible to support on other operating systems. Almost all general-purpose operating systems have a file system of some sort, as well as general operating system functions (such as memory management). Providing a fundamental *primitive* layer that NDS could depend on being there was all that had to be done. This is the purpose of the directory host (DHOST) engine.

To make those common primitives available, Novell designed a portable engine on which NDS could rely to provide the fundamental calls NDS needed. Rather than re-architect and rewrite NDS itself, a small portable engine was created. This engine (DHOST) is the *only* thing that must be ported to each operating system platform to provide the necessary NDS primitives. In other words, DHOST just provides basic operating system support for NDS for network communication and local file system storage of the NDS files. NDS itself must merely be re-compiled on each platform where the DHOST has been ported. *No* changes to NDS code were necessary to make it run on a platform where DHOST is present. As a result, Novell gains several advantages:

▸ Code changes to NDS are practically nonexistent across platforms.

▸ The code base for NetWare is *exactly the same* as the NDS code that uses DHOST on other non-NetWare platforms.

▸ DHOST is a small engine that translates general-purpose operating system calls, such as memory, network, and file I/O. DHOST is, therefore, easily and quickly ported to other operating systems.

NCPS-Based NDS Services versus DHOST-Based Services

When Novell embarked down the cross-platform path, the directory wasn't viewed as important as the file and print access. Therefore, Novell Cross Platform Services (NCPS) (the original cross-platform model) included directory, file, and print services in a single, monolithic product. While this extends Novell's directory and file/print services to other platforms, it does have minor disadvantages.

NCPS is a monolithic product, meaning that the *entire* NetWare operating system and services were ported as a single module. Any enhancements or bug fixes required revising the *entire* NCPS product—a difficult task! Also, NCPS duplicated functionality already found on the host platforms, such as file and print access.

NCPS-based products, which include NCPS for HPUX, IBM AIX, and SCO UnixWare, provide full NDS access and support. In reality, NCPS on these platforms allow the Unix server to "appear" to NetWare clients as a NetWare server, because, in fact, it was the NetWare server ported to the Unix operating system.

As time progressed, the importance of the directory became evident. Customers needed NDS functionality on their Unix servers, but were not as interested in file and print access. Customers also demanded a design that could be easily update—something more modular than the monolithic NCPS product. Hence, DHOST was born.

NDS for NT 2.0 Use of DHOST

DHOST provides the platform NDS uses to run on operating systems other than NetWare. NDS itself loads as a series of modules on DHOST. These modules include the following:

- *DS.DLL.* Equivalent to DS.NLM on NetWare, this is the main NDS module.

- *DSI.DLL.* Equivalent to DSI.NLM, this is used to install NDS initially. Usually it is not used after install.

- *DSLOADER.DLL.* Equivalent to DSLOADER.NLM, this provides some calls that NDS uses when loading.

Note that the NDS modules are much the same on DHOST as they are under NDS. This is because most of them *are* the same modules — they're just compiled under Windows NT as DLLs instead of NLMs! In addition, NDS modules are part of the DHOST memory space after they are loaded, just like NLMs under NetWare.

NDS for Solaris

Novell's NDS for Solaris uses DHOST rather than NCPS. As such, NDS for Solaris provides full NDS support, but not the NetWare file and print support found in the NCPS-based Unix products. NDS for Solaris includes several features that integrated the Solaris platform and services into the NDS directory. These features include:

▸ An LDAP-based install that creates or merges the Solaris users and groups into NDS.

▸ Authentication redirection of Solaris-based services (telnet, ftp, and so on) that allows a user to authenticate to the Solaris-based services with the NDS user name and password.

▸ Full NDS-database support that allows the Solaris server to fully participate in NDS partitioning and replication.

▸ NDS API access at the Solaris platform.

▸ Full TCP/IP support on the Solaris Server. In fact, NDS for Solaris doesn't include support for IPX.

Using NDS Cross-Platform

Now that you have a good understanding of NDS Cross-Platform, you should understand how it is used in a heterogeneous environment, as well as the requirements to implement and use NDS.

Client Requirements

NDS Cross-Platform requires one of three different types of clients to be used. You can combine client types as well, if you like. Client types are as follows:

- ▶ *A traditional Novell NDS client.* This could be either the older Virtual Loadable Module (VLM) client or the newer Novell Client32 client.

- ▶ *A Microsoft-supplied NDS client.* Microsoft NDS clients come with both Windows 95/98 and Windows NT. Windows 3.11 and below can use the Novell VLM client.

- ▶ *An LDAP-capable client.* This could be an application that requires LDAP access to a Directory (such as Netscape's Collabra Server), or perhaps an LDAP browser.

 NOTE **Microsoft's client API strategy, Application Directory Services Interface (ADSI), works with NDS on NT when installed, just as it works with NDS running on NetWare. If you are running a Microsoft client and an application that uses Microsoft's ADSI APIs to access a Directory, NDS on NT will work for you.**

Another option is running an LDAP-enabled management tool that enables creation, deletion, and data management of objects. In this case, an all-IP solution can be created because LDAP uses IP as its native protocol, and NDS for NT has an LDAP responder as part of the product.

Another tool provided to enable management of the NDS database is the same tool provided with NetWare: The NDS Manager tool NDS Manager provides administrators the capability to split the database (create partitions) and create multiple replicas for fault tolerance.

Server Requirements

Client access, as described, does require an enabled Directory client of some sort, either LDAP or a Novell/Microsoft NDS client. The server's requirements are actually slightly less stringent.

NDS to NDS communication can either be through TCP/IP or IPX, depending on your preference. That is, if you have an all-IP network, NDS for NT can use TCP/IP as its preferred method of communication.

Managing Services under NDS Cross-Platform

Once you have deployed NDS Cross-Platform, the matter of managing it *and* the services it uses still exists. Novell provides two different administration tools to help with this task.

Most administrators who have used NDS on NetWare are familiar with it. This is a graphical administration tool called the NetWare Administrator (NWAdmin). *NWAdmin* is a tool used for managing NDS and all its objects. It reads the configuration of NDS (for example, Schema) dynamically and enables rights management, as well as some graphical administration of objects. NWAdmin enables a drag-and-drop type of management for *any* created NDS object, regardless of whether the object is part of the base Schema. With the release of NetWare 5, Novell also provides a GUI Java-based NDS management utility called Console One. Console One runs on any JVM as long as native NDS APIs are available, which includes any client platform with Novell's NDS client (such as Windows 95/98 and NT) or any server platform running NDS, such as Sun Solaris and NetWare.

Managing Nonstandard Objects

When NWAdmin is packaged with NDS Cross-Platform (or NetWare, for that matter), it can fully manage base class objects. This includes Users, NCP (NetWare) Servers, Queues, Groups, and so on. Objects that are *not* part of the base class will show as a "?" object (see Figure 8.4). You can perform some management of the object, even though it is unknown to NWAdmin.

You can perform a significant amount of object management in NWAdmin even if no Snapin exists for the extended object type.

NOTE

The *NDS Schema* is a set of definitions of the types of objects that can be created in NDS. The default set of objects that can be created (as well as attributes) is called the *Base Schema*. The base Schema can be extended to include other objects and attributes. But the base Schema cannot be reduced. Base classes such as USER, for example, are part of the base Schema and cannot be removed.

Management options include:

▸ Moving the object to a new location in the NDS tree (drag-and-drop)

▸ Deleting the object

▸ Granting Trustee access to the object and its properties

▸ Revoking Trustee access to the object and its properties

You *cannot*, however, read or modify the object's properties. For this you'll need a custom management component, known as a *Snapin*.

NOTE **A good example may be a User object. If User objects were given a new attribute (such as "Shoe Size"), then you could not read or write to the attribute Shoe Size unless a Snapin existed to do so. If a brand new class were created (such as "NT Domain"), it would show as a "?" in the tree. You could not manage *any* of its properties, except who has rights to it or what rights it has to other objects.**

Summary

We've explored a great deal about NDS in this chapter. For those who already have worked with NDS, a new option of running NDS cross-platform exists, in addition to NetWare.

NDS Cross-Platform does *not* replace the native security or naming system in and of itself. Instead, NDS provides the directory that makes such services integration possible in the small network or the large enterprise.

With these topics, we can now discuss some other integration options available for the mixed network.

CHAPTER 9

Deploying Emulator Services in the Network

We have looked at a variety of ways to manage a heterogeneous system using server-side integration as well as client-side integration. This chapter deals with an emulator approach to providing client functionality and server access.

We discussed emulators and synchronizers in Chapter 4, and we've looked at some available synchronizers, such as Synchronicity and Novell Administrator for Windows NT. This approach is usually desirable from an administrator's perspective: It enables more integrated management of the system, although it requires two or more clients (SMB and NCP, for example) to enable the client to access services freely on either server.

In many cases, these emulator services aren't meant for a full-scale permanent network deployment. Many times, these services are necessary for a migration (noted in one of the following scenarios), but they aren't robust or scalable enough for a long-term solution.

When to Deploy Emulator Services

In some cases, deploying emulator services on the network does make sense. Such examples may be:

► Migration from other systems or network services

► Requirements for integration are noncomplex

► Cost prohibitive for a full-scale integration

► Multiple OS or other updates are forthcoming

With this list in mind, we'll go into more detail on what each means.

Migration

You may be migrating from LAN Manager, NT Server, or LAN Server to NetWare for file and print services (or perhaps just the opposite). This doesn't mean NT or LAN Server is going away for good. Instead, you may be using NetWare for File, Print, and Directory services while using NT Server for database service (such as Oracle). This means the clients need an Oracle Requester (for SQL access) and a NetWare client only in that scenario. If LAN Manager/NT Server file and print access had been in use up to this point, you might install the emulator services until the LAN Manager client has been removed from the workstations. The net gain would be twofold: less network traffic and one less thing to manage in the network.

Basic Integration Needs

Emulators usually only provide a basic level of integration, which may be all you need. A requirement for a deep level of integration may not exist. An emulator can provide basic services with minimal effort and management; most emulators, by the way, are not speed-demons. Because another protocol is being emulated, a performance loss usually occurs over using the native protocol. In a small network — or if the service being emulated is not called upon heavily — emulation will satisfy the integration requirements.

Cost of Full Integration Too Prohibitive

A fuller integration may be desired, but it may be cost- or time-prohibitive. Especially when the network may contain several thousand (or more) workstations. In other words, pursuing a synchronization strategy may be the desired result, but you may not have the people available to complete the integration in a timely manner.

Multiple Updates are Forthcoming

Another reason may be that an immediate update to the client or server operating systems may incur a duplicate cost if a new version of the OS is forthcoming. If you plan an upgrade in three months anyway, you may want to wait and deploy a temporary solution (such as emulation) until another round of updates is scheduled.

Emulation Options

With these issues in mind, we'll cover several emulation options available to a heterogeneous network. They include:

- File and Print Service for NetWare (FPNW)

- Gateway Services for NetWare

We'll cover the ins and outs, when to use them, and how to use them. You may ultimately choose to combine them or use them singly. Hopefully, we'll help you decide when to choose the right one for your environment.

File and Print Services for NetWare

Microsoft has created several services available to emulate NetWare on an NT server. We'll cover FPNW and Gateway services extensively. Simply stated, FPNW allows NT Servers to be seen and used as NetWare servers in a heterogeneous environment.

FPNW is a set of software services that are installed on an NT Server. NetWare volumes are then created as a part of the existing NT Server volumes (see Figure 9.1). Then NetWare clients can use a VLM client or earlier to access these emulated volumes.

NOTE

The Virtual Loadable Module (VLM) client is the latest client that works well with FPNW. Microsoft made a mistake when creating FPNW because the NT Server broadcasts it as a NetWare 3.x server. The level of file access it emulates, however, is only NetWare 2.x. As a result, a newer client (such as Client32) will try to communicate using NetWare 3.x/4.x file service NCPs and get errors when trying to MAP drives. This limits how this product can be used in existing mixed networks. You can get a workaround and an update from the Microsoft Web site to enable Client32 access.

The client must be using IPX to communicate over the LAN. This is because NT Server only understands TCP over NetBIOS (the way NT Server communicates) and does not support Novell's NetWare over IP (NWIP). In a network where NetWare clients need access to NetWare servers and services on NT Servers, while still storing files on NT Servers, FPNW can be a good solution.

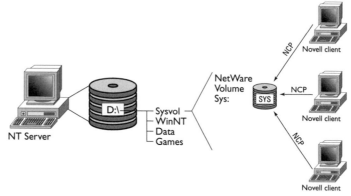

FIGURE 9.1

Volumes under NT Server can be exposed as NetWare volumes for Novell client access.

When to Use File and Print Services for NetWare

Several conditions exist where FPNW could be useful:

▸ A large number of NetWare clients exist (NETX, VLM, Client32) with NT Servers.

▸ A large number of NetWare servers exist.

▸ Services are being provided on NT Servers (such as SAP R/3).

▸ You do not want multiple requesters installed on client workstations.

▸ You wish to use some of the NT volumes for file storage or you want to use NT print sharing.

Another potential scenario: migration from a NetWare environment to an all-NT network. Although this seldom is the case, FPNW can prove a worthwhile tool for doing so.

Some caveats exist when using FPNW that restrict its usefulness. As a solution, FPNW has been targeted by Microsoft as a migration technology from NetWare to NT

Server, although many customer have found that FPNW can be an effective tool for migrating from NT Server to NetWare. Microsoft designed FPNW as a migration tool with a finite (short) lifetime within a customer environment, although customers often use it on a regular basis. Some of the limitations restricting its use include:

▸ Limited integration with Directory Services

▸ Cost of deploying FPNW

▸ Compatibility

▸ Deployment of FPNW in the network

No Integration with Directory Services

Even though the NT Server hosting FPNW appears as a NetWare server, it is only at a NetWare 2.*x* level of support. As such, single login to network services (a feature of NDS) is unavailable using FPNW. This means separate user's accounts must be created for each user of volumes on *each* NT server providing service (as illustrated in Figure 9.2). A user would single-login to the NDS tree, and then need to authenticate to each NT Server using FPNW.

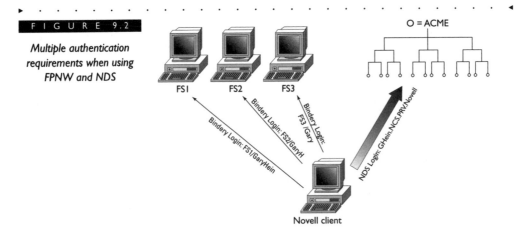

F I G U R E   9.2

Multiple authentication requirements when using FPNW and NDS

Cost of Deploying FPNW

FPNW is a charge item from Microsoft, sold on a per server basis. The cost of using FPNW as an integration product in a large-scale network, therefore, may prove expensive.

Compatibility

Earlier versions of FPNW didn't support the latest Novell client 32-bit technology, known as Client32. Make sure you're using the most current version of Microsoft's FPNW software if you need to support Client32 clients.

Deployment of FPNW in the Network

Any server you want to provide service must have the FPNW service installed and configured. This is better than installing new software on each client, but it still requires some time to update the servers.

Components of File and Print Service

Two options exist for installing File and Print Services. Primarily, the difference is in the packaging and the services included in the package. For example, *Services for Netware* includes several technologies in one box.

NT Server Version 3.51

Microsoft has a purchasable CD-ROM (File and Print Services for NetWare) that can be installed under NT Server 3.51 *only*. You do not need anything else to install and configure this service. You *do* need to install NWLINK IPX/SPX as a protocol option, however. This comes with the NT Server 3.51 CD. You *cannot* use this version with NT Server 4.0.

NT Server Version 4.0 — "Services for NetWare"

FPNW now comes with Directory Service Manager for NetWare as a single set of services called *Services for NetWare*. The specific components needed for FPNW are on the same CD; they are installed at each server that will provide NetWare services. Again, NWLINK IPX/SPX must be installed.

Installing File and Print Services

Installation of FPNW is relatively painless. Once you start the install, you need to answer only a few questions to get it to work. We'll cover a quick-step install:

1. Choose Add Software from the control panel/network in NT 3.51 or Services if you're using NT 4.0.

2. Choose Other to specify you will install from a CD-ROM other than the NT Server distribution CD-ROM.

3. Choose File and Print Services for NetWare (see Figure 9.3).

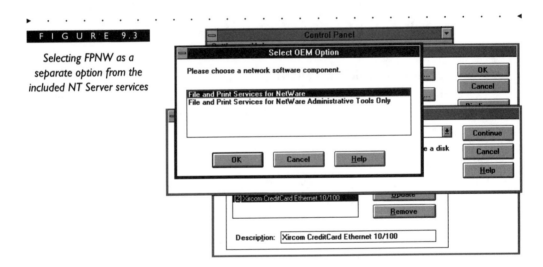

Selecting FPNW as a separate option from the included NT Server services

4. Provide a Supervisor password used for the Supervisor login (see Figure 9.4). Note, the place where the SYS: volume will begin is under the C:\SYSVOL directory on the NT Server volume.

5. Change the server name, if you wish. This can also be changed at a later time if desired (see Figure 9.4).

6. Specify a service password, as shown in Figure 9.5. When FPNW runs as a service under NT Server, it must logon like a user would. FPNW needs access to the file system and such. This is the password FPNW will use to

login to NT Server. If you look under User Manager after the install, you'll see the FPNW service account has been created.

After the install is complete, you can customize where the volume is exposed on the NT volume, as well as assign a shared NT printer to an exposed queue (see Figure 9.6). To customize FPNW, click the FPNW icon under Control Panel (see Figure 9.7). Control Panel can be accessed under the Start button.

FIGURE 9.4

Configuring the Supervisor password and exposed NT volume point

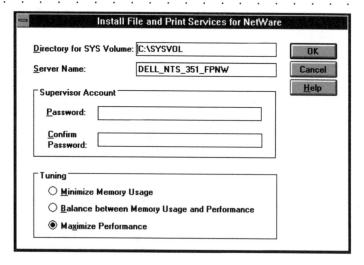

FIGURE 9.5

Entering the NT Service password used for FPNW

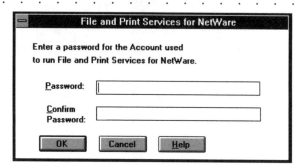

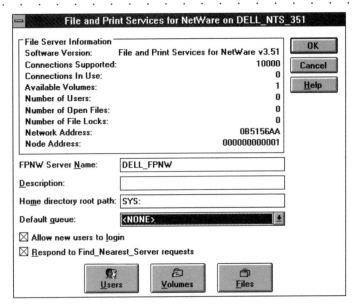

FIGURE 9.6

Renaming the FPNW server and assigning an NT Server as a queue

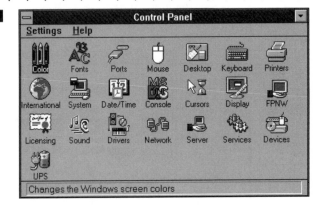

FIGURE 9.7

Configuring FPNW after installation

Using File and Print Services

Once installed, browse for the server name via Windows Explorer or use a command line utility to find and login to the FPNW server. You must define user names in the NT User Domain to login. These Domain user names can be mapped as NetWare account names, as well. The domain user name will then be seen as a Bindery user upon login.

If you do not also map a Domain user name as a NetWare name, the account can only be used for Domain logins. Mapping the Domain name as a NetWare name is accomplished through the User Manager utility on NT Server.

Mapping Drives

Microsoft provides a basic utility set (such as LOGON.EXE and MAP.EXE) for users who login to the FPNW server as their primary server. To MAP drives, use the standard MAP command or the Windows Explorer interface.

Using Printing Services

File and Print Services also enables NetWare users to CAPTURE (a NetWare command) to print queues exposed on the FPNW server. A printer on the NT Server is configured and designated as a shared print queue under FPNW. Once again, the client does not know the server is NT. You can use the standard methods to CAPTURE to the emulated NetWare queue (such as the CAPTURE command), as shown in Figure 9.8.

Managing File and Print Services under NDS

A slightly tricky way exists to manage an NT Server from within NWADMIN (the NDS graphical administration tool) by creating NDS objects and mapping them to the NDS server. Here are the steps to do this:

1. Create an NCP Server object in a container under the NDS tree. Name it the same as the File and Print (FPNW) Server (see Figure 9.9).

2. Create a Volume Object. Use the newly created server name as the host for the volume (see Figure 9.10).

3. You can see the volumes the FPNW server publishes once you have chosen the host server name created in Step 1 (see Figure 9.11).

4. Choose a Volume on the FPNW server you wish to manage.

5. Click the new server or volume object to manage it (see Figure 9.12).

► · ◄

"NET USE \\NTSERVER\HPLASER"

F I G U R E   9.8

A shared printer under NT Server can be mapped to a published NetWare queue name.

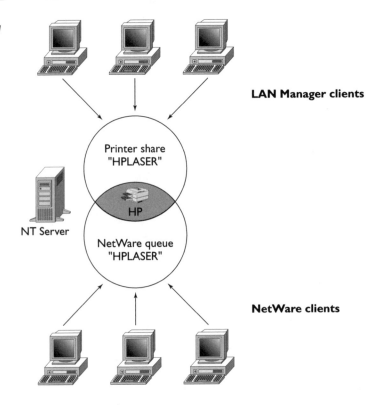

LAN Manager clients

NT Server

NetWare clients

"CAPTURE HPLASER"

FIGURE 9.9

You can create an NCP server object in the NDS tree that maps to the FPNW server.

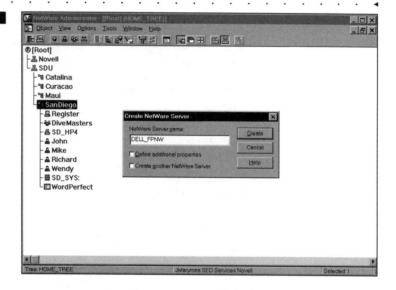

FIGURE 9.10

You can also create a volume object that references the newly created NCP server object.

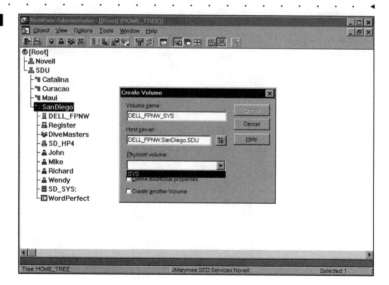

F I G U R E   9.11

Getting details on the NT shared volume that is now available

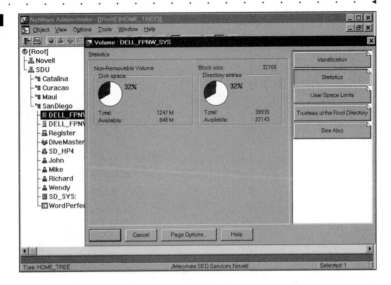

F I G U R E   9.12

You can also manage details on the FPNW server object.

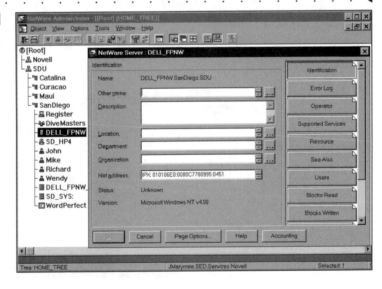

Your level of manageability will differ depending on whether you're using the VLM or Client 32 client (with the fix). Each time you want to manage the volume or server object, it will ask you to login first (because it is acting as a NetWare 3.*x* server).

Gateway Service for NetWare

Occasions will occur when you must have LAN Manager (NT) clients access resources on a NetWare server. This is especially useful when a migration (LAN Manager or NT Networking) to IntranetWare is taking place.

As we previously discussed, a large migration from LAN Manager or NT Server would warrant a staged migration because it's nearly impossible to change several thousand (or more) clients over to a new client in one night.

If you're more interested in Gateway Service from a purely integration perspective, be forewarned: Gateway Service is not designed to be a high-throughput solution. This is because *all* connections being serviced to the LAN Manager/NT Clients are coming through *one* connection going from the NT Server to the NetWare/IntranetWare server. This can be like trying to drink a milkshake through a coffee stir-stick: a lot of effort for little reward. But take heart! In smaller integration projects, this could be a workable solution.

One nice feature of Gateway Service is that it is included with NT Server 4.0 as an optionally installed service. To install Gateway Service, you need the original CD-ROM you used to install NT Server 4.0. Gateway Service is *not* included with NT Workstation.

When to Use Gateway Service

Typically, Gateway Service is used either as a migration tool or by workgroups where file and print services are handled by NetWare. Here are some examples where Gateway Service may make sense.

Migration from LAN Manager/NT Networking Environments

In this case, NT (Workstation or Server) may still provide the network services, but NetWare servers handle the main file and print services (no matter how hard we try, it seems most clients have to host two or more requesters, no matter what!). To access the NetWare server, therefore, the clients must have the newest requester installed.

NOTE

To use Novell Directory Services fully, the Novell client (VLM or Client32) should be installed. The Microsoft NDS client does not completely support the NDS specification. Consequently, using the Microsoft NDS client provides mixed results depending on what you're doing.

During the time when file and print access is still consumed using an SMB client, Gateway Service enables access to an installed NetWare server through the NT Server. This means newer clients can be installed on workstations as time permits, while still allowing the sharing of network resources.

Single Client Resource Sharing in the Workgroup

If your network follows the workgroup design, you may only have one or two file and print servers per workgroup. In addition, you may have one or more NT Servers hosting network services, such as database (SQL Server) or e-mail (GroupWise or Exchange, for example). In some cases, file and print services may be offloaded to an IntranetWare server (which may also run database or e-mail services!). If the workgroup is small enough, you could use Gateway Services as a solution to provide services from both servers, while only maintaining one file and print client (remember, you will probably need another requester for database or e-mail access). Figure 9.13 depicts such a solution. Remember, the Windows NT Server will do double-duty as a services platform and a gateway to NetWare services.

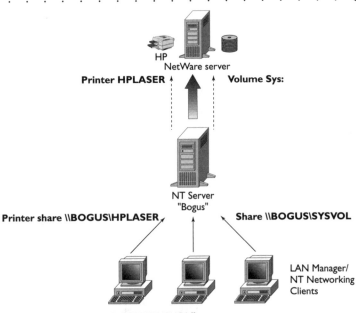

FIGURE 9.13

LAN Manager/NT Networking clients can access NetWare services through the Gateway Service.

To decrease the amount of client software needed at each workstation, supplying only *one* client at the desktop can be desirable. If you must provide services from Windows NT and NetWare, you typically need two clients. Using Gateway Services, File and Print from both operating systems can be provided from one SMB (LAN Manager/NT) client.

In either case, the benefit lies in the simplicity: only the NT Server acting as the gateway needs to have Gateway Services installed. The clients needn't be updated (unless you *are* performing a migration). The downside is limited performance due to translating NCP to SMB and vice versa (the job of the gateway).

Components to the Gateway Service

When you install NT Server, a variety of services can be installed. A few include

▸ FTP Service

▸ Domain Name Service (DNS)

▸ Dynamic Host Configuration Protocol (DHCP)

▸ Windows Internet Naming Service (WINS)

Once NT Server is installed, you can then choose to install the Gateway Service as another service option, like those previously mentioned. Gateway Service is actually two separate components:

▸ The Microsoft client for NetWare servers (this includes NDS client support for NetWare 4.*x*/5.*x*/NDS access)

▸ The Gateway Service that relies on the NetWare client

The Microsoft client software for NetWare is automatically installed when the gateway software is installed. This is a required component to talk to NetWare servers. When installing the Gateway Service, the client will be installed, followed by the Gateway Service itself. Note: Do *not* remove the NetWare client! If you remove it, the Gateway Service will cease to function.

Once installed, you can then configure the gateway to access the NetWare server and provide gateway access. This is *not* set up by default. A benefit to installing the Gateway Service is the Microsoft NDS client is installed on the NT Server. This enables basic client access to the NetWare server, even if you don't install the Gateway Service.

Installing the Gateway Service

Installing the Gateway Service is relatively easy. You'll need the NT Server or Back Office CD-ROM (disc one) to complete the installation.

The install at-a-glance entails these steps:

1. Under NWADMIN, create a group called NTGATEWAY.

2. Under NWADMIN create a user. This can be named anything, but usually you should make it descriptive, such as NTGATEUSER.

3. Ensure you create a password for the NTGATEUSER account.

4. Make the NTGATEUSER a member of the NTGATEWAY group.

5. Grant access rights to the NTGATEWAY group.

6. Install the Gateway Service under Services on the NT Server.

7. Select the Gateway option and enable it.

8. Create any Shares mapping you want to IntranetWare.

9. Create a normal printer under Control Panel, making it a network printer, but pointing it to an NetWare queue.

10. Enable sharing on the newly created NT Printer.

If you're somewhat familiar with NT installs, this should be fairly straightforward. If not, here's the play-by-play of what to do.

Create an **NTGATEWAY** User and **NTGATEWAY** Group

When the Gateway service is running on the NT Server, it actually logs into the IntranetWare server using the NDS client installed (automatically as part of the Gateway Service install) on the NT Server. It must do this to gain access, which it can then pass to LAN Manager clients in the form of Shares. This is also why you need to give access to the NTGATEWAY user account or NTGATEWAY group for this service to work properly. If the user or group does *not* have rights to the areas on the IntranetWare server you wish to share, LAN Manager users will be unable to see them.

NOTE

The reason for an NTGATEWAY group is unclear. The only clear thing *is* it MUST be created and named NTGATEWAY for Gateway Service to work. The user account can be named anything as long as it's a member of the NTGATEWAY group and specified in the configuration section of the gateway.

Install the Gateway Service on the NT Server or Servers

Installation of the Gateway Service and NetWare client is accomplished via the standard services install with Windows NT Workstation and Server.

1. Under the Network Neighborhood, you can right-click the mouse and choose Properties to install the Gateway Service. You can also go into the Control Panel from the START button and choose network/properties there.

2. Under the Services option, you can choose to add a service. Choose the Gateway Service for NetWare (see Figure 9.14).

3. After the install, you need to reboot.

4. After the reboot, NT will ask for user information to log in to the NetWare server. Use the user name, context, and password you created earlier (the NTGATEWAY user account), as shown in Figure 9.15.

FIGURE 9.14

*Selecting the Gateway/
NDS Client Service
when installing*

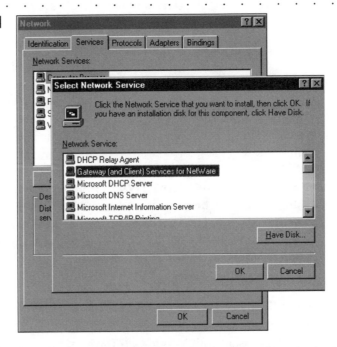

FIGURE 9.15

*Entering the NetWare
gateway account
information on reboot*

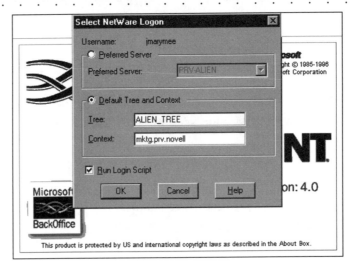

Configure the Gateway

At this point, you have the Microsoft NDS client installed and running, as well as the gateway, but you haven't shared anything yet. To do this:

1. Under Control Panel you'll now see a new option GSNW (Gateway Services for NetWare). Select it (see Figure 9.16).

2. Select the options you want (NDS context or NetWare 3.*x* server name, print options, and so on), as shown in Figure 9.17.

3. Select the Gateway button.

4. Click the Enable Gateway check box.

▶ · ◀

FIGURE 9.16

Configuring the Gateway Service under Control Panel

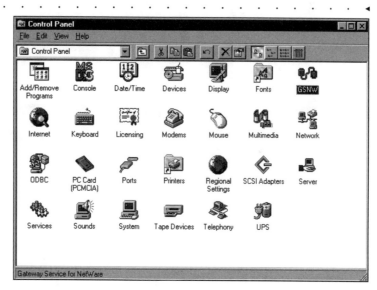

5. Put the account name you created into the Gateway Account box. Include the password (see Figure 9.18).

▶ · ◀

FIGURE 9.17

Entering Gateway Service required and optional information

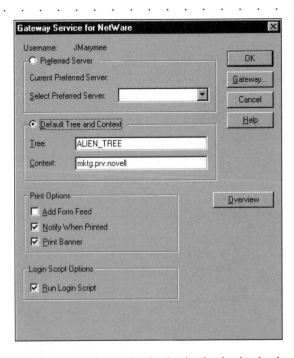

▶ · ◀

FIGURE 9.18

Setting up the Gateway account in NetWare

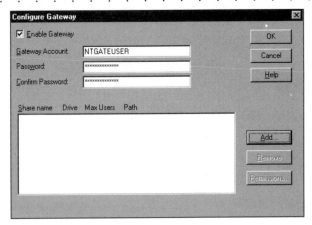

6. Choose Add to create a Shared Drive (see Figure 9.19).

7. Give the Share a name users will use to identify the resource. This name must be unique.

▶ • • • • • • • • • • • • • • • • • • • ◀

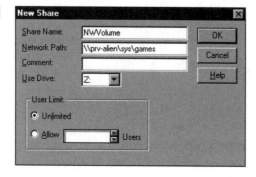

FIGURE 9.19

Entering the NT Share name to an NetWare path

8. Under Network Path, enter the server name and volume/path components of what you want to share on the NetWare server:

```
Example: "\\NWSERVER\SYS\GAMES"
```

9. Choose Permissions to change access for the LAN Manager/NT Networking clients (default is Everyone), as shown in Figure 9.20.

▶ • ◀

FIGURE 9.20

Setting additional permissions on the new Gateway Share

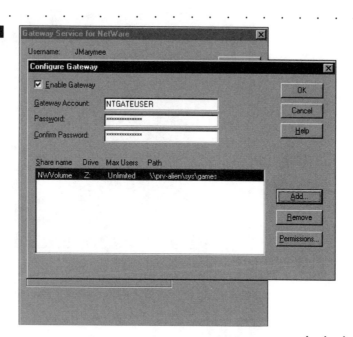

Once you complete these tasks, you can have LAN Manager clients NET USE or use the Network Neighborhood to attach to these shares and use them. That the server is actually NetWare is totally transparent. To use the share, a client will specify the NT Server name and the share name to access the NetWare server via a LAN Manager client.

Example: NET USE G: "\\NTSERVER\NWSHARENAME"

Create Printer Shares

This assumes you already have printer queues setup on the NetWare server. If you haven't yet, consult the online NetWare Documentation to do so. Once this is complete, return to the NT Server and complete these steps:

1. Under Control Panel, choose Printers.

2. Choose Add Printer (see Figure 9.21).

FIGURE 9.21

Creating a NetWare queue as a share

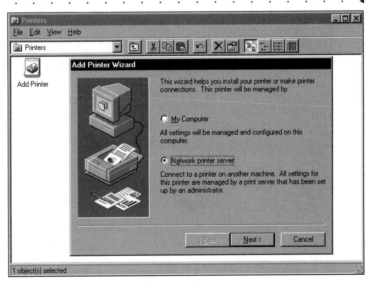

3. Select the Network Printer Server radio button (see Figure 9.21).

4. Browse the network to find the NetWare print queue desired. Note, both NT shared printers and NetWare shared queues can be seen from the same browser (see Figure 9.22).

5. Complete the remaining questions to install the print driver.

6. Once the install is complete, right-click the new printer icon and choose Sharing (see Figure 9.23).

7. Create a share name for the shared printer. Follow the normal rights assignments for shared NT printers as you would for an NT Server shared printer (see Figure 9.24).

FIGURE 9.22

Browsing NetWare queues to create an NT printer

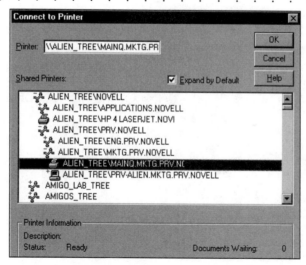

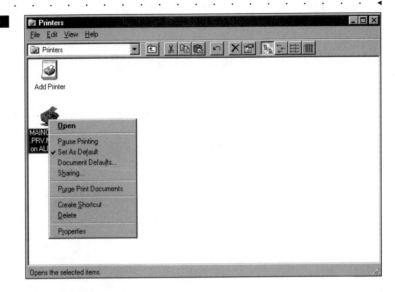

F I G U R E   9.23

*Enabling sharing of
the new NT printer
(NetWare queue)*

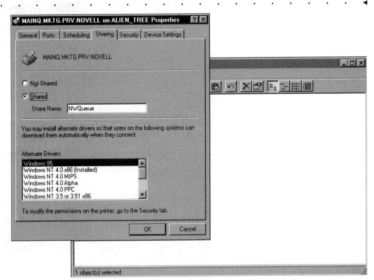

F I G U R E   9.24

*Giving the NT printer
a share name and
setting security*

Once complete, users can print to the shared device using its share name. If the
workstation is part of a Domain, you can browse and find the shared device (see
Figure 9.25). By clicking it, you can then attach and print to it. The print jobs will
be routed to the mapped queue and serviced by a NetWare print server. Users can

also get job information by clicking the printer icon in the *Printers* folder under Control Panel. As far as the user sees, it is only another NT Network-shared printer.

Administrators can also assign rights to the NT Networking/LAN Manager clients. This enables control to remain with the NT Administrator, even though the device is hosted on NetWare.

Using Gateway Services for NetWare

Now that Gateway Services has been installed, how to use it? Several tips will make Gateway Services the most effective when mapping resources:

F I G U R E   9.25

*Browsing the new
share under
Network Neighborhood*

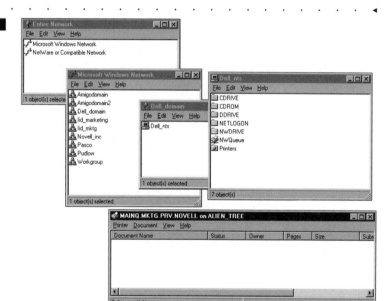

▶ If you're part of a Domain and using Windows 95/98, ensure that a Domain name has been selected under Network Properties. If not, you will *not* see these new gateway shares under the Network Neighborhood.

▶ If you are *not* part of a Domain and using Windows 95/98, you must know the names of the shares you wish to use. The browser (Network Neighborhood) will *not* show them, even if you are logged into the Domain under which they are hosted.

▸ Limit the amount of clients who use the shares pointing to NetWare. Remember, ALL the clients accessing the NetWare through the NT Server are doing so through ONE network connection.

▸ Ensure the Gateway account (NTGATEWAY) and/or the Gateway user have sufficient rights. If they do not, the users mapping to the share may not have enough rights, even though they have full control access to the share.

Summary

When it comes to creating useful junction points between NetWare and NT, some useful options exist. As we have shown, creating a perfectly flawless integration between the two can be reasonably difficult, but it is possible and it can yield some significant benefits.

As NT integration evolves, we will probably have even tighter integration between the two, especially in the area of services integration and NDS. This is clearly the case with NDS for NT. Let's see how some of these integration options broaden the integration horizon.

CHAPTER 10

Managing NT Workstations Through NDS: Z.E.N.works

When Novell first released NDS, it really only served one purpose — the management of NetWare file and print services. However, over the years, NDS has been extended far beyond the file server. NDS-enabled products greatly simplify management of all kinds of systems, from directory-enabled network devices such as routers, switches, firewalls, and printers, to applications, desktops, and other operating systems. The final result? By creating a user just one time in NDS, that user is enabled for a myriad of applications, services, and devices.

This chapter focuses on an extremely valuable NDS-enabled solution, known as Novell's Z.E.N.works. While some claim that Z.E.N.works is an acronym for "zero effort networking," everyone agrees that Z.E.N.works greatly reduces workstation management and application deployment.

What Is Z.E.N.works?

Z.E.N.works is actually a collection of several previous Novell technologies, combined to create an integrated solution. Z.E.N.works consists of three main areas:

▸ *Workstation Management.* Previously known as the NT Workstation Manager, Z.E.N.works can manage almost every component of both Windows NT and Windows 95/98 desktops. Workstation configuration, such as policies, profiles, printers, and workstation security, are all stored as objects within NDS and applied using standard NDS rules and inheritance.

▸ *Application Deployment.* Previously known as NetWare Application Launcher (NAL), Z.E.N.works can intelligently deploy applications through NDS. Unlike other software distribution products, Z.E.N.works can configure an application based on NDS information, customizing the application with NDS data. Z.E.N.works also leverages the distributed nature of NDS to deliver the same desktop configuration regardless of where the user logs in. Any application's usage can be controlled through NDS-enabled software licensing and software metering.

▸ *IT Helpdesk.* With Z.E.N.works' help-desk integration, an administrator can place a "panic button" on every user's desktop that is intelligently linked (through NDS) to that user's network administrator. Z.E.N.works also provides hardware inventory stored in NDS and a secure remote control that allows administrators to remotely manage and repair users' desktops.

▸ *GMT Software's Check2000.* Z.E.N.works includes a 5-user version of GMT Software's Check2000 client, a Y2K diagnostic utility. Check2000 has been integrated with NDS to simplify the information-gathering process. As a result, an administrator can use Z.E.N.works to check workstation hardware, software, and application data for Y2K problems.

Many of these concepts, such as software distribution and remote control, are not new technologies. Z.E.N.works has directory-enabled these technologies, blending the benefits of the directory with proven technologies. Although we'll focus on the Z.E.N.works features that simplify managing Windows NT workstations, most Z.E.N.works features also apply to Windows 95/98 and even Windows 3.1 desktops as well!

All of these Z.E.N.works features are provided in two different packages:

▸ Z.E.N.works includes everything mentioned above. Z.E.N.works is priced on a per-managed-user basis.

▸ Z.E.N.works Lite includes everything *but* hardware inventory, remote control, help-desk integration, software licensing, and software metering. Z.E.N.works Lite is "free" — that is, it is included with NetWare 5 at no additional cost.

There's a lot of material to cover here, so we've split this chapter into three main topics: installing Z.E.N.works, Z.E.N.works workstation management, and Z.E.N.works application deployment.

Installing Z.E.N.works

Z.E.N.works consists of three major components: extensions to the Novell desktop client, NDS schema extensions for Z.E.N.works objects, and a set of NWAdmin snap-ins for managing Z.E.N.works features.

All current Novell client software includes the necessary Z.E.N.works client components. Therefore, use either the client software included on the Z.E.N.works CD-ROM or download the latest client from www.novell.com.

Installing Z.E.N.works Server-side Components

Z.E.N.works isn't just a single technology; rather, it's a collection of several technologies compiled into a single solution. The version you choose (Z.E.N.works full version or Z.E.N.works Lite) determines which components are available for installation. Figure 10.1 shows these components, including:

- ▸ *Z.E.N.works 1.1.* This is the actual Z.E.N.works core software provided by Novell. It includes workstation management, software distribution, remote control, and hardware inventory.

- ▸ *Z.E.N.works Software Metering.* This new feature of Z.E.N.works provides the capability to use NDS as a software licensing/software metering system. Note that you must have either NetWare 5 or the latest service pack for NetWare 4.11.

- ▸ *Third-party products.* Z.E.N.works-enabled products, such as GMT's Check2000 Y2K diagnostic utility, are found here.

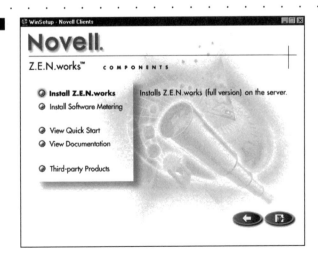

FIGURE 10.1

Additional Z.E.N.works-enabled products may be installed after you install Z.E.N.works.

Be sure to install Z.E.N.works before adding more features such as software metering and Check2000.

You may choose which components of Z.E.N.works to install, depending on your environment (see Figure 10.2):

▸ *Application Management.* Previously known as NAL, Application Management provides distribution of any software to the client's desktop. This feature also allows customization of the application package with NDS information.

▸ *Workstation Maintenance.* Remote control, hardware inventory, and help-desk integration features.

▸ *Desktop Management.* NDS-enabled workstation policies and profiles.

▸ *NWAdmin32.* The latest version of NWAdmin. No need to install onto NetWare 5 servers (it is already included), but required for NetWare 4.1*x* servers.

▸ *Copy Clients To Network.* Useful if outdated clients must be upgraded to a Z.E.N.works-enabled client, but it does consume quite a bit of server disk space.

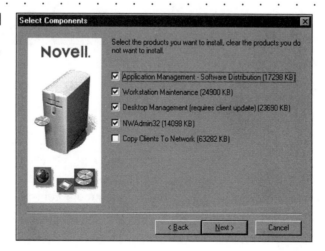

FIGURE 10.2

Choose which Z.E.N.works components will be installed on the server.

Z.E.N.works must extend the NDS schema during the first installation. If you're the first person to install Z.E.N.works into the NDS tree, you must have *write* rights to the [ROOT] of the NDS tree. The NDS schema is extended only during the first installation of Z.E.N.works. A subsequent installation of Z.E.N.works does not require extending the schema.

Finally, if you're planning on storing workstation information in NDS (a key feature of Z.E.N.works!), the NDS tree must be configured so that workstations can "register" their object within NDS. NDS, by default, doesn't give *anyone* write access to the NDS database. However, a workstation must somehow write its information into NDS. This is accomplished by giving [PUBLIC] write rights to a selected property on organizational unit objects (see Figure 10.3). The net effect? Workstations can register their object in NDS (more on this later).

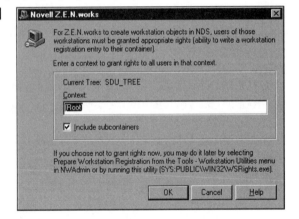

FIGURE 10.3

The NDS tree must be configured so that workstations may register their object in NDS.

Installing Z.E.N.works Client-side Components

Now that the server is Z.E.N.works-ready, it's time to update the clients. The Z.E.N.works client installation features can be added during the initial client install or after the client has been installed. (See Chapter 5 for more details on workstation clients.) The Z.E.N.works client installation offers Typical and Custom installation package choices, as shown in Figure 10.4. The Typical installation installs all necessary Z.E.N.works components *except* remote control features. The Custom installation package prompts the installer for more information, but allows customization of the various client features (see Figure 10.5).

FIGURE 10.4

Choosing Typical installs the most common Z.E.N.works features. Choose Custom if you require the Z.E.N.works secure remote control capability.

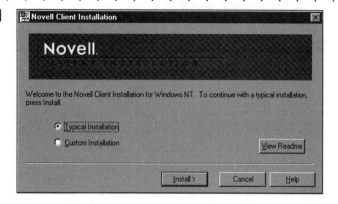

FIGURE 10.5

Choosing Custom allows a wider variety of client installation options.

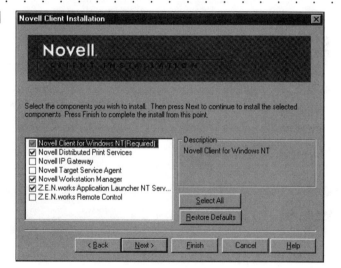

Z.E.N.works Workstation Management

As previously mentioned, Z.E.N.works isn't necessarily new technology—just an NDS-enabling of existing technology. NT Workstation provides key workstation management features, such as profiles and policies, that are difficult to use in a network environment. Z.E.N.works simply integrates these features into the directory, greatly simplifying desktop management and integration.

Z.E.N.works Policy Packages

Z.E.N.works uses the concept of "policy packages" for managing the desktop. A policy package is a collection of configuration information. For example, a package may consist of printer configurations and drivers, a desktop background bit map, and client configuration settings. Packages are divided by *users* and *computers*:

▸ *User Policy Packages.* User packages follow the person as he or she moves from computer to computer. For example, a user package could ensure that the user always has proper printer configuration (and drivers), regardless of which machine the user accesses.

▸ *Computer Policy Packages.* Computer packages remain with a computer or groups of computers, regardless of who logs into the computer. For example, a computer package may restrict desktop access for a computer placed in a non-secure area (such as a lobby or kiosk).

Packages are also defined by operating system. In other words, since there's quite a bit of feature variation between Windows 3.1, Windows 95/98, and Windows NT Workstations, the Z.E.N.works policy packages must reflect these differences, as shown in Figure 10.6.

▸ · ◂

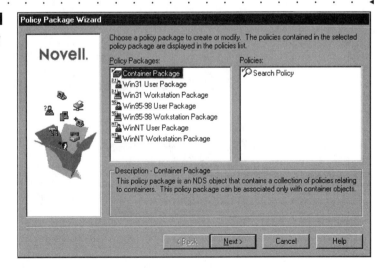

F I G U R E   10.6

Policy packages are defined both by type (user or computer) and by operating system.

Applying Policy Packages

Once a policy package is defined, it must be associated with NDS objects to impact desktops:

▶ *User Policy Packages.* User policy packages can be associated to one or more users, groups of users, and containers (such as NDS organizational units).

▶ *Workstation Policy Packages.* Workstation policy packages can be associated to one or more workstations, groups of workstations, and containers (such as NDS organizational units).

Z.E.N.works searches all appropriate objects for policy and applies the cumulative policy to the user or computer object. Special policy packages, called container search policy packages, specify how policy is applied. For example, the default container policy package first applies object policy (user or workstation), then group policy (groups of users or groups of workstations), and then container policy.

Using Z.E.N.works User Policies

So, now that we've spent a bit of time reviewing how Z.E.N.works policies are created and defined, how can they be used to integrate NT Workstations into an NDS environment? Let's take a closer look by starting with user-specific policies (see Figure 10.7).

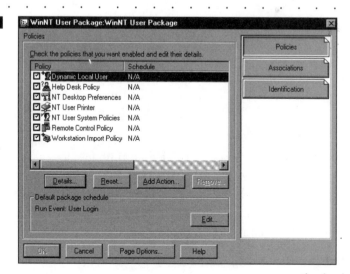

FIGURE 10.7

The Z.E.N.works user policies manage the user's desktop environment regardless of where they log in to the network.

Dynamic Local User   NT Workstation is a secure desktop. Before users can access the desktop's resources, they must authenticate to the local NT workstation. In a pure NT environment, there are essentially two ways to accomplish this task:

► *Create the user locally.* Using User Manager, create the user in the local workstation's SAM database. While this is fine for a single user or single machine, a network introduces much greater complexities. For example, if 500 users must be able to access 500 different machines, the administrator must create (500 users × 500 accounts =) 250,000 accounts! Now try to keep these passwords synchronized!

► *Create an NT Domain.* Install an NT Server. Create all the users in the NT domain, and add all the workstations to the domain. Users then authenticate to the domain, and "pass through" to use the local workstation's resources.

Novell was approached by many customers asking for a third alternative. Customers wanted the advantages of the secure NT desktop without the need to deploy NT domains, which are difficult to design, deploy, and manage. Hence, Novell's Workstation Manager (now part of Z.E.N.works) was born!

The dynamic local user settings work as follows (see Figure 10.8). If a user is a valid NDS user, dynamically create the user in the local SAM database on the workstation, and make the user a member of the listed workstation groups. When the user is finished with the workstation, either delete the account (Volatile User) or keep the user's account in anticipation that the user will log on to this workstation again (Manage existing NT account). If the user saves files to the local workstation's hard drive, it's probably a good idea to make the account permanent (non-volatile) and enable Manage existing NT account. If, on the other hand, all user files are stored on the file server, it's probably a good idea to remove the user's account after login (Volatile User), which keeps the workstation's SAM database free from clutter.

NT Desktop Preferences   NT Desktop preferences allow customization of the desktop interface (see Figure 10.9). For example, an administrator could configure a background bitmap by selecting the Display icon, or reverse the left and right mouse buttons for a group of NDS users called "lefties." The NT Desktop Preferences also control how profiles are handled in a network environment.

Dynamic local user settings affect how a user's account is created and maintained on NT Workstations.

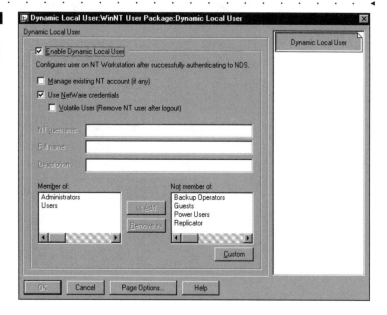

NT Desktop Preferences allow customization of the NT desktop interface through Z.E.N.works policies.

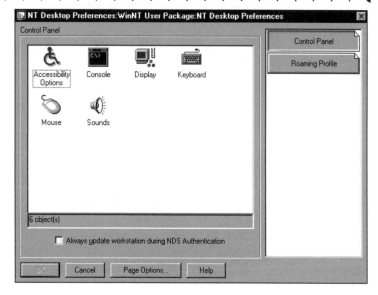

NT User System Policies   Aha! You're about to discover one of the neatest features of Z.E.N.works workstation management. NT Workstations (and Windows 95/98, to a lesser degree) can be controlled through desktop policies. NT Workstation policies are normally configured with the Microsoft POLEDIT utility. Z.E.N.works simply NDS-enables POLEDIT, as shown in Figure 10.10. Here's just a *brief* sampling of what an administrator can do with Z.E.N.works user system policies:

▸ Restrict users from editing the local workstation registry (no more registry security holes!)

▸ Restrict users from Control Panel (no more accidentally deleted LAN cards!)

▸ Hide local drives in My Computer (no more accidental shares!)

Keep in mind that these policies can be given to an individual user, groups of users, or an entire NDS container structure. This allows an administrator to apply multiple desktop policies to a wide range of users within the NDS tree.

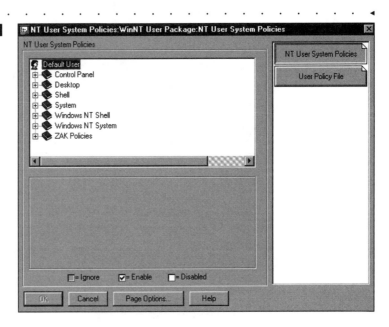

F I G U R E   10.10

NT User System Policies set desktop restrictions that follow users wherever they log in.

NT User Printer   Z.E.N.works policies can also define printing configuration. By creating an NT User Printer policy, both the desktop printer object *and* the printer driver can be installed on the user's desktop. Here's a great example of how this technology could be used:

1. Create a Z.E.N.works policy for the Accounting group.

2. Define the NT User Printer settings for the accounting department's check printer. Configure the printer to appear on the desktop, along with the special driver required to print checks.

When anyone from the Accounting group logs into *any* NT workstation on the network, the printer appears on the user's desktop along with the proper printer driver!

Remote Control Policy (Z.E.N.works full product only)   Z.E.N.works didn't invent remote control — it just makes remote control better by integrating with the directory. Remote control software packages, in general, have two major limitations:

1. Advertising remote control capability — How does a workstation advertise that it's capable of being remotely controlled? Most remote control agents will broadcast their presence to the network. Broadcasts are generally bad in medium-to-large environments. Broadcasting not only increases network traffic, but many larger networks also filter broadcasts between routers.

2. Remote control security — Most remote control agents use a single password for all desktops. If someone should happen to find that password, the administrator must visit every desktop to change the password.

With Z.E.N.works remote control, workstations do not broadcast that they are capable of being remotely controlled. Rather, the directory is used to locate workstations that can be remotely controlled. NDS also manages remote-control session rights. Before a workstation can be remotely controlled, NDS checks the workstation, logged-in user, and administrator's rights to determine whether the administrator has sufficient rights to remote-control both the user and the workstation.

Workstation Import Policy Many Z.E.N.works features such as remote control, hardware inventory, and the Check2000 Y2K diagnostic utility require a workstation object in NDS to function properly. The Workstation Import Policy, as shown in Figure 10.11, determines where workstation objects will be created in NDS, how the objects will be named, and whether or not the workstation will be added to any workstation groups.

Note that the workstation really can't create its own object. If it could, you'd have a *major* NDS security hole, because then anyone could create objects within the NDS tree. The Z.E.N.works workstation import policy simply creates a "hint" in NDS that a workstation would like to register in NDS. To create the workstation object, an administrator (or someone with sufficient NDS rights) must use a special tool launched from the NWAdmin Tools menu to import workstations (see Figure 10.12). This scans NDS for any new workstations and creates the workstation object in the correct NDS location (see Figure 10.13).

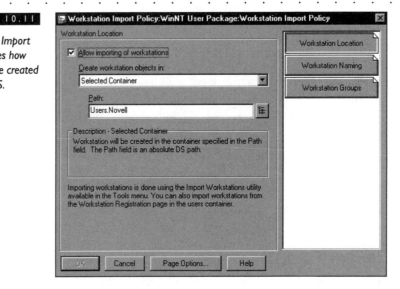

FIGURE 10.11

The Workstation Import Policy determines how workstations will be created within NDS.

You can also import workstations by running the WSIMPORT.EXE program found in the SYS:\PUBLIC\Win32 directory.

TIP

▶ • ◀

FIGURE 10.12

When you launch the Import Workstation command from the NWAdmin Tools menu, NDS is searched for any new, unregistered workstations.

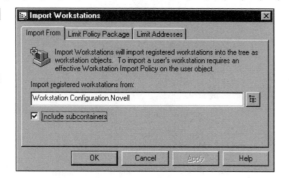

Help Desk Policy (Z.E.N.works full product only) Z.E.N.works also provides a limited help-desk capability. A Z.E.N.works help-desk policy determines whether users can launch help-desk tickets (through GroupWise or a standard MAPI mail-client), and if so, who should receive their help desk requests. By associating these help-desk policies with NDS objects, such as groups and containers, it's easy to establish location-based or task-based help systems. For example, a help-desk policy could be called "New York." By using a Z.E.N.works help-desk policy, users in New York would be referred to their local IS professional instead of an international help-desk agent.

▶ • ◀

FIGURE 10.13

In this example, three new workstations were found, but only one was added to NDS.

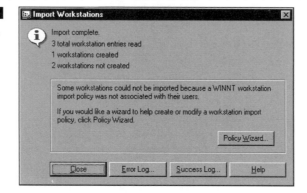

Using Z.E.N.works Workstation Policies

Z.E.N.works understands that users and computers are different. As such, Z.E.N.works tracks user and computer policies differently. This enables Z.E.N.works to apply user policies anywhere a user authenticates to the network, or computer policies regardless of who is logged into the computer. Let's take a close look at Z.E.N.works computer-specific policies (see Figure 10.14).

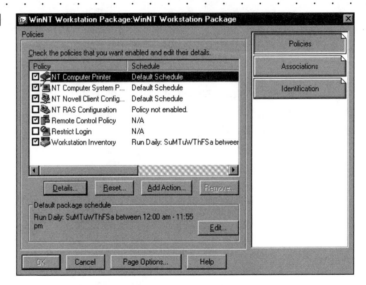

F I G U R E 1 0 . 1 4

Z.E.N.works also maintains workstation-specific policies.

NT Computer Printer   The NT Computer Printer policy settings are identical to the User printer policy settings, except that they are specific to a particular workstation or group of workstations. For example, consider a lab environment where many users share a common computer, but want to print to a printer at the end of the aisle. With the NT computer printer policy, a printer is automatically configured, complete with printer driver, regardless of who logs into the machine.

NT Novell Client Configuration   Have you ever needed to update the Novell client settings on 1,000 workstations? Rather than visiting each desktop individually, or using an ACU script, the NT Novell Client configuration policy allows mass workstation client configuration (see Figure 10.15). Any client configuration change would affect all workstations where this policy is applied.

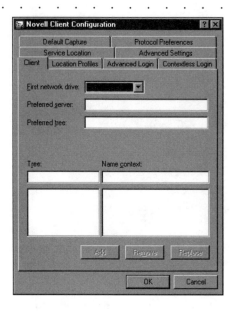

The NT Client Configuration enables an administrator to remotely update any NT client configuration through simple Z.E.N.works policies.

NT Computer System Policies   The NT Computer System policies are similar to the NT User System policies, except that they apply to computer-specific settings rather than user-specific settings. Just as Microsoft's POLEDIT has user and computer configurations, so does Z.E.N.works. Computer system policies are used to configure SNMP traps, customize shared folders and start menus, and so forth.

NT RAS Configuration   Z.E.N.works can automatically update the local workstation's dial-up networking configuration if dial-up networking is installed. While this may not apply to most corporate desktops (who brings their entire PC home for the night?), it's a great tool for remote users. For example, you can create an NT RAS configuration for the "New York" container that configures dial-up networking with the local New York telephone number.

NT Remote Control Policy (Z.E.N.works full product only)   Z.E.N.works differentiates remote control settings for users and computers. This enables network administrators to define certain computers that may *never* be remote-controlled regardless of who is currently logged into the machine. The NT remote control policy also provides a choice of protocol for remote control (either IP or IPX). (See Figure 10.16.)

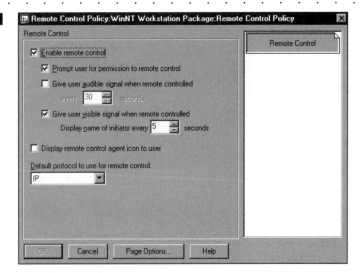

F I G U R E 10.16

Remote Control settings can be applied to either the user or the computer. Note that only the Workstation Remote Control settings allow you to specify the preferred protocol (IP or IPX).

Use IP for Z.E.N.works remote control. It's faster!

TIP

Restrict Login Because every workstation is an object in the directory, Z.E.N.works can manage who can access your NT workstations through the Restrict Login feature. To enable this feature, add user, group, and organizational units to either the permit or deny list (see Figure 10.17). Note that this workstation policy can apply to a single workstation or a group of workstations.

Hardware Inventory (Z.E.N.works full product only) If every workstation is an object in the directory, why not keep the NDS workstation objects updated with hardware information? Z.E.N.works can read every workstation's hardware configuration and upload this information into NDS. The result? When diagnosing a user problem, an administrator can simply look at the user's workstation object in NDS to get a better understanding of the user's hardware and software configuration.

FIGURE 10.17

The Z.E.N.works Restrict Login feature enables NDS to manage NT workstation access.

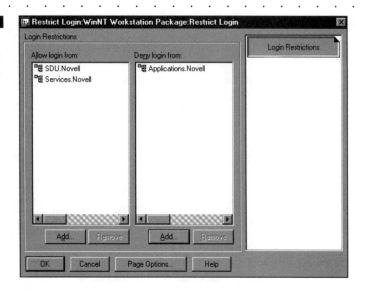

The Workstation Object

All the Z.E.N.works user and workstation policies combine to result in a highly manageable system that leverages NDS. By storing both user and workstation configuration information in NDS, Z.E.N.works can deliver a highly tuned desktop for a particular user, group of users, groups of machines, location, division, or entire company.

One obvious Z.E.N.works benefit is that users can have their optimal working environment regardless of where they log in to the network. However, Z.E.N.works is more than just a one-way, user configuration management product. With Z.E.N.works, a two-way relationship is established between the workstation objects and the directory. The result is that workstations actually update the directory with important information.

Consider the workstation object in Figure 10.18. The Z.E.N.works import policy specified that the workstation be named by its NT computer name plus its IP address. Therefore, the object in NDS is called MICRONNT WKS137_ 65_215_252. Choosing Effective Policies (see Figure 10.19) quickly displays all Z.E.N.works policies that affect this particular workstation. Also, by selecting User History, an administrator can quickly determine who has used this machine (see Figure 10.20).

FIGURE 10.18

A Z.E.N.works workstation tracks information about usage, hardware, and effective policies.

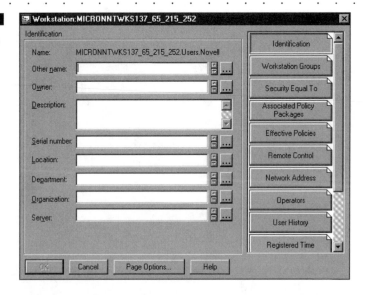

FIGURE 10.19

By selecting Effective Policies, an administrator can determine which Z.E.N.works policies apply to this workstation.

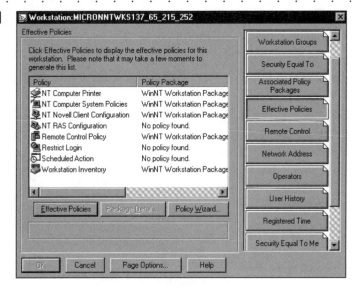

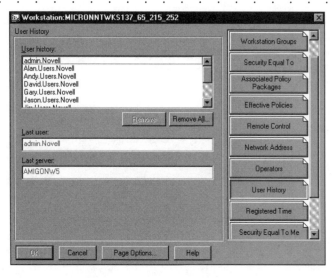

F I G U R E   10.20

The User History tab displays all users who have used this workstation.

Selecting the Hardware Information tab enables an administrator to quickly determine CPU type, memory information, and operating system information (see Figure 10.21). If more details are required, simply click View Advanced Information (see Figure 10.22) to see detailed information about services, IRQs, DMA, display adapters, and so forth.

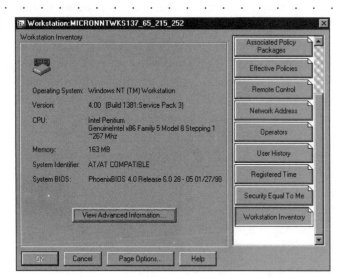

F I G U R E   10.21

Basic hardware information is displayed on the Workstation Inventory tab.

F I G U R E   10.22

*Advanced Workstation
Inventory displays detailed
workstation hardware
information.*

Exporting Hardware Information   What if your boss asked you "How many workstations are running NT Service Pack 3?" or "How many machines have CD-ROMs?" With Z.E.N.works, all the necessary hardware and software information is in NDS, though you probably don't want to examine each individual workstation object. Don't worry—Z.E.N.works can export all workstation inventory information to a standard, tab-delimited file. Simply choose an NDS container at the top level of your tree, and select the Workstation Inventory Extract option (see Figure 10.23).

Z.E.N.works has directory-enabled many common desktop technologies, such as remote control, NT policies, NT profiles, and hardware inventory. By using the various Z.E.N.works technologies, an entire desktop configuration can be defined in the directory and applied to users, groups, workstations, and even entire corporations, based on standard NDS rules. The result is a directory-integrated solution that significantly reduces the costs of managing NT Workstations and users on an individual basis.

But that's just barely one half of Z.E.N.works. . . .

F I G U R E   1 0 . 2 3

Z.E.N.works includes utilities for exporting workstation inventory information.

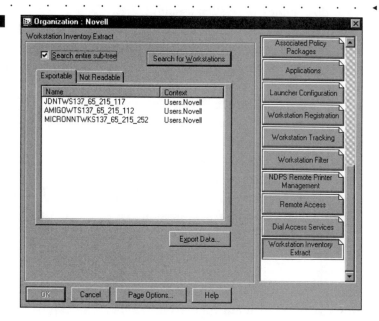

Z.E.N.works Application Distribution

Z.E.N.works enables users to run applications whose definitions (Application Object Templates) are stored in the NDS tree. Z.E.N.works automatically displays the icon of any application if the user meets the administrator's predefined workstation prerequisites, and if the administrator has given permission for that user to run that particular application. At launch time, Z.E.N.works dynamically connects to all required resources (such as network drives, printers, and so on), pushes down any components that must be at the workstation, updates any registry settings, and generally does whatever is necessary to get that application to run.

Network administrators do many things as part of their network management job: They perform simple, mundane tasks such as replacing printer toner cartridges and paper, chasing down lost print jobs, and resetting user passwords.

They do complex work such as adding new users, deleting terminated users, and shuffling potentially thousands of permissions to respond to a reorganization. Then they do the really awful stuff, such as manually deploying workstation operating system upgrades, patches, and new applications to entire divisions or possibly even the entire company.

It isn't that this work itself is inherently uninteresting, but it *is* highly repetitive, slow-going, and complex — and you must concentrate hard because the work is prone to errors. If *any* time or budget is left, administrators must scour the weekly periodicals to keep up with the blinding changes in technology, because they rarely, if ever, receive formal training.

As a fully distributed and replicated directory service, NDS solves the complex work by enabling entire reorganizations to be accomplished through a single drag-and-drop operation. All permissions that should be lost because a user is no longer in the old area, plus all permissions that should be gained because the user is in the new area are recalculated automatically through a process called *inheritance,* which is automatic, immediate, and maintenance-free. NDS was a great break-through; it freed administrators' time so they could work on many other overdue tasks. It also made the network more secure and reliable, because manually processing a reorganization involved potentially thousands of changes in permissions — all of them subject to failure, since humans can make mistakes.

But what about the most time-consuming, error-prone tasks? These tasks are dauntingly expensive. Imagine one of the simpler ones: Place a new Web browser on 10,000 workstations, configure it for security and proxy, and predefine several bookmarks. You could possibly do this automatically, if all the workstations were fairly similar and every user in an area needed the same customizations. Now let's make this more realistic: Not all users get the new application, users are running multiple versions of the operating system, the application does not have the capability to install in an unattended mode, users like to customize their desktop and have it follow them, and the application requires certain support files to run (which, of course, are not on *every* machine). Yet, a user should be able to sit at any workstation and have *all* applications run flawlessly.

That's quite a set of requirements. And this is an example of a *simple* application deployment project. You'll agree this will be an expensive undertaking. Let's try to put a price on it.

Application Deployment Example

You're good — really good. So good that you can instantly teleport to any location within your company for free. This enables you to eliminate any traveling costs. You also are perfect. You can install applications over and over again without a single mistake.

However, each machine still takes 30 minutes to install, configure, and test the application, not counting the time for the machine to boot *twice* — once for the initial boot-up when you arrive, and again at the end of the product install. Figure half an hour multiplied by 10,000 workstations, for a total of 5,000 hours (or 2.5 work years). Bad news: even if you start now, you can't finish in time to start the year 2000 bug project (maybe you'd better skip lunch).

Assuming your fully burdened salary is $75,000 per year (when is your boss going to give you that raise?), the project would cost nearly $185,000. But what is the employee doing while you're staring blindly at the screen, waiting for this product to install? Probably nothing. So, you'd better add in the employee's time to the cost of installation. Let's assume the employee makes the same amount of money as you do (which is terribly unfair). This would double the cost to $370,000, plus the cost of the actual software.

What's the alternative? If you used Z.E.N.works, you could create an Application Object Template (AOT) for each operating system you wanted to support, copy the AOT information to major sites within your corporation to speed product installation, and use inheritance and groups to grant permission. Then you could have Z.E.N.works automatically install the application when the user logs in (or selects the icon — the choice is yours). You can even spread out the installation automatically over a week to avoid overloading the network. This should take approximately three to five days. This represents a huge savings of 5,000 hours, divided by 40 hours (five days), which equals 1,250, or three orders of magnitude.

Z.E.N.works Application Distribution

Are you convinced that you need Z.E.N.works ? Are you interested in hearing more about how Z.E.N.works can distribute your applications to your users' desktops? Please read on.

Z.E.N.works application distribution consists of three components:

- *NDS schema extension.* Z.E.N.works defines new NDS objects that represent applications. Z.E.N.works also provides the necessary snap-ins for managing applications within NWAdmin.

- *Application object creator.* Z.E.N.works provides a utility (snAppShot) for automatically creating NDS application objects.

- *Desktop application launcher.* A small desktop application that accesses NDS to determine which applications should be visible on the user's desktop.

How does Z.E.N.works application distribution work, in a nutshell?

1. The administrator creates an application object in NDS that represents a particular application. The administrator can either manually configure all application settings (such as registry settings, .INI file parameters, and so on) or use the snAppShot utility to automatically configure application settings.

2. The administrator associates the application object to a user, group, or organizational unit.

3. The client workstation periodically checks NDS to determine which applications to display on the user's desktop. The workstation checks the user's individual object, the user's group membership, and all parent OUs above the user. All applications are displayed on the user's desktop.

That's the "nutshell" version. However, we omitted some features—such as fault tolerance, dynamic load balancing, application scheduling, force run, application foldering, launch nearest, and automatic assignment of file rights. Z.E.N.works application distribution can be either a very simple install or a highly tuned install, depending on an organization's needs.

Creating the NDS Application Object

You're tasked with deploying Office 97 to 5,000 NT Workstations. You know that Z.E.N.works can do the job, but were you aware that there are over 3,500 registry settings for Office 97? How in the world are you going to get these correct?

Never fear — the engineers at Novell have included a nifty utility that monitors any application installation. snAppShot carefully monitors a workstation as an application is installed and configured. When the application installation is finished, snAppShot creates a file with all the necessary installation information (see Figure 10.24).

Here's how to use snAppShot:

1. Start with a generic workstation that's representative of the workstations that will receive this application.

2. Start snAppShot (SYS:\PUBLIC\SNAPSHOT\SNAPSHOT.EXE). snAppShot will examine all computer files, registry settings, .INI files, and so on, to set a "baseline" workstation configuration *before* the application is installed.

3. Install the application(s). Customize the application as necessary.

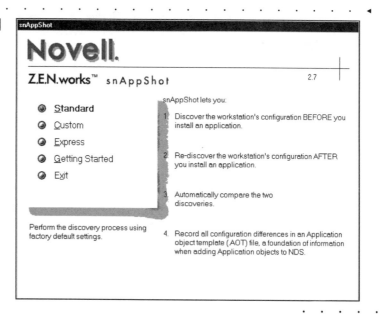

snAppShot monitors an application installation for distribution with Z.E.N.works.

4. When the application is completely installed and configured, restart snAppShot. snAppShot discovers all changes that occurred during the application installation, and saves these changes to an .AOT file.

5. You may now use the .AOT file to create application objects in NDS for this particular application.

Wait a minute! When you created the snAppShot, you were logged in as Fred. Some application settings, such as e-mail address and user name, were tailored to Fred and do *not* apply to the general user population — but if you distribute this application to your users, everyone's e-mail address will be Fred!

NDS Mass Customization   Z.E.N.works provides a very clever way around this problem. After taking the snAppShot, the software distribution can be customized with NDS data. For example, using the Search and Replace feature from the NWAdmin Toolbar, it's possible to search the application object for all instances of Fred and replace them with an NDS macro, %CN% (see Figure 10.25). The result? When the user Gary uses Z.E.N.works to install this application on his desktop, "Gary" will be placed in all locations instead of "Fred." The same goes for every user on the network.

▶ · ◀

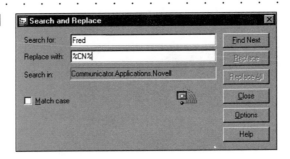

F I G U R E   10.25

NDS macro substitutions facilitate application customization with the user's NDS data.

Check out www.novell.com/coolsolutions/zenworks**! It has all the latest information on Z.E.N.works, with in-depth, technical discussions on snAppShot — often hosted by the Novell engineers who wrote Z.E.N.works.**

TIP

Associating the Application After the application has been defined with snAppShot, it must be associated to users, groups, and NDS organizational units that should receive the application (see Figure 10.26). The application can appear on the desktop in four different locations: within the App Launcher window, on the Start Menu, as an icon on the desktop, or in the system tray (lower right-hand corner). The application can be configured as "force run," meaning that no user intervention is required to start the application.

You must run NALEXPLD on client workstations before applications can be distributed to the desktop, Start menu, or system tray.

TIP

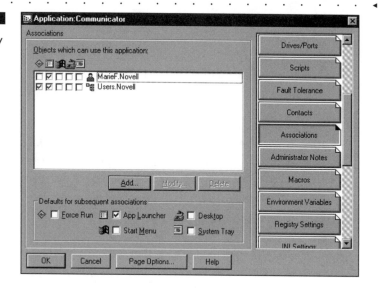

The application object may be associated with NDS users, groups, and organizational units.

Advanced Z.E.N.works Application Distribution

Literally over 200 different customizations may occur on any given application object. In fact, we've only scratched the surface of possibilities with Z.E.N.works Application Distribution. The Z.E.N.works product is worthy of an entire book unto itself. Without going into too much detail, however, a few advanced features of Z.E.N.works should be mentioned, and left to the reader as an exercise. (Does this bring back memories from your school days?) Those features are as follows:

▶ *Systems requirements.* Before the application appears on the user's desktop, the desktop must meet minimum hardware and software requirements. For example, you may specify a minimum OS version, minimum RAM requirements, or minimum disk space before the application icon will even appear on the user's desktop. This feature prevents users from running applications that their workstation can't run.

▶ *Fault tolerance/load balancing.* If an application is distributed across multiple servers, Z.E.N.works can provide simple fault tolerance and load balancing. For example, if servers A, B, and C all have the same application, Z.E.N.works will distribute client application requests across all three servers (using a round-robin approach). Furthermore, if server B is unavailable, new application requests will be directed to the remaining servers (A and C).

▶ *Application Site List.* What if every site or location uses the same applications, such as Microsoft Word and Excel? Doesn't it make sense for mobile users to get the application from the nearest server, instead of traversing the WAN for their home server? With the Application Site List setting, Z.E.N.works will automatically direct the user to the *nearest* server that contains the application.

▶ *Termination.* Have you ever tried to back up a database while users were still connected — especially users that forgot to log out at night? With application termination, an administrator can specify when and how users should be disconnected from a particular application. For example, Z.E.N.works could automatically close an application on a user's desktop at a predefined time.

▶ *Software metering.* Definitely a worthwhile enhancement to Z.E.N.works! Software licenses are defined in NDS, and distributed to NDS users, groups, and containers. Before applications are launched, Z.E.N.works checks NDS to see if a valid software license is available. For example, a software license called AutoCAD could be defined in NDS, and be associated with the Engineering group. Z.E.N.works would distribute the application to the engineer's desktop, but a valid license must be available before Z.E.N.works allows AutoCAD to start.

Controlling Applications Hosted on NT Server

Because of Z.E.N.works' capability to support UNC (see Chapter 11), applications and resources may reside on either NetWare servers or NT servers. The difference between NT application objects and NetWare application objects is that when creating application objects, many users like to browse for the exact path to the desired executable. In Figure 10.27, clicking the browse button next to Path to executable file enables you to do this. This browsing feature is limited to NetWare resources, however. You must manually type the exact UNC path (\\Server\Share\Path) to the NT resource to create the application object successfully.

F I G U R E 10.27

Z.E.N.works can launch applications hosted on NT Servers through UNC naming.

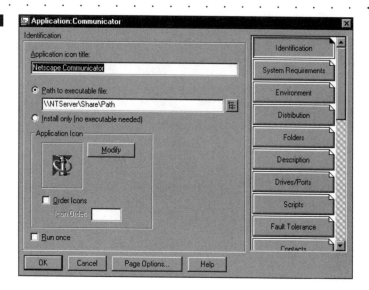

Summary

We've only just scratched the surface of Z.E.N.works, but hopefully we've shown you how Z.E.N.works provides significant value in environments with Windows NT workstations and NDS. In a Z.E.N.works environment, complex, mundane management tasks are reduced to a few simple mouse clicks.

Scripting an Integrated Environment

An important aspect of managing an integrated NetWare and Windows NT environment is providing transparent, automated access to the resources across both platforms. This chapter details how scripting can be used to automate the access to network resources in an integrated environment. Its purpose is to provide a basic understanding of common problems in an integrated environment and to suggest ways to overcome them. In this chapter, we will cover the following:

- Methods available to refer to resources (naming syntaxes)

- Microsoft's login script and permanent connections

- Novell's multilevel login scripts

In addition, we will provide you with examples of real-world scripting solutions. Specifically, this chapter provides details on the following topics:

- Naming syntaxes

- Permanent connections

- Drive mapping

- Printer mapping

- Using variables

- Multilevel scripting

- Conditionals

- Locating the "nearest" server

By the time you have completed this chapter and Chapter 10, you will be able to map drives and printers, deploy new applications, move existing applications to different servers, upgrade workstation O/Ss, apply service packs, control desktops, and make registry changes (when applicable) company-wide in a few minutes.

Naming Syntaxes

Administrators face several new complexities when working in an integrated environment. One of the problems is how to refer to Novell resources properly. Another problem is that the proper way depends on what you are doing. Both problems are easily overcome, though, as we show you in this section. But first, let's review the different naming conventions (syntaxes) available.

When managing an integrated environment, three naming syntaxes are used:

- Bindery mode

- NDS mode

- Universal Naming Convention (UNC)

Most NetWare administrators are already familiar with bindery and NDS modes, while most NT Administrators are familiar with UNC.

Bindery Mode

In bindery mode you refer to resources using the server name and the object name, such as:

```
FS1/SYS:
```

In this example, SYS: is an object located on server FS1.

NDS Mode

In NDS mode, you refer to objects using their Directory Services distinguished name. NDS object naming names objects from the least significant location in the tree to the most significant. For example:

```
FS1_SYS.MARKETING.BOISE.WIDGET_CO
```

In this case, FS1_SYS is the object name residing in the MARKETING.BOISE. WIDGET_CO context.

Universal Naming Convention (UNC)

The third naming syntax is Universal Naming Convention (UNC), invented by Microsoft to solve the problem of naming in a multivendor environment. UNC uses the syntax of:

```
\\COMPUTERNAME\SHARE
```

For example,

```
\\NT_SERVER\C$
```

or,

```
\\NOVELL_SERVER\SYS
```

NOTE

When naming volume objects using UNC naming, a colon does not follow the volume name as with bindery or NDS naming.

By comparing the UNC syntax with Novell's bindery mode syntax, you will see a strong resemblance. This is because both syntaxes are designed for workgroup constructs.

How would you make an NDS resource assignment using the UNC convention? By simply extending the syntax like this:

```
\\TREENAME\WIDGET_CO\BOISE\MARKETING\FS1_SYS
```

Which one should you use? This depends on your environment. DOS users will have to use NDS and bindery syntaxes to reach Novell resources, and UNC to reach Microsoft resources. Windows users (3.1, 95/98, and NT) should use NDS mode for Novell MAP statements (because MAP is actually a DOS command) and UNC for all desktop uses.

Permanent Connections

Permanent connections are drive mappings and printer assignments made at the Windows desktop that have the "Reconnect at logon" box checked as shown in Figure 11.1 and Figure 11.2. One might find them attractive on the surface because they are easy to understand and they easily access both NT and NetWare resources by using UNC or by browsing.

Creating a permanent drive mapping in Windows 95/98

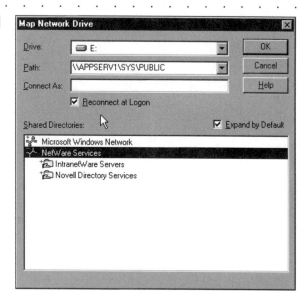

Creating a permanent printer assignment in Windows 95/98

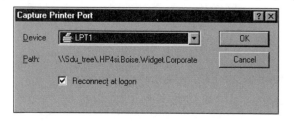

Permanent connections are convenient for a one-time resource assignment, but they have many limitations:

▸ Users can cancel them at logon time.

▸ No concept of nearest exists, such as nearest copy of Microsoft Word.

▸ They are difficult to manage centrally.

> ▸ They result in slow login times.

> ▸ Users can create/delete them at will.

> ▸ The resource must be available at login time or it is unavailable for the rest of the login session.

> ▸ There is no capability to load balance users across several identical servers.

For these reasons, permanent connections are not recommended.

Scripting Basics

A better alternative to permanent connections is scripting. Login scripts are essentially batch files that execute at login time. Scripts have several advantages over permanent connections, such as centralized administration and conditional execution. Remember the following when you choose Microsoft's or Novell's scripting system.

> ▸ How rich are the scripting commands available?

> ▸ What is the multilevel scripting capability?

> ▸ How will I locate the "nearest" copy of a resource?

> ▸ How will scripts be replicated across multiple-servers (script fault-tolerance)?

> ▸ Can I move an application to a different server without having to touch all my scripts or user desktops?

> ▸ Can the scripts be controlled, but still enable users to have some ability to customize their own environment?

Microsoft Scripting

In a Microsoft NT network, users' login scripts are configured on a user-by-user basis; no way exists to associate a script with a group of users or to the entire Domain itself. Each user can be configured to run only one login script, which is placed in the \WINNT\SYSTEM32\REPL\IMPORTS\SCRIPTS directory of the Primary Domain Controller (PDC). Then scripts must be replicated to all the Backup Domain Controllers (BDC); otherwise users will be unable to locate the script when the PDC is down or if they connect to a BDC for authentication. Microsoft's built-in file replication utility can be used to maintain login script consistency across servers.

With Microsoft's scripting language, you can do the basics—map a drive or map a printer. That's about it, though. There is no concept of load balancing, fault-tolerance, location independence, or locating the nearest server. In a pure Microsoft NT network, you would have to find other means to accomplish these things.

NOTE

Mapping drives and printers in a Windows NT login script is done using the standard NET USE command.

Table 11.1 shows a few variables available for use with Windows NT login scripts that provide some flexibility.

TABLE 11.1	DESCRIPTION	VARIABLE
Summary of Microsoft Login Script Variables	Login server	%LOGONSERVER%
	User name	%USERNAME%
	User domain	%USERDOMAIN%
	Home drive	%HOMEDRIVE%
	Home share	%HOMESHARE%
	Home path	%HOMEPATH%

Novell Scripting

Novell login scripts are typically not done on a user-by-user basis because Novell recognized long ago that anything done user-by-user is time-consuming and, therefore, costly to implement.

In an NDS environment, login scripts are stored in the NDS tree as attributes, just like a user object's last name, location of home directory, permissions to files and other objects, and so on.

Many NDS objects can contain login scripts including the following:

▶ Organizations

▶ Organization Units

▶ Profiles

▶ Users

When you create login scripts, make certain you take advantage of the inheritance capabilities built into your NDS tree. When a user logs in, three login scripts will, by default, be automatically executed if they exist. They are:

▶ The Organizational Unit that is the parent of the user logging in (parent is a term given to the container that holds the actual object)

▶ The profile's login script

▶ The user's login script

Knowing the parent container and the user object both have a login script is fairly intuitive, but what is a profile? A profile is an object whose purpose is to enable you to assign a login script to a group of users. If a user is associated with more than one profile, one profile is designated the default profile whose script is executed, and the rest are secondary profiles whose scripts are not executed.

Note, too, that login scripts are NDS properties. They are not physical files as with bindery-based versions of NetWare (3.11 and below). NDS login scripts are automatically self-replicating. What this means is they exist anywhere a replica of the user's partition exists. So, having login script unavailable is virtually impossible, because they are replicated and automatically distributed across the NDS tree. Administrators simply define the script; the rest is handled automatically through NDS's inherent replication capabilities.

Figure 11.3 shows how login scripts are executed in an NDS environment.

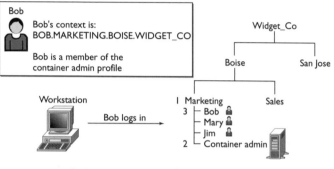

FIGURE 11.3

NDS login scripts process in the following order: (1) Container Script (2) Profile Script (3) User Script.

Login script processing order:
1. Marketing container script
2. Container admin profile script
3. Bob's user login script

In Figure 11.3, when Bob logs in to the network, the Marketing Container Login Script executes first. Then, if Bob is assigned to a profile (in this case, the Container Admin Profile), the profile script will run followed by the individual user script. Any parameters set in a login script can be overwritten in the scripts that follow. For example, if the profile script maps drive letter G: to SYS:DATA\ADMIN, Bob's user script could remap that drive to SYS:DATA\BOB.

Using the login script inheritance in this fashion simplifies login script administration. Unless a user needs some custom scripting different from all other users in their container and from their profile, no user level scripting must be written at all.

Normally users share many characteristics with other users who are in the same department or location. For our example, assume DEMO-USER is a user in the MARKETING.BOISE area of WIDGET_CO's tree. You can reasonably assume most scripting for DEMO-USER will be the same as other MARKETING users, such as knowing DEMO-USER wants to access the marketing printer.

By placing all the common resource assignments in the MARKETING container's login script, you have solved the entire common scripting problem for the marketing group. If you need more granular control, you can create a profile to represent a subset of the marketing group, such as those marketing people who need access to the color laser printer. In this case, you would create a script for the profile that provides a mapping to that printer. By taking advantage of NDS login scripts in this way, you will only be required to address exceptions at the individual user level.

In some companies, network administrators will take care of the management of the container and profile level scripts and enable users to manage their personal login scripts. This enables each user to customize his or her scripts, if desired.

Drive Mapping

Mapping a drive in a login script is accomplished with the MAP command. MAP supports Bindery, NDS, and UNC naming conventions. Although UNC is supported, MAP does not support NDS UNC mode. Examples of using MAP with each of these syntaxes are shown as follows.

NDS Example:

```
MAP F:=.FS1_SYS.MARKETING.BOISE.WIDGET_CO:
```

Bindery Example:

```
MAP F:=FS1/SYS:
```

UNC Bindery Example:

```
MAP F:=\\FS1\SYS
```

MAP enables you to assign drive letters to network resources, such as NetWare volumes, volume aliases, and to Directory Map Objects (discussed later in this chapter).

You can also use any environment variable or one of the built-in identifier variables in any script command. For example,

```
MAP F:=%HOME_DIRECTORY
```

In this example, the identifier variable %HOME_DIRECTORY equates to the user object's home directory attribute (property). Variables will be covered in greater depth later in this chapter. For more information on the MAP command, see the NetWare documentation.

Printer Mapping

To provide access to network printers, printer mappings should be established in login scripts. This is done with the CAPTURE command. CAPTURE also supports NDS and bindery naming syntaxes. CAPTURE commands using these naming syntaxes are shown in the following examples.

NDS Example:

```
CAPTURE /Q=HPLJ.MARKETING.BOISE.WIDGET_CO
```

Bindery Example:

```
CAPTURE /S=FS1 /Q=HPLJ
```

For more information on the CAPTURE command, see the NetWare documentation.

Using Variables

Two types of variables are supported in Novell login scripts: built-in and environment. Built-in variables are special keywords the Novell login processor inherently understands. Environment variables are those variables set in the AUTOEXEC.BAT file (DOS, Windows, and Windows 95) or the System Registry (Windows NT).

Built-in Variables   Built-in variables, or login script variables, were created to assist the administrator in accessing resources based on complex criteria. Novell has a rich list of login script variables for virtually every conceivable need (see Table 11.2).

	DESCRIPTION	IDENTIFIER VARIABLE
TABLE 11.2 *Novell's Login Script Identifier Variables*	Access Server	%ACCESS_SERVER
	Account Balance	%ACCOUNT_BALANCE
	Administrative Assistant	%ADMINISTRATIVE_ASSISTANT
	Allow Unlimited Credit	%ALLOW_UNLIMITED_CREDIT
	Certificate Validity Interval	%CERTIFICATE_VALIDITY_INTERVAL
	CN (Common Name)	%CN
	Description	%DESCRIPTION
	E-Mail Address	%EMAIL_ADDRESS
	Employee ID	%EMPLOYEE_ID
	Equivalent To Me	%EQUIVALENT_TO_ME
	Fax Number	%FACSIMILE_TELEPHONE_NUMBER

Continued

	DESCRIPTION	IDENTIFIER VARIABLE
T A B L E 11.2 *Novell's Login Script* *Identifier Variables* *(continued)*	File Server	%FILE_SERVER
	Full Name	%FULL_NAME
	Generational Qualifier	%GENERATIONAL_QUALIFIER
	Given Name	%GIVEN_NAME
	Group Membership	%GROUP_MEMBERSHIP
	Higher Privileges	%HIGHER_PRIVILEGES
	Home Directory	%HOME_DIRECTORY
	Initials	%INITIALS
	L (Locality)	%L
	Language	%LANGUAGE
	Last Name	%LAST_NAME
	Locked By Intruder	%LOCKED_BY_INTRUDER
	Login Context	%LOGIN_CONTEXT
	Login Disabled	%LOGIN_DISABLED
	Login Maximum Simultaneous	%LOGIN_MAXIMUM_SIMULTANEOUS
	Login Name	%LOGIN_NAME
	Machine	%MACHINE
	Mailbox ID	%MAILBOX_ID
	Mailbox Location	%MAILBOX_LOCATION
	Mailstop	%MAILSTOP
	Message Server	%MESSAGE_SERVER
	Minimum Account Balance	%MINIMUM_ACCOUNT_BALANCE
	Network Address	%NETWORK
	Object Class	%OBJECT_CLASS
	OS	%OS
	OS Version	%OS_VERSION
	OU (Department)	%OU
	Password Allow Change	%PASSWORD_ALLOW_CHANGE

TABLE 11.2

*Novell's Login Script
Identifier Variables
(continued)*

DESCRIPTION	IDENTIFIER VARIABLE
Password Expires	%PASSWORD_EXPIRES
Password Minimum Length	%PASSWORD_MINIMUM_LENGTH
Password Required	%PASSWORD_REQUIRED
Password Unique Required	%PASSWORD_UNIQUE_REQUIRED
Physical Station	%P_STATION
Postal Office Box	%POSTAL_OFFICE_BOX
Postal Code	%POSTAL_CODE
Private Key	%PRIVATE_KEY
Profile	%PROFILE
Requester Context	%REQUESTER_CONTEXT
Requester Version	%REQUESTER_VERSION
Revision	%REVISION
S (State)	%S
SA (Street Address)	%SA
Security Equals	%SECURITY_EQUALS
Security Flags	%SECURITY_FLAGS
See Also	%SEE_ALSO
Server Holds	%SERVER_HOLDS
Shell Version	%SHELL_VERSION
Station	%STATION
Supervisor	%SUPERVISOR
Surname	%SURNAME
Telephone number	%TELEPHONE_NUMBER
Title	%TITLE
User ID	%USER_ID

How can these variables help you to manage an integrated environment? One problem you may face is the need to update client software automatically whenever a new version has been approved for deployment by your IS staff. You could walk around manually updating every workstation (guaranteed job security) or you could have more important things to do. If time is limited, why not allow Novell to do the work for you?

The following simple example shows how this can be accomplished using variables in a login script:

```
IF "%OS" == "WIN95" THEN BEGIN

    #SETUP /ACU

END



IF "%OS" == "WINNT" THEN BEGIN

    #SETUPNW /ACU

END
```

TIP

A powerful command is available that is hidden away in the Novell documentation. This variable enables you to query any value of any NDS object attribute for use in a login script. The variable syntax is %objectname;attribute.

You should acquaint yourself with the many login script variables, which were created to solve most common problems Novell customers face.

Environment Variables   Another common need in scripts is the ability to query environment variables. Querying is most often used to guide execution based on workstation specifics. For example, you could need to launch an application with a command line switch indicating the brand of workstation. Here's an example of how you can use variables to accomplish this:

I. At the workstation in AUTOEXEC.BAT or the System Registry (as appropriate), set the following environment variable:

```
WS=BRANDNAME
```

2. In the login script use the command

```
#program_name /<WS>.
```

The variable is in "<>" to tell the login script processor this is an environment variable, not one of the built-in script variables.

Another need you may have is to map a drive to the nearest application server. Setting an environment variable at the workstation is one method you can use to locate the nearest server automatically. For detailed information on how to locate nearest resources, see the section, "Locating Nearest Servers," later in this chapter.

Launching Applications

Any application can be launched in any of the three levels of scripting by using the following command:

```
"#programname"
```

The path to the program can be specified using the traditional path method, such as

```
#F:\APPS\OFFICE97\WORD
```

Or, you may use UNC to specify the path. For example,

```
#\\FS1\SYS\APPS\OFFICE97\WORD
```

Many people are moving to the UNC naming conventions for consistency reasons and because you needn't have a drive mapped prior to executing the command.

In general, a login script is not the correct place from which to launch applications. We strongly recommend you use Novell's Application Launcher (NAL — part of the Z.E.N.works product) instead. NAL was designed and built exclusively to solve the unique problems associated with launching applications. Login scripts are typically used to launch special-purpose applications, such as updating the client requester software or NAL itself. The reason behind this is actually quite simple. Commands in login scripts execute one at a time, with the script processor waiting for the current command to complete before starting the next one.

The following example of a login script misuses the execute program capability:

```
MAP ROOT Z:=FS1\SYS:\PUBLIC

MAP ROOT P:=FS1\APPS:


#P:\OFFICE97\WORD

#P:\GAMES\SOLITAIRE
```

In this example, Solitaire would not load until after the user exited out of Word. Clearly, this was not the intended effect.

For this reason, Novell recommends limiting execution of applications within a login script to utilities such as MAP and CAPTURE. For all other applications, use NAL. For a complete explanation of NAL, see Chapter 10.

Conditionals

As shown in previous examples, conditionals are an important part of login scripts. Building a usable network without them is almost impossible. They allow action to be taken based on a condition, or conditions, being met. Administrators could use this, for example, to check if the user's workstation is running Windows NT and upgrade the client, if necessary.

The login script for this might look like the following:

```
IF "%OS == "WINNT" THEN BEGIN

    #SETUPNW /ACU

    END
```

Novell supports checking for the following conditions: "==", "<>", "<", "<=", ">", and ">=".

Conditionals allow multiple statements to be executed if the condition is met. In addition, the conditionals can be nested.

For example:

```
IF "%OS" == "WINNT" THEN BEGIN

    IF "%OS_VERSION" == "4.0" OR

    "%OS_VERSION" == "3.51" THEN BEGIN
```

```
        WRITE "NT client upgrade starting ..."

        #setupnw /ACU

        END

    ELSE BEGIN

        WRITE "Unsupport version of NT. Contact Help Desk"

    END

ELSE BEGIN

    WRITE "Unsupported OS. Contact Help Desk"

END
```

In this example, we first check to see if the operating system is Windows NT and if it is, we then proceed to check the version number. If all of the conditions are met, we start the upgrade process; otherwise, we display the appropriate error message.

▶ · ◀

Locating "Nearest" Servers

Difficulty locating the "nearest" server must be one of the most commonly expressed problems. The problem starts with "nearest" meaning different things to different people and the method of determining "nearest" is different in an IPX versus an IP world. Add a mix of NT and NetWare servers and you have a real headache.

Why Care About "Nearest" At All?

With the ever-growing sophistication of today's applications comes the need to consume (read/write) an almost unimaginable amount of code and data. This demand places a heavy burden on the network infrastructure in terms of both speed and reliability. So learning administrators want to minimize the load (traffic) in both quantity and distance should come as no surprise. By distance, we refer to the general mantra of the computer industry, "Keep resources as close to the users as possible." This means loading Office 97 across the LAN is one thing, yet loading it across the WAN is quite another. It should be obvious that loading Office 97 across the WAN will entail significant delays, impact the performance of other critical operations that need to send data across the WAN, and may raise operating costs, as many WAN solutions charge by the packet.

The solution to this problem is launching the application — in this case Office 97 — from a local server.

Another common problem is the roaming user. Consider the traveling employee who is normally based in Los Angeles, but who traveled to New York today. His login script would traditionally be configured to launch all applications from the Los Angeles file server. He shows up in the New York office, sits down at an available workstation, logs in, and proceeds to launch Office 97. What will happen? Office 97 will come from the Los Angeles file server, even though an identical copy is local in New York.

Let the Network Determine "Nearest"

Many people suggest determining the "nearest" server should be done automatically without human intervention. We like to say, "That's not automatic, that's automagic." Unfortunately, the technology to do this entirely automatically is not yet available. Meanwhile, consider the following problems:

- ▶ How can the network automatically know all locations where a particular application resides?

- ▶ How can the network decide "closest" in a transport-independent fashion?

- ▶ What occurs if I need to move a copy of the application to a different server? Do I need to rework all the existing scripts?

- ▶ How can the network determine if the "nearest" server is too busy to support another user?

- ▶ How can the network automatically locate all the NT locations where a particular application resides?

▸ How does the network select between a "close" NT server and a NetWare server?

▸ What would a login script look like to connect automatically to the nearest resource?

Fortunately, the engineers at Novell do practice red magic and they have created (conjured up) the Novell Application Launcher (NAL) (a core component of Novell's Z.E.N.works product), which addresses each of these issues well. Although it isn't quite 100 percent automatic, it is close. (For a complete explanation of Z.E.N.works application distribution capabilities, see Chapter 10.)

Scripting Three Solutions to the "Nearest" Problem

For those of you unwilling to use Z.E.N.works, we present Alternative #1. This solution is based on three key concepts:

▸ All versions of Client32 and the VLMs support a concept known as Requester Context.

▸ Login scripts can read and act on the value of an environment variable.

▸ Login scripts can read and act on any value of any NDS attribute of any NDS object.

The solution works like this. When one of the clients previously listed starts up, a login script variable called Requester Context is set to the NDS context of the server to which the client first connected. With that information, we know where we are physically in the NDS tree. With this in hand, we read the description attribute of the container and use that information to map to the correct server. Obviously, beforehand someone had to use NWAdmin to edit the description attribute of the container and place the name of the server to which you want users to connect. At this point, an example would be enlightening.

Suppose three file servers (FS1, FS2, and FS3) are in the San Jose branch of the Widget Company in the Marketing, Sales, and Engineering areas, respectively. The fully qualified names of these servers quite possibly could be:

```
FS1.MARKETING.SAN JOSE.WIDGET_CO

FS2.SALES.SAN JOSE.WIDGET_CO

FS3.ENGINEERING.SAN JOSE.WIDGET_CO
```

Then, to make things difficult, let's assume you want them to connect to the San Jose NT server, NT_APPSRVR_1, and use the sharename, APPSHARE, because this is where your application resides.

You would launch NWAdmin and go to the Details page of the Marketing, Sales, and Engineering containers in the San Jose portion of the tree. Next, you would erase any text in the description field and replace it with

```
\\NT_APPSRVR_1\\APPSHARE
```

Finally, in the login script, you would place the command

```
NET USE G: %REQUESTER_CONTEXT;DESCRIPTION.
```

When a user from Boise sat at a San Jose workstation, the user would, by default, initially attach to one of the San Jose file servers and, therefore, his or her requester context would be set to a location in the San Jose container. Which location the context is set to is irrelevant because the description field of all three containers points to the NT server.

NOTE

This works for both NT servers and NetWare servers because the NET USE command can map a drive to either NT or NetWare resources, provided you use the UNC name.

Figure 11.4 summarizes the process used to map to the nearest application server.

Alternative #2 is for NT workstations. This method is necessary when using the NT Requester version (4.11). That version does not correctly support the parameter "Requester Context." This method does work for DOS, Windows 3.x, and Window 95; it's less desirable because more typing is required for those operating systems.

In this method, the administrator sets a system environment variable at each NT Workstation indicating the nearest application server. (Remember, in an NT environment, variables are stored in the registry and can be remotely managed.) At startup, the login script does a NET USE to map the drive to the nearest application server. Consider the following example.

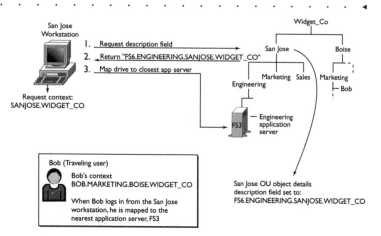

FIGURE 11.4

Login process to locate and map a drive automatically to the nearest application server. Notice how the normally unused description field is used to store the correct server name.

All users in the San Jose office are supposed to map to the San Jose application server, NW_LA_APP_SRVR. The administrator has created an environment variable — "NEAREST" — for all the NT Workstations. In the login script, only the following line is needed:

```
MAP G:=<NEAREST>/SYS:
```

The nearest server could easily have been an NT server instead of a NetWare server.

Figure 11.5 shows an example of using a system environment in an NT workstation to map a drive to the nearest application server.

FIGURE 11.5

Example using a system environment in an NT Workstation to map a drive to the nearest application server.

San Jose Workstation

Bob (Traveling user)

Workstation Environment
OS = WINNT
TEMP = C:\TEMP
APP = FS1.FINANCE.SANJOSE.WIDGET_CO

Login process using system variables:
1. Bob logs in from San Jose workstation
2. "App" variable is read
3. Drive is mapped to nearest application server, FS1

Alternative #3 is for those customers who have an IP stack at the workstation and support Dynamic Host Configuration Protocol (DHCP).

Most administrators who must support Internet Protocol (IP) are familiar with DHCP, a specification and a protocol for centrally managing IP addressing-related information. What is not generally known is DHCP has an optional construct called custom tags. Custom tags support enables administrators to define special information they want sent to the workstation at boot time, which the IP protocol itself does not need. For example, in addition to sending out the IP address, network mask, DNS address, and name, you could also send out the administrator's phone number to call if things do not work properly or, more important in this scenario, the nearest application server. With this information you could then use the technique in Alternative #2 to map the drive correctly. This is shown in Figure 11.6.

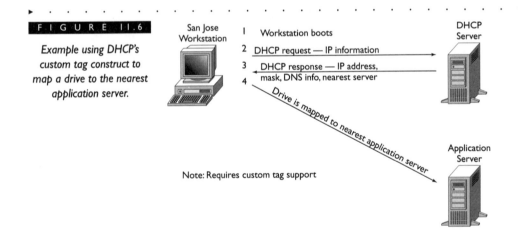

FIGURE 11.6

Example using DHCP's custom tag construct to map a drive to the nearest application server.

San Jose Workstation

1 Workstation boots

2 DHCP request — IP information

3 DHCP response — IP address,
4 mask, DNS info, nearest server

Drive is mapped to nearest application server

Note: Requires custom tag support

DHCP Server

Application Server

Fictional Case Studies

In this section we present several examples indicative of the kinds of problems companies are trying to solve today.

Study #1: First Intergalactic Bank (FIB)

This first case study involves a company that has already made significant cuts in its network support costs by using NDS, but faces the challenge of making further cuts.

Problem

First Intergalactic Bank has been instructed by upper management to pull the reins in on the spiraling costs of supporting its network. It has standardized on Novell's NDS to reduce the time and costs associated with creating, deleting, and shuffling users whenever the company goes through a reorganization. Now it needs to reduce costs further by addressing the following items:

1. How do we support roaming users?

2. How do we enable the user's desktop to follow the user anywhere in the world?

3. How do we automatically locate and use the closest copy of an application?

4. How do we minimize the work necessary when hiring/firing a new user?

5. How do we minimize the work necessary to deploy a new application?

6. How do we enforce licensing for the applications?

7. How do we locate an alternate server if the closest one is unavailable?

8. How do we spread the workload across multiple identical servers (load balance)?

9. What would the login script look like for such a solution?

FIB has ambitious, but entirely realistic, goals that are achievable today. Due to the scope of the project, though, it will take more than login scripts to make this happen.

Solution

To meet the previously stated needs, FIB will require the following:

1. Modern workstation operating system — Windows 95/98 or Windows NT

2. Novell's Z.E.N.works, which provides workstation management and application distributions services

3. Proper login script

Proposed Login Script

```
'

' Sample login script

'


IF "%OS" == "WINNT" THEN BEGIN
   #SETUPNW /ACU ' This ensures client is always
                   current
   #NALEXPLD      ' Starts Z.E.N.works Explorer

                   Desktop integration component
      EXIT
END


IF "%OS" == "WIN95" THEN BEGIN
   #SETUP /ACU   ' This ensures client is always
                   current
   #NAL           ' Start Z.E.N.works application

                   distribution Window
```

```
              EXIT

        END
```

```
  WRITE "Your operating system is too old. Please contact
  the Help Desk for assistance upgrading to currently supported
  version"
```

Limitations
None. This solution will meet all goals previously listed, including being able to support fully any or all applications residing on NT.

Case Study #2: First Interstellar Trust of Zimbabwe
The second case study involves a situation where a company wishes to add a number of significant enhancements to its network without upsetting the status quo or restructuring its staff.

Problem
The First Interstellar Trust of Zimbabwe (FITZ) is a competitor of FIB. It has a corporate culture, where the larger a group you are within the company, the more power you wield. It does not see any reason to change the status quo. To its IS department, reducing costs means, in the long run, reducing staff. It does, however, need to deploy new applications, provide roaming user support, and allow access to NT and NetWare servers.

FITZ has decided NAL is too big a change to make. It already has a team of people who are tasked with visiting each workstation to deploy new applications or client patches occasionally, and the team members feel they are becoming efficient.

The team wants to address the following items:

1. Roaming User Support

2. Locating "Nearest" Server

3. Minimizing changes to existing network with little or no retraining of network support staff

Solution

1. Enable Roaming Profile Support in Client32 for Windows 95/98 and in Workstation Manager for NT.

2. Review existing login scripts for functions that could be removed from the individual's script and placed in the container or profile script.

3. Standardize on a drive letter that will always be mapped at login time to the nearest application server.

4. Proper login scripts.

Login Script

FITZ will need to include the following login script fragment into its container login script:

```
'

' login script for mapping to nearest application server

'

IF "%OS" = "WINNT" THEN BEGIN

    MAP P:=<NEAREST>     ' Use system environment variable

END


IF "%OS" = "WIN95" THEN BEGIN

    MAP P:=%REQUESTER_CONTEXT;DESCRIPTION

    ' Use description attribute of parent container

    END
```

Limitations

None. This solution will meet all goals previously listed.

Summary

With the explosive growth in interest in Windows NT, customers are asking how they can use Novell's rich scripting capability to access both vendors' network resources. In this chapter, we have presented the key concepts and working examples of how to accomplish the most common tasks — properly referring to resources, supporting roaming users, keeping client requester software current, and locating "nearest" application servers.

We also briefly touched on the newest concepts in desktop management — dynamic mapping, load-balancing, and fault-tolerance, which are not suited for login scripts, but for which Novell's Z.E.N.works was exclusively written. For details on Novell's Z.E.N.works, see Chapter 10.

NDS Versus Domains

Is it a directory service or is it a name service? NetWare includes a global distributed resource database known as Novell Directory Services (NDS). Windows NT Server also includes a resource database most commonly called NT Server Domain Services. However, Microsoft has frequently referred to Domain Services as NT Server Directory Services (implying that it, too, is a directory service). With the seemingly never-ending debate between the two companies, each with their point and counter-point marketing propaganda, the distinction between the two is quite murky. Off the battleground, the real question becomes: What sets a directory service aside from a name service? And, more important, does it make a difference in my network? To help answer these questions, let's define directory services in general and compare Novell's and Microsoft's services.

What Is a Directory Service?

Directory services are some of the most fundamental, yet least understood, components of today's networks. Directory services are specialized databases designed to store information about network resources. The ultimate goal of a directory service is to provide users with full transparent access to all network resources and other users throughout the network. Although the implementations of directory services vary from vendor to vendor, the X.500 standards represent the only standard for directory services to date.

X.500

X.500 was developed by the International Standards Organization (ISO) and Consultative Committee for International Telegraphy and Telephony/International Telecommunications Union (CCITT/ITU) to provide a standard that enables the creation of an interoperable, distributed, worldwide directory service. To achieve this, the standards indicate that a directory service should provide the following functions:

- ▸ Transparent access to all network resources, regardless of the location of the user or the resources being accessed

- ▸ A unique naming method for all network resources that allows the sharing and access of data across multiple organizations

▸ High availability providing fault-tolerant login and administration from anywhere on the network

▸ Extensible attribute information supplying useful network information to users and applications

▸ Extensive query and searching techniques beyond simple mapping of network names to addresses

If standards are important to you, and your goal is to create an interoperable, enterprise network, then you will want a directory service that meets these criteria. Even if you're not building an enterprise network, these features provide ease of use and administration, as well as a platform for future interoperability.

Meeting the Standard

No PC-based directory services on the market today are fully X.500-compliant. NDS is probably the most X.500-like, because Novell used X.500 as a model when designing NDS. All the features and functions described by X.500 are implemented in NDS. However, Novell implemented proprietary lightweight protocols in place of the more heavyweight Open Systems Interconnection (OSI) protocols defined by X.500. A gateway is required to provide X.500 interoperability.

An emerging standard that has caught the eye of many administrators is Lightweight Directory Access Protocol (LDAP). The attraction has been that through LDAP, the directory itself doesn't matter as much as the access protocol. Even this can be a confusion point of sorts; LDAP is merely an access protocol, not a directory specification in and of itself (at least not today). LDAP is a good middle ground between heavyweight directories and directory access (full X.500), and the plethora of directories that seem to become more plentiful each day.

NDS, Domains, and X.500

Both Novell's NDS and Microsoft's Domain Services provide functionality described by X.500 to a certain degree. Yet their individual implementations differ greatly as described in this section.

NDS Provides Single Login, Global Access

Meeting the first X.500 objective of transparent access, NDS provides users with global access to an entire enterprise network with a single login. With a single login ID, a user logs in to the NDS Directory tree and can automatically view the entire network as a single information system. User access to resources will vary, based on the security access the user has been given. For users who travel, NDS provides a consistent view of the network, regardless of their login location.

To provide a unique naming method across an enterprise network, NDS resources are organized in a hierarchical fashion through the use of container objects. This hierarchy ensures that object names are unique throughout the network and provides a basis for simplified administration and use of the network. NDS trees can be administered from any location on the network, either in a centralized or distributed manner.

Container objects can be used to organize network resources based on geographical location, department, or other administrative unit. Typically, container objects are referred to as Organizations (O) or Organizational Units (OU). Some NDS add-on products extend the NDS Schema to add different types of container objects, however. An example of this is the Novell Administrator for Windows NT, which adds a Domain or Workgroup container to NDS.

Figure A.1 shows network resources in an NDS tree.

The important distinction of NDS is it provides a scalable design, which enables it to be implemented in networks of all sizes with minimal administration effort.

NTS Provides Domain-Based Single Login

NT Server also provides users with a single point of access to the network, but with a quite different implementation. NT Server uses a basic unit of administration known as a Domain. Domains are flat-file databases — as opposed to hierarchical — which generally represent a single workgroup. Each Domain is administered independently. Small networks may only require one Domain, so single login is not an issue. For medium or large networks, generally more than one Domain is required. The Domain architecture only guarantees unique naming within a particular Domain, thereby requiring the administrator to be aware of all resource names within all Domains to avoid redundancy.

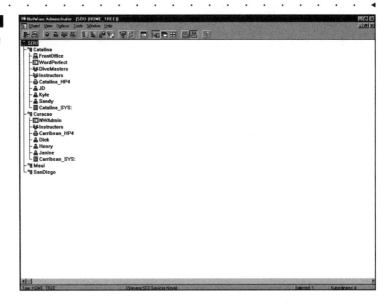

FIGURE A.1

NDS objects are organized in a hierarchical fashion through the use of container objects.

To provide single login, trust relationships must be established between each Domain. Trust relationships enable the users in one Domain to access the resources in another Domain. In Figure A.2, the Sales Domain trusts the Marketing Domain, providing users in Marketing with access to resources in Sales.

Trust relationships are unidirectional. So, for the users in the Sales Domain to access resources in Marketing, an additional trust relationship must be created. Users can have location-independent access to all network resources if trust relationships are established between every Domain throughout the enterprise network. Although this is possible, it is administration-intensive. This type of configuration is known as a complete trust relationship. In the past, Microsoft has recommended against deploying this as a practical solution.

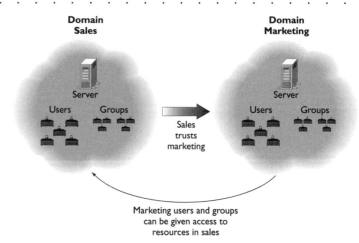

FIGURE A.2

NT Server requires trust relationships to be established between Domains to provide single login to network resources.

The approaches recommended by Microsoft to provide single login and naming include Single Master and Multi-Master Domain implementations. These implementations are illustrated in Figure A.3 and Figure A.4.

In a Single Master Domain configuration, one Master Domain is set up that contains all the user accounts. Multiple Resource Domains are set up that contain individual group and departmental resources (such as printers and servers). The result is resources can be managed locally by groups that own them and central MIS can maintain one global user account for each user in an organization.

The Multi-Master configuration uses the same concept of Master User Domains and Resource Domains; the only difference is Multi-Master User Domains are set up. This configuration will generally be seen in large organizations.

While these options do not remove the requirements for multiple trust relationships, they minimize the number of trust relationships required, thereby reducing the administrative burden.

The key difference between NT Server's Domains and NDS in this area is NDS provides a hierarchical design that automatically accommodates transparent global access. NT Server also provides users this type of access, but at the expense of additional administrative efforts.

FIGURE A.3

Single Master configurations consist of one Domain deployed as the Master and any number of Domains deployed as Resource Domains linked by a one-way trust.

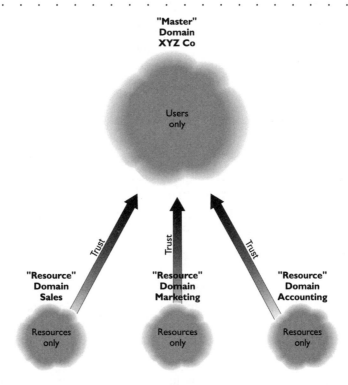

"Master"
Domain
XYZ Co

Users
only

Trust   Trust   Trust

"Resource"
Domain
Sales

"Resource"
Domain
Marketing

"Resource"
Domain
Accounting

Resources
only

Resources
only

Resources
only

FIGURE A.4

A Multi-Master is like a Single Master tied together into a large network. Many trusts may exist, depending on how accessible the resources must be to all the users.

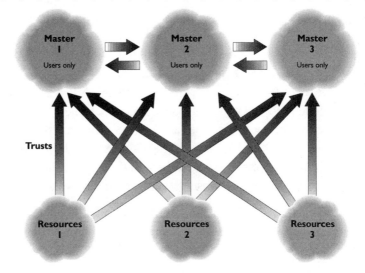

Master
1
Users only

Master
2
Users only

Master
3
Users only

Trusts

Resources
1

Resources
2

Resources
3

NDS Provides Fault-Tolerant Access

The NDS database is distributed and replicated across the network to provide fault-tolerant login and administration from anywhere on the network. The NDS database can be partitioned into manageable pieces and distributed to file servers across the network. Any container object can be created as a partition and partitioning can be done on the fly. In addition, NDS data can be placed close to the users who use it, providing load-balancing and ensuring optimal performance when accessing the network.

NDS partitions are copied or replicated across the entire network as many times as necessary to provide fault tolerance and performance. NDS has three types of replicas: Master, Read/Write, and Read-Only. The original copy of a partition is, by default, the Master. Read/Write and Read-Only replicas are created as backups. Any backup copy can be changed to a Master with a simple click of a button. File servers on the network can store as many replicas as required and they do not require re-installation to store a replica.

Authentication to the network and administration can be performed through any writable replica (Master or Read/Write). To maintain database consistency, NDS replicas are synchronized automatically.

If a Master replica is lost, the network instantly and automatically reconfigures itself to use a Read/Write, without the need for administrator intervention. This further increases reliability of the network and allows for construction of a system where failure, maintenance of a file server, or temporary loss of a communications link need not affect operations.

NT Server PDCs and BDCs

For fault-tolerance and load balancing, NT Server uses Primary Domain Controllers (PDCs) and Backup Domain Controllers (BDCs). When an individual server is configured to be a PDC, it contains the Domain's user account information. Other servers in the Domain can be configured as BDCs. If the administrator wants a server to be a PDC or BDC, the server must be configured as such at the time of installation. Existing servers must be re-installed to be configured as a PDC or BDC.

BDCs contain copies of the Domain information. For fault tolerance and load-balancing, users may authenticate to a BDC. Any changes to the Domain's information, however, must occur on the PDC. The PDC then synchronizes any changes to the BDCs.

For example, if the server containing the PDC goes down, users can still log in to that Domain through the BDCs. Changes to the Domain information cannot take place until the PDC comes back online, however, or until a BDC is promoted to a PDC. Promoting a BDC to a PDC does not take place automatically; it is a manual process that must be done by the administrator.

Because of the flat structure of Domains, no partitioning capabilities exist. With no granularity in the Domain architecture, large Domains must be replicated in their entirety.

Customizing the NDS Database

The NDS database is customizable, which allows any intelligent device to be attached to the network. The NDS database is extensible, which enables customers to modify it to fit their needs. For example, a User object can be extended to include properties such as a social security number or an emergency contact name and telephone number. Independent software vendors (ISVs) can integrate new services into the network by adding new objects to NDS. For example, an ISV could add fax server functionality to the network by adding a fax server object to the NDS tree. This extensibility also allows other network services (such as an e-mail or fax server) to use the NDS database as their user database, instead of maintaining a separate individual database. This provides users with a single login not only to NetWare, but also to applications. It also reduces the number of network databases that must be administered, providing a single point of administration.

Domain Database is Static but Well-Integrated

NT Server's Domain structure is static. The Domain database contains information about basic networking objects (such as users, groups, printers, and file servers). Extension of the Domain database is not available today.

NT Server, however, integrates well with the applications in the Microsoft BackOffice suite. Applications such as SQL Server, SNA server, Microsoft Mail, and SMS, are all integrated with the Domain database. Although each application maintains its own database, it is loosely coupled with Domains, providing single login to those services.

Searching for Resources

The hierarchical structure of NDS makes searching for resources on the network easy. Resources can be located through browsing the tree or through initiating a search either of the entire tree or a selected container. NetWare 4 provides administrator and user tools for searching and querying network resources. These include NWAdmin, NETADMIN, NWUser, NETUSER, and numerous command-line utilities.

The Domain architecture in NT Server makes searching for resources a bit more difficult.

Limited querying and viewing of network resources can be accomplished through Network Neighborhood (Win95/98) or File Manager (Windows NT Workstation and Server).

Managing Network Resources

When it comes to managing network resources, the hierarchical nature of NDS, once again, gives it a tremendous benefit. NDS provides the ability to manage network resources "by exception." What this means is all management (granting rights, managing login scripts, establishing account restrictions, and so on) can be done on a container level. Making the change to the container object affects all users in that container. If a specific user in the container requires different access, then this "exception" is managed on an individual level. This type of management saves significant time by enabling you to perform bulk management operations on a department or workgroup level. In addition, the container inheritance described here is automatic — just by creating a user in a container the user obtains the rights of the container. Move a user out of the container and he or she loses the rights of the old container and inherits the rights of the new.

The flat structure of NT Domains does not allow for this type of functionality. NT enables you to perform limited bulk management through the use of groups. Unfortunately, this process is not automatic — the groups must first be created and then the appropriate users are added to the membership list. This process is time-consuming and cumbersome. In many cases, the desire to manage a department's resources independently is often the driving factor in deploying additional domains.

▶ . . . . ◀

Summary

So — is it a directory service or a name service? By the X.500 definition, NDS is a true directory service. NT Server provides a service that is close, but it doesn't quite meet all the criteria of a true directory service. Does this really matter? Probably not. What is important is how it affects your network.

Although Microsoft has made some enhancements to the domain architecture to make it more scalable in an enterprise environment, NDS still surpasses it in scalability, usability, and accessibility of network resources in the enterprise. In smaller environments, the differences between the two are negligible. Where it becomes apparent is when you are dealing with larger, enterprise systems.

So, if you're dealing with a small local network, take your pick; either will suffice. If you're dealing with a large enterprise environment, you may want to take a closer look at NDS.

Solutions Guide

This book presents the many methods of integrating NetWare and Windows NT, as well as the products available to accomplish this integration. The sheer number of integration possibilities and solutions can be mind-boggling for even the most seasoned network professional.

Table B.1 has been designed to help you determine which products you should implement in your environment and which chapters in this book to refer to for more information.

TABLE BI	IF YOU WANT ...	YOU WILL NEED ...	REFER TO ..
Product Implementation	Single-sign on to both NT Workstations and NetWare without a Domain	NetWare Client for Windows NT	Chapter 5
	NT Workstations to have full access to all NetWare services including NDS	NetWare Client for Windows NT	Chapter 5
	To manage NT work-stations centrally with-out having to deploy an NT Server domain	Z.E.N.works work-station management	Chapter 10
	To use synchronization to manage NT domain users and groups through NDS from a single utility— NWAdmin	Novell Administrator for Windows NT or NetVision Synchronicity for NT	Chapter 6
	A Single point of admini-stration and access for NT Workstations and NDS	NetWare Client for Windows NT Z.E.N.works work-station management Novell Administrator for Windows NT	Chapter 5 Chapter 10 Chapter 6
	To store NT domain information in NDS creating a single, common directory for network access and management	NDS for NT	Chapter 7

TABLE B1	IF YOU WANT …	YOU WILL NEED …	REFER TO …
Product Implementation (continued)	To deploy an NT Server-based application (such as Exchange) that requires an NT domain without the complexities of deploying and managing domains	NDS for NT	Chapter 7
	To reduce significantly or completely remove all NT domain trust relationships	NDS for NT	Chapter 7
	A single point of access and management for directory, file, and print services for UNIX, NT, and NetWare	NDS for NT	Chapter 8
	To manage centrally and deploy applications to Windows desktops	Z.E.N.works application launcher	Chapter 9

Microsoft Active Directory Services

Microsoft has announced a new direction that Windows NT will take, starting with its next release (Windows 2000) due out sometime in late 1999 or early 2000. This new direction is to move the existing Domain-based directory service to a true X.500-based directory similar in many ways to Novell's NDS. Active Directory Services (ADS) is a pathway to a more scalable, extensible directory structure that can enable Windows NT to participate in the enterprise networks at a higher level.

This appendix provides a cursory overview of ADS and what it offers to Windows NT. In addition, we'll briefly discuss possibilities of integration with NetWare networks going forward.

Domain Services Today

Microsoft has had significant input (so we're told!) on improvements to the existing Domain services. As a result, one of the goals of ADS is to solve some of the top issues with Domains that exist today, including:

- Management of trust relationships

- Scaling to large number of objects in the directory database

- Traffic associated with NetBIOS

- A plethora of utilities to manage the system (User Manager, Server Manager, Profile Manager, WINS Manager, DHCP Manager, SQL Manager, and so on)

As described in this book, NDS and technologies, such as SAM Replacement, have been designed to address many of the same issues Microsoft is also attempting to solve with ADS.

Maintaining the Domain

ADS does not replace the current Domain architecture. Rather, ADS addresses some of the major issues with administrating Domains (such as trusts) and hierarchical naming. When ADS becomes available, a migration strategy will occur to move existing Domains into ADS-supported Domains and trusts.

Replication Challenges with Domains

Another major issue addressed with ADS is the challenge of database replication. Currently, a Domain replicates the entire user/object data associated with a Domain database (the Primary Domain Controller, or PDC) to all the backup databases (Backup Domain Controllers, or BDCs), as shown in Figure C.1. If the PDC fails, manual intervention is required to bring management of the system online. This entails promoting a BDC to a PDC or fixing the PDC server that went down.

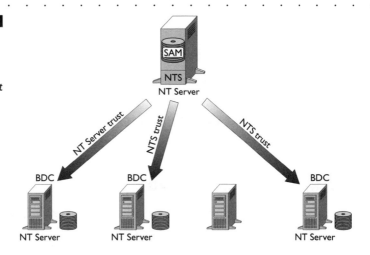

ADS uses the concept of a multi-master replication design. The limitation of keeping a PDC online was caused because Domains today use a single master replication design. Any changes to the Domain database *must* be issued to the PDC. Changes are then replicated down to the BDCs. In ADS, each database can accept changes and forward them to the other database copies. This removes the need to have any *one* server up constantly to perform administration of the network. Figure C.2 shows an example of using the ADS multi-master replication.

For this to work, *all* servers must be upgraded to Windows 2000. This is because a Windows NT 4.0 server doesn't know how to do multi-master replication, only single master. The logic of how to do multiple-master replication is found only in Windows 2000.

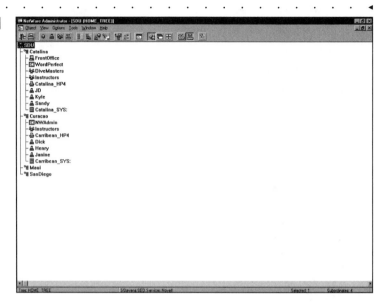

FIGURE C.2

*ADS uses a multi-master
update strategy to
propagate changes to each
Domain Controller (DC).*

Components of ADS

ADS is an add-on to the Windows NT environment. In moving forward to a 2000 revision, Windows NT will contain a significant number of enhancements, none so important to the Windows NT future as ADS. Coexisting with Windows NT 4.0 is paramount to the success of Windows 2000. Therefore, Microsoft is taking great care to ensure a smooth migration wherever possible.

New Features for Windows 2000 Directory Service

Similar to NDS, ADS has a list of new features that make it a more viable choice when choosing directories. These options include

> ► An extensible Schema (for adding and managing new objects such as a *SQL Server* or *Exchange Server* object)

- The ability to search for resources (nonexistent in Windows NT 4.0 today)

- A much more scalable underlying database (based on the Microsoft Exchange database, also known as JET)

- Automatic trust relationships (manually assigned and maintained today in NT 4.0)

- Better graphical-management utilities (using the Microsoft Management Console)

- Interoperability with Internet directory standards, such as Lightweight Directory Access Protocol (LDAP)

New APIs (ADSI) Enabling Access to Directories

In addition, Microsoft has created a set of Application Programming Interfaces (APIs) to simplify programming to a directory (including NDS). This initiative is called Active Directory Services Interfaces (ADSIs).

 NOTE **Originally, ADSI and ADS were named OLE-DS. OLE-DS included a number of technologies, such as a set of common programming interfaces, a directory service, and so on. In renaming many Microsoft initiatives with the word *Active*, OLE-DS was similarly renamed to *Active* Directory Services.**

ADSI enables a programmer to code to one set of APIs, which, in turn, can access a multitude of other directories via their native protocols (such as NDS APIs, LDAP, and so on). The intent is to abstract programmatic access to directories down to one API provided by Microsoft.

This technology has been available since March 1997 and is a core technology Microsoft is championing to the developer community. Predominately, LDAP is the access method of choice today for programmatic access to directories.

Services Integration with ADS

Paramount to the usefulness of a directory is the amount of application/services integration with that directory. This means the ability for a service (such as e-mail, database, or business workflow application) to use a directory for naming and authentication.

NDS and Bindery Emulation

When NDS originally shipped, NetWare had (and still has!) a feature called *Bindery Emulation*. Using Bindery Emulation, an application could continue to function even if it had not been made Directory-aware. In this way, Novell provided a way to aid applications toward a true Directory migration. Microsoft is also doing a similar backward-compatibility strategy with the current SAM technology when ADS becomes available.

BackOffice Integration with ADS

Today, BackOffice services (such as SQL Server and Exchange) use the Domain database for some naming and authentication. As ADS becomes the preferred way to store services information, BackOffice applications must be migrated to use ADS natively. Meanwhile, a way must exist to provide backward integration. ADS will do this by providing old API calls to the existing SAM-based Domain until a majority of applications natively use ADS.

Interoperability with NDS

Of great concern is the interoperability of ADS and NDS going forward. ADS is publicly stated to be released sometime in 1999 (late-year) as part of Windows 2000. Companies that move forward with NetWare and Windows NT integration projects may have a real concern as to the possibilities of continued integration between the two (NDS and ADS).

Overlapping Functions of NDS and ADS

NDS and ADS provide some of the same functionality. When running side-by-side, what are the possibilities? Here are some potential scenarios where the two might be co-deployed:

- ▸ Using NDS as the Directory to manage any services that have been written to NDS. Deploy ADS, if required, when Windows 2000 ships.

- ▸ Use NDS and NDS for NT to provide continued management of Windows NT from NDS. Backward compatibility in Windows 2000 ensures this will work well after Windows 2000 becomes available.

- ▸ Use NDS or ADS as a Meta-Directory. Allow changes in NDS to be synchronized to ADS or vice versa.

Issues of Compatibility

No one can guarantee that NDS and ADS will be compatible when ADS ships. In fact, Microsoft has a vested interest in championing ADS as the main directory service for Windows NT wherever Windows NT is installed.

Novell, being aware of this issue, has written NDS for NT and SAM Replacement using published Microsoft APIs and tools. As a result, unless intentionally broken by Microsoft, those products will continue to run on Windows 2000 as companies choose to migrate.

Index

Continued

Continued

Continued

Continued

Continued

T

U

V

W

Continued

X

X.500 standard, 400

Y

Y2K diagnostic utility, 341

Z

NOTES

NOTES

NOTES

NOTES

NOTES

my2cents.idgbooks.com

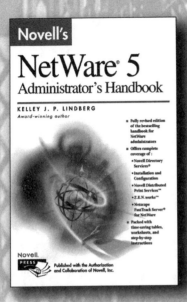
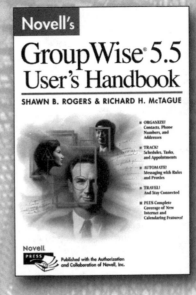
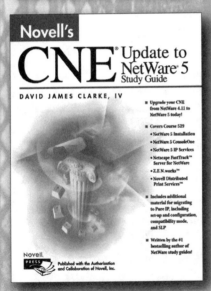

MORE BOOKS FROM NOVELL PRESS™